75 QUID AND AN AXE

Julia Matthews

75 QUID AND AN AXE

This is a TRUE STORY.

75 QUID AND AN AXE
Copyright © December MMXI by Julia Matthews.
Julia Matthews has asserted herself as the author of
75 QUID AND AN AXE, an original work.
© ACASHIC™ INTELLECTUAL CAPITAL PTY LIMITED

All rights reserved including the right to reproduce this book or
a portion thereof in any form is strictly prohibited,
unless you have contacted the writer to obtain permission.

Published and distributed by

ACASHIC™ INTELLECTUAL CAPITAL PTY LIMITED
PO Box 8030, Subiaco East
WA 6008, Australia
+618 9324 4455
www.acashic.com
acashic@acashic.com   acashic@gmail.com

Font size—14pt Dutch801 Rm BT Roman, Paper type—60gsm Norbook White
Editor in Chief: Michael Garcia
Cover Design & Book Formatting: Chi-Ting Chan and Evonne Hew

Printed in the USA

ISBN 978-1-4477-8612-2

PUBLISHER'S DISCLAIMER

Acashic Intellectual Capital Pty Limited ("the Publisher") asserts the following in regards to the book ("the Work") and the cover ("the Cover"):

The views expressed on any aspect of the Cover and in the Work are solely those of the Author ("the Author"), other writers and or individuals providing them, and do not reflect the opinions of the Publisher, its parent, affiliate or subsidiary companies. Caution is advised when reading or using the Work. The Publisher is not responsible for any damages sustained by the Reader ("the Reader") or User ("the User") of the Work, when reading or using the Work. The Publisher shall not be responsible for any aspect that may result in claims of defamation and invasion of privacy. In all instances the Publisher has relied on the expertise of the Author and has not investigated the matters provided by the Author. The Publisher has no duty to investigate the factual or other basis of the material provided by the Author.

Protection is deemed to include all of the Publisher's products which includes but is not limited to books, web sites, CD-ROMs, DVDs and other media ("the Products") that give advice or provide instructional information – all of which are protected in their own right under appropriate, legally drafted Disclaimers.

Copying or disseminating any information published by the Publisher, electronic or otherwise is strictly prohibited. The Reader should be aware that the text of the Work is subject to change at any time. Uploading of the Work and its Cover without permission of the Publisher is unauthorized and may lead to a conviction as a result of a piracy suit.

The work is provided by the Publisher on an "as is" basis. The Publisher makes no representations or warranties of any kind, express or implied, as to the operation of the Work, its website(s), the information, content, materials or products, included in the Work. To the full extent permissible by applicable law, the Publisher disclaims all warranties, express or implied, including but not limited to, implied warranties of merchantability and fitness for a particular purpose. The Publisher will not be liable for any damages of any kind arising from the use of the Work, including but not limited to direct, indirect, incidental punitive and consequential damages.

The Author and the Publisher specifically disclaim any implied warranties of merchantability or fitness for any particular purpose and shall in no event be liable for any loss or profit or other commercial damage, including but not limited to special, incidental, consequential, or other damages incurred as a result of specific decisions made by the Reader and or User.

Publisher does not take responsibility for any Author- or third-party websites or their contents.

It is assumed that a Reader and or User reads books front to back and therefore start at the front flowing through the Disclaimer. This means that the Reader and or the User of the Work has entered into a "contract" with the Publisher that includes that the Reader and or User read and or used the contents and its information in the Work with full knowledge of and agreement with the Disclaimers.

Acting affirmatively or continuing to read and or use the Work is deemed by the Publisher that the Reader and or User accepts the terms and conditions of the Work and or its Disclaimers. If the Reader and or User of the Work refuse to accede to the terms of any of the Disclaimers contained herein, then it is agreed by the Reader and or User that the Reader and or User shall immediately return the Work. If the Reader and or User do not so act, the Publisher may argue that a "contract" was formed with the Reader and or User making the Reader and or User bound by the terms of the Disclaimers.

If the Disclaimers are defective in some way, or that the Disclaimers are defectively placed, the use of all Disclaimers will nevertheless in all instances still act as a claim to a defense.

If a claim, action, or proceeding is brought against the Publisher, its licensees, or any seller of the Work, based on facts which, if true, would violate any of the warranties or representations in this Agreement, Publisher may defend the same through counsel it chooses and may settle the same in its sole discretion.

Copyright © MCMXCVI-MMVI/MMVII/MMX/MMXI/MMXII Acashic Intellectual Capital Pty Limited. No portion of the Work including its Disclaimers may be copied, transmitted, retransmitted, posted, reposted, duplicated or otherwise used without the express written approval of the Publisher.

The sale of a book without a Cover is un-authorized.
Books sold without a Cover have not been paid for by the retailer and have been reported as unsold and destroyed. Please report books with no Cover to Acashic Intellectual Capital Pty Limited.

AUTHOR'S DISCLAIMER

The Author asserts the following in regards to the book ("the Work") and the cover ("the Cover"):

Caution is advised when reading or using the Work. The Author is not responsible for any damages sustained by the Reader ("the Reader") or User ("the User") of the Work, when reading or using the Work. The Author shall not be responsible for any aspect that may result in claims of defamation and invasion of privacy. In all instances, and as far as is reasonably possible, the Author has relied on third party representations and expertise.

It is assumed that a Reader and or User reads books front to back and therefore start at the front flowing through the Disclaimer. This means that the Reader and or the User of the Work has entered into a "contract" with the Author that includes that the Reader and or User read and or used the contents and its information in the Work with full knowledge of and agreement with the Disclaimers.

Acting affirmatively or continuing to read and or use the Work is deemed by the Author that the Reader and or User accepts the terms and conditions of the Work and or its Disclaimers. If the Reader and or User of the Work refuse to accede to the terms of any of the Disclaimers contained herein, then it is agreed by the Reader and or User that the Reader and or User shall immediately return the Work. If the Reader and or User do not so act, the Author may argue that a "contract" was formed with the Reader and or User making the Reader and or User bound by the terms of the Disclaimers.

If the Disclaimers are defective in some way, or that the Disclaimers are defectively placed, the use of all Disclaimers will nevertheless in all instances still act as a claim to a defense.

If a claim, action, or proceeding is brought against the Author, its licensees, or any seller of the Work, based on facts which, if true, would violate any of the warranties or representations in this Agreement, the Author may defend the same through counsel it chooses and may settle the same in their sole discretion.

CONTENT

...Chapter 1   9
  ...Chapter 2   24
...Chapter 3   36
  ...Chapter 4   45
...Chapter 5   54
  ...Chapter 6   61
...Chapter 7   68
  ...Chapter 8   74
...Chapter 9   76
  ...Chapter 10   82
...Chapter 11   93
  ...Chapter 12   98
...Chapter 13   107
  ...Chapter 14   112
...Chapter 15   127
  ...Chapter 16   138
...Chapter 17   150
  ...Chapter 18   165

...Chapter 19	**173**
...Chapter 20	188
...Chapter 21	**198**
...Chapter 22	206
...Chapter 23	**222**
...Chapter 24	227
...Chapter 25	**232**
...Chapter 26	237
...Chapter 27	**244**
...Chapter 28	252
...Chapter 29	**256**
...Chapter 30	259
...Chapter 31	**263**
...Chapter 32	268
...Chapter 33	**270**
...Chapter 34	274
...Chapter 35	**281**
...Chapter 36	290
...Chapter 37	**295**
...Chapter 38	304

...Chapter 1

"You won't need to put *this fellow in nappies Mrs Challis. He can go straight into working clothes.*" These were the words of the doctor who greeted my arrival on the 1st December 1914 in the small English village of Faulkbourne in Essex. Weighing in at eleven pounds, my parents must have decided I needed a name to match my size and so I was given the handle of George Joseph Alexander. I was the third son of a family that would later grow to nine - six boys and three girls. Many years later I was told that for the first week of my life I wouldn't suckle from my mother, so she starved me, but after a week, she realised it was either the bottle or let me die, so she gave in. That stubborn streak has remained with me all my life - the need to never let anything beat me and always do my best at whatever I tackle.

My earliest memory is of the day I started school, which was only a stone's throw from our house. I finished the morning session and when I went home for lunch, I decided to take off my boots and return to school without them. I must have looked like a turkey amongst ducks because I remember the other kids staring at my feet. It didn't worry me much, but the lovely teacher we had quietly told me to go home and put them on again. Ever since I can recall, I have loathed wearing shoes. I grew to have the flattest feet some doctors had ever seen and the most relief I got was when I was barefooted. I doubt whether this condition affected my early years and if so, it didn't matter - I duly had to wear my shoes to school every day, much to my disgust.

Of my two elder brothers, Bill and Les, I was closest to the second one, Les. We were best mates and if a fight started, we fought as one. Needless to say, we got into a bit of mischief.

My father, Frederick Challis, worked on a farm owned by Mr Speakman. It was quite a mixed farm with cattle, sheep, pigs, crops, vegetables and an orchard. It was in the orchard that an incident occurred which remains etched in my memory.

One Saturday, Les and I went to the orchard which grew near a big shed that housed the wagons and machinery. We climbed through a hedge and sneaked to a tree laden with fruit. Les always did the climbing while I stood, pommie cap in hand, ready to catch the spoils. When we had picked enough for a good feed, we slipped inside the shed, climbed into a wagon and devoured the lot. We thought we could perhaps find room for a bit more, so returned to the orchard. Again Les climbed the tree and proceeded to drop the fruit in my outstretched cap. All was going well, when I happened to glance up and see a face looking over the gate near the house.

Quietly, I whispered to Les, "*We're being watched by Mr Speakman.*" Thinking quickly, we pretended we were examining the fruit to see how good the crop would be. We thought our performance may have been convincing, because Mr Speakman said nothing and left. I must say, the fruit did not taste quite as nice as the first lot and we worried over the weekend, waiting for something to be said.

It was a practice during the fruit season for Mrs Speakman to bring a box of fruit to the school and leave it on the porch for the children to take a piece as they left the classroom. Monday arrived and with it Mrs Speakman and a box of apples. She placed the box on the porch, then said to the class, "*Now I've got something to say about two very, very naughty boys in the class.*" It didn't take much for Les and I to figure out who the naughty boys were. She continued, "*On the weekend, Mr Speakman saw these boys stealing fruit from the orchard.*" She carried on for a while, then said, "*So, for their punishment, every child can take an apple except Leslie and George Challis.*" We were greatly relieved to be getting off so lightly and what with a few bites from apples of generous friends we did not really miss out at all.

We didn't have much in the way of toys or board games so our leisure time was filled by inventing all sorts of activities. Though harmless enough, some were nevertheless annoying to others! A prank we enjoyed immensely was played on an old chap who used to arrive home inebriated from a pub in a nearby village. One day, the old man was wending his way home when he came across a parcel on the road. Les and I had made this package and attached it to a string which we were holding on the other side of a hedge. As he bent to pick up the parcel, we pulled the string so that it moved just out of his reach. Much to our delight, he tried several times to grab the elusive bundle. Finally he gave up, uttered a few well chosen words and kicked the offending article down the road.

Another trick a group of us liked to play was to knock on someone's door, hide, wait for the person to answer the knock, then repeat the procedure again. Somehow, I was always the one chosen to do the knocking and on one particular day, I knocked on our teacher's (Mrs Beardwell) door. Her husband was a nice old chap and after coming to the door a few times, he realised what was going on and decided to ferret us out. I remember squeezing under a little culvert that crossed over a ditch and lying there trembling because he was standing on top of it. Luckily, I wasn't caught but it sure curbed my enthusiasm for knocking on doors.

In the lands surrounding our village were areas of woodland, left purposely for game hunting. Every hundred yards or so a track ran from one end of the wood to the other. The shooters would stand along the first track, shoot whatever the beaters flushed out, then move on the next tract and so on. I recall being a beater on only one occasion and it stands out mainly because I was the youngest one there. Having finished my job, I lined up with mostly grown men for the distribution of a collection taken by the shooters. As I stood with outstretched hand, an old gentleman placed a shilling in it. To me a shilling was like having a fortune. In fact, I doubt whether I had ever handled a shilling till then. I was ready to bolt home to my mother with my spoils when the old chap told me to stay where I was for a minute. Along he came again and placed sixpence in my hand, then on the third pass, I received a further threepence. One and ninepence - I could hardly believe it! I clung tightly to those coins and flew home. This was a big win for my mother as she was, by now, raising six children on thirty shillings a week, the younger three being Winnie, Harry and David.

The woods were patrolled by a gamekeeper called Mr Wheeler. Luckily for us, he had a crippled leg and was therefore unable to run very fast. Many times, we managed to collect chestnuts, blackberries, crab-apples and mushrooms for our mother without being caught. From the crab-apples, she would make jam and a type of cider. Things changed when Mr Wheeler retired and a new chap took over. Through the grapevine, we heard that he was physically very fit, carried a double barrelled shotgun and was accompanied by two huge dogs. The story was that he did not mess around by asking questions. If he caught you, he shot you and fed you to the dogs. For kids our age, this was very frightening, but obviously not enough to deter Les and I from planning a raid on a crab-apple tree. We worked out that between the times the gamekeeper made his rounds, we would be able to collect the apples and be gone before he arrived on the scene. With great confidence, we entered the woods with a basket and made for the tree. As usual, Les climbed it and started dropping apples in my cap. Suddenly, a loud voice said, "*Hey! What are you doing there?*" I froze. I cannot remember in all my life being so terrified. There was no escape. In the background I could hear Les still in the tree, howling his eyes out. Next came the command, "*Come here!*" Somehow I walked shakily toward the keeper, then had to crawl under a fence near where he was standing. The sight that greeted me from that position was even more nerve shattering. I was staring down the barrels of his gun and into the slobbering, panting mouths of two large, shaggy dogs which looked like they were just about ready for their next meal. The absolute terror I was feeling must have been conveyed to the keeper. "*Now look,*" he said sternly, "*I'm going to let you go this time, but don't ever let me catch you near these woods again.*" With that, I took off like a jack rabbit. I don't think even Herb Elliott would have caught me. As I ran, I could hear Les calling out to me, but brother or no brother, I was not about to stop till I reached the safety of our house. Eventually, Les returned home with the basket of apples which the keeper had made him take. I'm afraid even that kind gesture did not alter the image that remained with me of the shot gun and two man-eating dogs.

For a bit of entertainment, Les, another boy and I sometimes crushed rocks under a grating in the road. The grate was hinged and rested on steel ledges. Les and the other boy would lift the grate and I would place rocks on the ledges. When the grate fell, it smashed the rocks to pieces which we found very satisfying. One day, as I was inserting rocks, the grate dropped just before I had completely removed my arm and it landed across my wrist. The gash was so wide that my mother placed her thumb in it to stop the bleeding. Still, blood spurted all over her. The local nurse was called. She rushed in and her first comment was, "*By Jove, is it broken?*" In those days, stitches were not commonly used so padding and bandages were applied instead. It healed very nicely but I still think now, as I look at the scar, how lucky I was not to have lost my hand.

When my eldest brother Bill was about twelve years

of age, he attended a school in another village. Once a week he had the job of carting water for the teacher from the village pump and for this he was paid sixpence. His pay day was eagerly looked forward to by me and several other boys because he would go to the shop and purchase three twopenny packets of Willy Woodbine cigarettes. We would then find a spot behind the hedges and out of sight. Me and Len Thoroughgood, my old school mate who was my age, were posted as lookouts while the rest had a big smoko. After, as a reward, we were each given one half of a cigarette. Little did I know that this would be the start of a habit that would last for approximately fifty six years.

Another job Bill had was to clean the stable of Mr Otley, the local shopkeeper. Apart from the shop, he also baked bread which he delivered by horse and cart. For his efforts, Bill was paid twopence. He had been working there for quite a while when he came across a bad penny. A bad penny was just a worthless coin and Bill recognised it as such but as the shop stayed open till dusk, Bill planned to wait till it was dark enough to pass the penny over the counter in exchange for four pear drops, his favourite lollies. When the time came, he entered the shop, asked for the peardrops and gave the coin to Mr Otley, who placed it in the till. Later, when Mr Otley was checking his takings, he discovered the coin and worked out who the culprit was. Nothing was said until Bill failed to show up for his job. Mr Otley couldn't understand why he hadn't turned up as we lived close by, so when next he saw Bill, he said, *"Listen Bill, you haven't been in to clean the stables."* Bill replied, *"No Mr Otley I'm not going to clean them."* *"But why?"* asked Mr Otley. *"Because I don't feel like it,"* said Bill. *"I don't*

75 QUID AND AN AXE

want to clean them." Rather stunned, Mr Otley asked, "*But what has happened to make you stop Bill?*" "*If I clean them,*" Bill replied, "*You might not pay me.*" Being almost an open admission of guilt, Mr Otley twigged that Bill was afraid of being docked a penny from his next pay. Hiding a smile, he asked Bill if he would continue the job if paid in advance. "*Oh! Yes!*" said Bill quickly, "*I'll do them straight away if I get paid first.*" From then on, Mr Otley had to produce twopence before Bill would venture into the stable. It became quite a standing joke between Mr Otley and my father.

As I mentioned before, my father worked for Mr Speakman who was a very mean person. One of the reasons we migrated to Australia was because Mr Speakman refused my father's request for a rise in pay which would have amounted to one shilling a week. Several draft horses were kept on the farm and one of them developed lockjaw. The vet, Mr Young, was called in to give his opinion. According to my father, the poor horse was completely paralysed except for its tongue. The vet said, "*Look Fred, I'm afraid we'll have to put him down. I've seen a lot of cases in my day and I've never seen one survive, especially one as bad as this.*" My dad was very attached to animals and hated the idea of the horse being shot so he asked the vet if he'd mind leaving the horse in his care for a while. Mr Young was quite happy to oblige. To feed the animal, my father made a funnel which he placed in its mouth. He then poured very fine, smooth linseed down this funnel and into the horse's throat. After a week of this, my father entered the stable to find the horse turning its head slightly to greet him. He knew from that moment he had won the battle.

Mr Speakman had been getting a bit irate about

the time Dad spent with the horse and said to him, "*Why didn't you have it put down in the first place?*" Dad answered, "*I'll have that horse down at the pond drinking in the next day or so.*" Mr Speakman laughed his head off and said, "*That'll be the day, Fred.*" Sure enough, a couple of days later, my father led the horse to the pond where it started to drink. Mr Speakman was speechless. When Mr Young, the vet, heard the news he was absolutely delighted and congratulated dad on his success. He said he'd never seen a cure like it in all his career. He was so thrilled, he gave dad two shillings and said, "*There's a little something Fred, and if Speakman thinks anything of you, he'll put another two shillings with it.*" If my father had been a cynical type, he would have laughed as Mr Speakman had and said, '*That'll be the day!*', because not one threepenny bit was forthcoming for the effort he had put in to save the horse.

Along the road from the school lived two lovely young ladies called Hilda and Katie Hills. They were in their twenties when I was at school but I always reckoned that Katie was my girl. They used to sew beautifully and would sit either side of a big window that fronted the road. It was close enough for us to be able to speak to them if we were passing. Occasionally, they would go to the village of Wigham in a donkey cart. One day, they asked Les if he would like to go with them. This was considered a major event, so Les dressed in his Sunday best for the outing. When he arrived home, I wanted to know every detail. He related the events of the trip and how he had stayed to tea at the sisters' house afterwards. I can't recall if I pestered them a little or if they just took pity on me, but eventually my turn came and I was invited on one of their excursions. I sat between them in the cart, feeling very excited. Arriving at Wigham, they asked me to stay in the cart and hold the reins while they did their shopping. Some big boys came along and teased me, which made me a bit frightened but I sat it out till the ladies returned. As we started for home, I silently hoped and prayed that I would be asked to tea. Thankfully, I was invited in. I couldn't believe my luck when I saw butter on the table. We were so hard up, we rarely saw butter. Added to this was fresh bread, jam, jelly and other assorted foods, all of which were absolute luxuries to me. I felt on top of the world and tried to display my best manners as I tucked in to the delights on the table. To finish, the ladies insisted I have some bread and jam. I remember it was raspberry jam, something I had never tasted before. It was so delicious, I can still taste it today. I got rather carried away, asking for seconds and then thirds. Thanking Hilda and Katie several times, I dashed home to have a little skite to the others about my day out. It was one I look back on with great fondness. As far as I know, those lovely girls never married and their only brother died when he fell on shears which pierced his heart.

Once a year, the children and some of their parents were taken by bus to South End for a day by the sea. Although none of us could swim, dad always had a wallow in the ocean while we paddled in the shallows. My greatest joy on these occasions was to buy a small plate of cockles with a penny my mother had given me. I would make those cockles last half a day by slowly eating one at intervals throughout the morning. Forty eight years later, I had the pleasure of buying cockles again at South End and they tasted just as good as they had then.

Every day after school, I joined my father on the

farm and stayed with him till he finished work. Dad was a softly spoken, gentle man and I worshipped him. We had a very close relationship, more like pals than father and son. I would have walked over hot coals for him and I know the feeling was mutual. He always carried a quart bottle which was curved slightly to fit close to his body. During milking he would fill the bottle with milk, place it in a large inside pocket of his coat and take it home. This helped supplement our meagre supply.

An old chap call Isaac, (Ike for short), worked on the farm and had the job of collecting eggs. As he was getting old, I often did his job for him. He was always saying, "*You're a good boy. I'll give you something for this one day.* If someone promised you anything in those days, it never left your mind. As the weeks passed, I started to worry that he may have forgotten his promise, so I jogged his memory. "*You haven't forgotten what you were going to give me have you Mr Isaacs?*" "No, no boy," he replied, "*I haven't forgotten. You'll get something, don't you worry about that.*" Finally, the big day came. I didn't quite know what to expect, but I was very excited and thought it would have to be pretty fantastic. Into his pocket went his hand. He fumbled and fumbled for ages and eventually pulled out one half penny. While I was a little disappointed, I knew that I could at least buy two pear drops, but I was never over anxious to collect the eggs again.

I helped my father with many jobs on the farm. One was chopping mangles which are similar to large sweet turnips. I dropped them into a hand turned machine which sliced them for cattle feed. My dad added treacle to the mangles before putting the mix into troughs. This was the main diet for most of the farm animals during winter. Another job was to crush large blocks of linseed cake for the sheep. Into a long trough in the paddock, dad tipped bags of this cake. Wanting to feel important and useful, I spread it along the trough which was, by now, surrounded by pushing and shoving sheep. One day I was busy doing my job when a ram took exception to my presence and butted me squarely in the backside, lifting me straight over the trough! My father saw the funny side and laughed his head off but I was not at all amused and nursed a very sore behind for the next few days.

Winter was always a good time for the children of the village. We used to make huge snowmen by rolling snow into balls, stacking one on top of another and then decorating them. Of course, we could not afford skates but a good run up and slide over iced puddles in the road gave us just as big a thrill. There was one particular pond that sometimes iced over and would then become our skating rink. One day, I dashed onto the ice, my feet slipped from under me and I came down hard on the back of my head. It really knocked the stuffing out of me and I howled my eyes out.

During spring, we made a few coppers by picking bunches of wild flowers for anyone who would buy them. The posies mainly consisted of primroses, bluebells and peggles, which were yellow and similar to a kangaroo paw. When I visited the old country many years later, no-one except one cousin had heard of peggles. She took me to a place where they grew. This reassured me that my memory was still pretty sharp.

Once a year we made a special visit to our relations in the village of Finchingfield. I looked forward to this event as I got to play with all my cousins but mainly, I loved to see my favourite Aunty Ruth who thought as much of me as I did her. She had a son, Bill, who we used to call Bill-a-Ricky — heaven knows why! He was a little older than me and slightly superior. While playing around in a paddock we came across a wasp nest in the ground. They were quite common and we never thought of them as dangerous. Bill had a golf ball which he had pulled to pieces. Inside was a ball made of elasticised rubber strips wound tightly together. Bill had unwound quite a lot of it and handed pieces to several of the boys, but I was left out. I was dying to get a piece and must have made it quite obvious because he said to me, "*I'll give you a chunk if you stand in the wasp nest till I count to ten.*" I was in it like a shot. Pulling my pommie cap down over my eyes and thrusting my hands in my coat pockets, I stood bare legged over the nest. He was a bit slack in the counting and really took his time but I held my ground. About to step off unscathed, I was suddenly bitten under the eye on the count of ten. I let out a big yelp and howled loudly with the pain. This drew a generous response from Bill, who offered me the whole ball, just as long as I didn't spill the beans to Aunty Ruth. I came away sore, but vindicated.

   At the time of year when the swallows were due to return from their migration, our teacher would promise sixpence to the first child who spotted one. This became a real contest and a lot of time was spent watching the eaves of the school where the nests were built. I recall winning twice. School never really held much interest for me. I preferred the open spaces and physical work. I suppose I held my own during the first few years, mainly because the teacher was so kind and encouraging but later on - in Australia - I couldn't wait to leave.

Not long before I turned eight, brochures and pamphlets started arriving advertising a group settlement scheme in Western Australia. They read of sunshine, beaches and wealth, the land of milk and honey. Photographs boasted well developed farms, ready and waiting for us to take up residence. As my father was working seven days a week for thirty shillings with no prospect of a raise or hope of buying a house of our own, he and my mother decided to start a new life in Western Australia. The premier of Western Australia at that time was James Mitchell. The scheme was his idea to re-develop the south west of the state. Earlier, in the 1800's, there had been thousands of people living in the area. The Davies had set up timber mills at Karridale and Boyanup, employing hundreds of families. They had built the Flinders Bay and Hamelin Bay jetties and the lighthouse which still stands at Cape Leeuwin. When the timber ran out, the mills closed, people left and the south west more or less fell back into its former undeveloped state until the 1920's. Now land was to be allotted to families who, as they progressed, paid for their properties by instalments. We became the news of the village for quite a while before our departure. Mr Speakman was most upset that my father was leaving but did not offer any incentive for him to stay. The ship fare for the eight of us was thirteen pounds. After that was paid, the only money we possessed came from the sale of our furniture and other odds and ends. The rest of our belongings were stored in large packing cases which later played a large part in providing us with furniture.

On the day of our departure, the villagers wished us well and said their goodbyes. We were picked up by relatives from Finchingfield and taken by wagon to the nearest station. The electric train was quite a novelty for us. We enjoyed the trip to London where we stayed overnight with another relative. Next day we travelled to Tilbury docks, ready to board the "Barrabool", one of the P&O ships. Along with many other migrants, we were shunted onto a rather small boat which started off from the dock. Such was our ignorance of distance and sea travel, we kids thought this was the Barrabool and happily accepted that this vessel would transport us to our destination. When we pulled alongside the real thing, anchored out in the harbour, our eyes nearly popped out of our heads. The ship was 13,500 tons which was considered a large vessel in those days. Having transferred to the ship, we were shown to our cabins. My mother, Winnie and David were put with a Mrs Marshall, dad had to share with several men and the four boys filled another cabin. Everyone was very excited and time till departure was spent exploring the ship and generally settling in. Meals were preceded by a loud gong - a very welcome sound to us. The food was excellent and quite a good deal better than what we were used to, so there were never any complaints. Early next morning the anchor was raised and the Barrabool headed for the open seas.

...Chapter 2

None of us were prepared for the effects a rolling ship has on the human body. What a terrible few days followed! I remember being violently ill, unable to raise my head from the bunk The whole family suffered as did nearly everyone on board. A couple of days later, on entering the Bay of Biscay, we ran into a raging storm. It hit during the night. Amazingly, we children slept blissfully through it. Next day we found out how bad it had been when word went around that the Captain had readied the crew for lowering the lifeboats. Thankfully it hadn't come to that and the ship ploughed on towards Africa. As we gained our sea legs, we settled in to a routine. Days were spent playing games, running all over the ship and eating our eagerly awaited meals.

The first stop was the Canary Islands. We anchored off the coast and no one was allowed ashore. Small boats owned by the locals came out laden with goods - pineapples, bananas, fruits we'd never seen before, cigarettes and many other items. Our eyes were like saucers. Anything bought by the passengers was hoisted on board by ropes that had been dropped over the side. It was then a matter of trust for the buyers to lower their money down to the locals. One passenger refused to pay for his goods and left a poor old chap loudly protesting below. My mother purchased some fruit and a few little things for us - a very welcome treat.

By now we were seasoned sailors, settled in to shipboard life. My mother never seemed to worry as to our whereabouts. I suppose we were relatively safe as there were always adults around and everyone looked out for each other. One chap used to play the banjo during the day. He was a big, thick set fellow who really enjoyed music. He would entertain us for hours. One song I especially loved and have never forgotten was "Margie". At night, straight after tea, we kids were put to bed. Mum and dad would then join the other passengers for a chat or some dancing or whatever happened to be the entertainment of the night. Around nine o'clock, biscuits and cheese were distributed for supper. The biscuits were hard and large and the cheese was served in big chunks. Every night, Bill, usually alone but sometimes with Les or I in tow, would run the gauntlet to snaffle some biscuits and cheese for the kids. We had to be very careful not to get caught and to know where the food was going to be placed and how to get to it. Always successful, we would sneak back to the cabin with our spoils. The biscuits were real jawbreakers, but delicious. Broken into pieces and eaten with the cheese, they became a wonderful nightly treat for us.

A couple of young fellows on board who were obviously lacking in the financial department employed me to gather up any cigarette butts I could find on the deck or in the little gutter that ran along the outside of the deck. Every day I would do my rounds and managed to keep them supplied with smokes all the way to Capetown. They said I was the greatest kid ever. Continually, they promised me the world when we docked. They were going to buy me all sorts of things and take me places. Naturally, I believed them. It got to a stage where I expected huge and wonderful rewards for the work I had done. When the ship docked at Capetown, the two left the ship without so much as a goodbye. I had had no idea Capetown was their destination. Even though we were allowed to disembark, I never sighted the two chaps again. My only consolation was that they had allowed me a few puffs of their smokes made from the butts I had collected.

Black people were few and far between in England, so it fascinated me to see dozens of tall, strong Zulus on the docks. Their job was to refuel the ship with coal. They entered the lower side of the vessel on one ramp carrying baskets full of coal on their shoulders, then exited with empty baskets by another ramp One continuous stream of men flowed on and off the ship till the hold was full.

My parents planned to go to Tabletop Mountain which overlooks Capetown but were advised that it was too dangerous a venture. I expect the only access to the top in those days was by road and may be it was a treacherous one. Whatever the reason, my parents decided it would be wise to heed the advice given. We amused ourselves for a couple of days while the ship was re-stocked with fuel and supplies, then set off for Fremantle in Western Australia. In all, the journey from England took six weeks, ending in October 1923.

The first glimpse of land was greeted with great excitement by everyone on board. The main part of the journey was over. We were about to enter the so called "land of milk and honey". The ship slowly made its way into the harbour and docked alongside the wharf. Eventually, after a short wait while the gangplank was lowered, we left the ship for the last time and walked to an immigration house situated close to the wharf. It was a pretty rough and ready place, I recall, but at least the food was good. The building was huge, large enough to accommodate the many immigrant families and their belongings. I can't remember if my parents were allowed outside the fenced yard into Fremantle but I know us kids remained inside for two or three days prior to our departure for the South West. We departed Fremantle by train, headed into the city of Perth, then left for Busselton situated approximately one hundred and fifty miles away. Today the journey can be done by car in two and a half hours but by steam train, it took around fourteen hours. The only impression I have of Busselton as it was then is of a large building standing quite desolate in a paddock some distance from the station. It was called Sussex House, and provided guest accommodation for those passing through. It was run by a lady who, after we were settled, served a meal. The one thing about that meal that I can recall was the wonderful soup. To this day I still enjoy a bowl of hot kangaroo tail soup. Next day, we boarded a lorry for the final leg of the journey. Accompanying us was a family named Hall. We had already made their acquaintance on the ship. Mr Hall had become very unpopular during the voyage with his arrogance and stand over tactics. One day he bragged to my father, *"You've no need to worry about Australia.*

You'll love it. I've got a big property out there and I've just been back to England to pick up my wife and boys. I've got everything ready for them when we arrive." Everyone on the ship was under the impression he was a wealthy farmer. During our stay at the immigration home, this same chap approached my father and asked if he would buy a sixpenny stamp from him. Dad paid the money realising the so called wealthy farmer was not as well off as he had made out. Now here they were again, bumping along with us on a rough bushtrack through thick virgin bush. My mother and David sat in the front of the truck but the rest of us were slotted in amongst the mountain of goods and chattels on the back. The track, if you could call it that, was rutted and uneven, causing the truck to sway precariously from side to side and narrowly missing the huge trees that lined the edges. We kids thought it was great fun. Suddenly, one of us spotted blackboys, a native plant of Australia. We shouted with excitement, *"They must be banana trees."* Turning to Mr Hall for confirmation he said, *"Yeah, that's right, they're banana trees."* It was quite a long time before we discovered their true identity. Having heard Mr Hall's stories on the ship, we all expected to see him and his family dropped at a prosperous looking farm. Somewhere along the track, the truck pulled up. There was nothing but thick bush in all directions - no buildings - no people - nothing. It was here that the Halls were unloaded with their belongings. We left them standing at the side of the road in the middle of nowhere. I expect someone met them later but by that time we were out of sight, left speechless by what we had just witnessed.

On we rattled, marvelling at the abundance of "banana trees" and the size and density of the bush - all so very different from the soft English country side. Finally we reached our destination - Kudardup! Unlike the Halls, we were dropped at a building about twice the size of a toilet - a weatherboard structure which proved to be the post office. The next sight that greeted us was of a horse, cart and driver wending their way towards us from a side track. The lad on the cart was Jack Rowe, today a man of around eighty who still lives in the area at Margaret River. He was in charge of the only transport in our group settlement and had the job of collecting and depositing new arrivals plus delivering goods or whatever other errands a cart was needed for. He helped load our gear and then informed us that he could only take my mother and the youngest children on the first trip. He said he would come back for the rest of us later. As usual, Les and I had to challenge this statement. With no idea of the distance we might have to go, we decided to walk behind the cart, holding on to the tailgate. It was a decision we sorely regretted. The track was covered in palms and prickly bushes which whipped our lily white legs, causing us to howl with pain. We were frightened to let go of the cart as day light was fading so we followed along, crying with every step. No way would Jack allow us on the cart. We had gone against his instructions and we were paying for it. For three tortuous miles we travelled like this. When we finally reached the end we were complete wrecks. Our legs were torn and bleeding and we were exhausted. The only comment from Mum was, "*It serves you both right. You should have stayed with your father!*" The "end" was in front of a house, one of the few erected in the area. Having unloaded our belongings, Jack headed back for dad and Bill.

The house was new and had been built out of green

75 QUID AND AN AXE

jarrah. As the jarrah dried, the floorboards had shrunk leaving wide gaps between them. When young Harry ran inside, his legs went straight through the cracks. There were two bedrooms, a kitchen and a verandah. The kitchen contained a Metters wood stove and an open fireplace. Apart from that, the place was bare. White sand surrounded the building and huge trees leaned dangerously over it. As we stepped between the cart and the house, fleas attacked our legs, giving us the appearance of wearing long socks. Having never encountered fleas before, we jumped around madly trying to escape but they covered the ground in countless millions. We discovered later that everyone in the district was plagued with these vicious insects, ours more so because the house had lain dormant, giving them a chance to breed undisturbed. As time went by, we managed to control them by pouring kerosene around the house but for quite a while we all suffered badly. Somehow, in the confusion, my mother managed to prepare a meal from bread and jam bought in Busselton and arranged makeshift bedding for us on the floor. We slept fitfully, our bodies bitten and crawling with fleas - a wonderful start to our farming life.

    The next day we were visited by our nearest neighbour - a Mrs McDavid. She arrived via a narrow bush track, introduced herself and offered to show my mother how to make yeast. This was essential as there was no such thing as a baker in the area and bread made up the bulk of our diet. I remember later on when mum started producing yeast, she used to stand the bottles on the trimmers of the unlined kitchen. Now and then we would hear gun like explosions as corks popped from the necks of the bottles. Mrs McDavid demonstrated the method of baking bread and scones which was completely new to us. My mother was extremely grateful to be given such useful information. A day or so later, we were paid another visit. From a different bush track emerged Mrs Fisher and her mother, Mrs Rowe. Having been settled in the area for twelve months or more, they had a well established vegetable garden from which they had brought a chaff bag full of fresh vegetables. I think their main reason for calling was to cheer up my mother who, as you can imagine, was not feeling very happy about the situation in which she found herself. The worry and responsibility she felt for her young family must have weighed heavily on her.

In the days that followed, we slowly got organised. Kerosene boxes and our packing cases were used for furniture and it was surprising how versatile they could be. Stacked one above the other, they became cupboards and shelves. Placed around a table, they made excellent seats. Our only lighting came from a wick lantern brought from England. Beds were set up in the bedrooms and on the verandah where Bill, Les and I slept. Washing was done in a kerosene tin placed over an open fire. A thousand gallon tank of water beside the house soon emptied, so my mother was forced to carry the laundry to a well situated about two hundred yards from the house. Dad set up a line nearby on which the washing was hung to dry before being carted back again - a very back breaking job for any woman let alone one of my mother's small stature. Two flat irons, heated on the stove, were used to press our clothes. Bathing was done in a bathtub which had been used as a container for some of our gear on the journey out.

Before we left Perth, the government had supplied us with some tools. They included an axe, shovel, mattock, crowbar and a cant hook; an instrument used for rolling logs. My father also received three pounds a week which accrued as a debt to be paid back once the farm was operational. This was a very small amount on which to support a wife and six children, but somehow we managed. The nearest shops were one about a mile north of the Kudardup post office and another opposite the hotel in Augusta which was a few miles from our place in the opposite direction. The hotel and general store were owned by a Mr Staines. There was a garage and a few other buildings - about eleven in all that made up the town. Of course, being without transport of any kind, all visits to the stores or neighbours were done on foot along winding tracks through dense bush. We were always very careful not to venture from the paths for fear of becoming lost.

At first it was Les's and Bill's job to walk to Augusta for stores. They carried them home in thirty six pound sugar bags slung over their shoulders. I was as usual, rather envious, and it wasn't long before I wheedled my way into going along with them. I considered these trips big events - just seeing the town and a shop was quite a novelty after being stuck out in the bush.

Soon after our arrival, my father commenced work with other men in our group. Each group consisted of about thirteen families. We were in group four. The men worked together on one block at a time, overseen by a foreman. The aim was to clear and fence twenty five acres on each property. Clearing was not as it is today. Some trees were ringbarked and left to die. The dead leaves and bark eventually fell to the ground where they were collected and burnt. Crosscut saws and axes were used to fell smaller timber. I remember a chap called

Sweeney who was our local powder monkey. He was supplied by the government with fracture which he used to break large fallen timber into manageable pieces. With an auger, he drilled holes in the trunk at regular intervals then filled them with explosives. He had a set time for blasting so the area could be cleared. Bill, Les and I looked forward to these times as we were allowed to watch from a distance. We thought it was great to see wood flying in all directions into the air. After blasting skids were used to stack the sections of trunk into piles for burning. Fires were constantly going day and night for weeks. Land between the trees was cleared and worked over in preparation for planting pasture. It's sad to think now of the thousands of beautiful timbers that were killed because we had the mistaken idea that trees left alive would take all nourishment from the earth.

It wasn't long before our turn came to have land cleared. In the meantime, Les, Winnie and I were enrolled at the school in Kudardup. Bill did not continue his schooling after reaching Australia. Instead, he worked on the block for a small wage. On our first day of school, Mum prepared a basket of sandwiches for us and, accompanied by the ever present fleas, we trekked three miles through the bush to be greeted on our arrival by a not too receptive bunch of kids. Being lily white and speaking with heavy English accents, we were really put through the mill. The school was more like a galvanised tin humpy. A few wooden slats provided a floor and boxes had been adapted for desks. There were no windows and being summer, the place was like an oven. With about two dozen kids crammed in together we, who had not yet adapted to the heat, nearly stifled. Mr Jones was the teacher and quite a nice chap he turned out to be. When lunch time arrived, we made a bee line for our basket - but somebody had got there before us. The sandwiches were crawling with maggots. We had never seen maggots before, let alone heard of their depositors - blow flies. "*You can't eat that!*" cried the other kids, "*You'll get sick if you eat that.*" Then, without any fuss, they all clubbed together and provided us with lunch - we were accepted! It was like that all through my school days - one minute you'd be fighting tooth and nail with someone then five minutes later you'd be best mates.

A treat we enjoyed either going to or from school was provided by dear Mrs Fisher who lived beside the track we walked each day. Without fail, she met us and handed out cakes or sandwiches. On one occasion she gave us tomato sandwiches. We had been led to believe by dad that tomatoes were like poisonous berries. It stemmed back to England, the reason for which I am not sure. Not wanting to appear rude, we accepted the offering but waited till we were out of sight before disposing of the tomatoes and eating the bread. It was a long time before any of the family could be persuaded to try tomatoes but thereafter they became a favourite. Another time, Mrs Fisher asked if we'd like some lollies. Not knowing what they were but willing to accept anything, we said yes. When handed beautiful pillow shaped objects, we cried delightedly, "*Sweets, look! They're sweets!*" Lollies was a foreign word to us.

All our time outside school was spent working. There were always things to be done - picking up bark and sticks, preparing ground for a vegetable garden, carting water - just anything and everything we were capable of. Once our acreage was cleared, dad planted clover. Because the ground was sour and lacking in trace elements, it wasn't a great success but enough to support a horse and cow. Kate came first, a strong, unpredictable draft horse. She was put to work, dragging logs and pulling out blackboys. Her strength was incredible and she proved a great asset but we had to be careful not to touch her rear end as she would lash out with her large hooves. A horse we got three years later called Billy was the complete opposite. He was so docile, I could walk up and down his back and often three or four of us kids rode him together.

After Kate came Daisy, a lovely animal with a white face. She was a cull cow, which means she was amongst other milkers that had been taken to market from different farms, bought by the government, then sent down to the group settlers. Most were delivered to Charlie Lowe's place as he was the only one with a cattle yard. A ballot system was used to allocate the cows, so it was just a matter of drawing lots. As it was dad's first ballot, he was only allowed one cow. Daisy was an excellent milker. Mum scalded quite a lot of the milk and after it cooled, she would scrape the cream from the top to use for cooking or for us as a treat with bread and jam. Later on, we extended our "herd" by eight or nine more cows and a bull, the only one in the district. Being an old stockman, everyone considered dad to be the best person to handle a bull. Cows from other blocks were driven to our place for servicing. As time passed, herds increased and bully calves were used for meat. Until then, we had our meat delivered by Mr Sutton, the butcher in Augusta. The next acquisition was some fowls and now we had plenty of eggs. A large vegetable garden produced all the vegies we could eat. It was only a matter of twelve months since we had arrived and we were progressing well.

...Chapter 3

To give an idea of how thick the bush was in those days, we were informed about two weeks after our arrival that there was a nice river situated about four hundred yards from the house. One Sunday, dad decided to have a look for it. He was told that if he walked directly out from the front of the house and kept in a straight line, he'd have no worries. So that he would not lose his way, he blazed a trail by marking trees with an axe. On his return he confirmed that there was indeed a river close by and it was beautiful. The Blackwood River, as it was called, turned out to be three miles wide where we were situated. Our property fronted the Hardy Inlet, the biggest basin on the river. We kids got really excited at the news and it wasn't long before there was a well worn little track through the bush and paperbarks to the water's edge. At first, we just paddled around as none of us were swimmers, but on one particularly hot day, we decided to take the plunge. Stripping off all our clothes, we splashed and frolicked in the water. Later, as we tired, we lay on our fronts near the banks. There the water was only about six inches deep, leaving our backs and bottoms exposed to the sun. We thought it was just marvellous - until the next day! It was as if we had been put in an incinerator. We were nearly cooked. And the pain! For days we suffered, hardly daring to move. A lesson had been learned the hard way. Our only consolation came when the pain stopped and we started peeling. We derived great pleasure out of stripping sheets of skin from each others backs.

Our family swelled to seven with the birth of Joan, the first true Aussie among us. My mother never missed a beat during the pregnancy. She worked just as hard as ever. On the day of Joan's impending arrival, mum was busy washing. We had dug a second well near the house thus saving her a lot of foot slogging. She followed this chore with the cooking, then ironing and finally retired to bed. Around midnight, dad rushed onto the verandah where Bill, Les and I slept, shook us awake and said, *"You've got to go and get the horse. I have to take your mother into hospital."* Bleary eyed we crawled out of bed. It was pitch black and we had an area of about thirty acres to search for Kate. We lit a hurricane lamp, spread out and started across the paddock, keeping in contact with each other by yelling back and forth. It wasn't long before we caught Kate and harnessed her to the cart. By this time mum was in labour and Karridale Hospital was still eight miles away. She climbed aboard and sat on the seat with dad. The lamp was hung under the front of the cart and away they went. There was only one track to Karridale which made it almost impossible to become lost and a good thing it was as the light from the lamp was

75 QUID AND AN AXE

of little use. Dad hurried Kate as much as possible with Mum saying at intervals, "*I don't think I'm going to make it Fred.*" Normally you could travel that road at night and never see a soul but on this night, about three miles from Karridale, a set of headlights appeared ahead as if sent from above. Dad hailed the driver, a chap by the name of Hooley. He was a carting contractor and was driving a large truck. As dad quickly explained the situation, my mother entered the final stages of labour. "*Don't worry about a thing,*" said Hooley. He managed somehow to turn his vehicle round on the narrow road, helped mum into the cab and took off at full speed. Dad followed up with the horse and cart and by the time he reached the hospital, he was informed he had a healthy daughter.

After the trouble we'd all been involved in to make her entry into this world a safe one, we were lucky, when she started crawling, not to lose her. This particular day we were using old Kate, our horse, to snitch logs. Knocking off for lunch we led Kate to the house yard for a feed and left her to it. She must have finished her hay and wandered round the side of the house to a green patch of grass. The next thing, we heard a scream. Racing outside we discovered Joan lying about five feet from Kate's rear end, crying her heart out. We worked out that she must have crawled up and wrapped her arms around Kate's leg. Naturally, Kate kicked but only succeeded in tossing Joan away from her. If she had struck Joan before then, it would have killed her instantly. Joan came out of it without a scratch.

Another episode concerning Kate's volatile nature occurred several years later after a visit I paid to Charlie Lowe's farm. He was carting wood with his beautiful horse, Jim, between the shafts of his cart. I arrived as he backed Jim and the cart up to the woodheap. Releasing the girth and breeching straps holding the shafts and pad, he allowed the cart to tip up and deposit the wood. Chains still connected Jim to the cart so when the pad shafts dropped down on to his back, Charlie only had to reconnect the girths and straps to be ready for another load. I was fascinated by this procedure and thought I'd really show the family how easy wood carting could be. Time couldn't pass quickly enough till I got the chance to get my first load. I harnessed Kate and leading her into the bus I stacked the cart full of wood. Hoping I had an audience, which I now doubt, I steered Kate to the woodheap. When I let go the girth and breeching straps, the shafts lifted into the air and the wood slid off as planned but the sudden movement must have unnerved Kate. As the pad came down and hit her back she took off before I could secure the straps. Connected to the cart by just the chains and with me running alongside clinging to the reins, she galloped off in a big circle. My mother had washing on the line, kerosene tins full of soaking clothes and a long cast iron type of copper neatly arranged outside the yard. To my utter dismay, as Kate came past, a wheel of the cart went right through the centre of it all. The washing line hit the ground, the tins and copper were crushed. On Kate went regardless, with me still holding on for dear life. I stuck with her till she ran into a dead end chute we used for the cows. Unable to go any further, she let fly with her hooves. Bits of cart flew in all directions. My big moment had ended disastrously. Mother did not see the funny side at all and I was branded "a dill". It was my first and final attempt at using the new method with only Kate available to pull the cart. Any other horse and it could have been my shining hour!

A year had passed and I was ten years old. A new school was erected near the old one. It was a great improvement on the tin shanty and a lot cooler. The school still stands today, renovated, extended and used as a kindergarten. Number one on the list of after school activities was fights. These usually resulted from the desire of one or more boys wanting to be "top dog" at school. Starting with verbal abuse, metered out during school hours, the challenge was inevitably given - "*I'll see you after school!*" Three roads led off in different directions from the school and by following the crowd, one could tell straight away on which road the brawl would take place. Attendance was always good and the events thoroughly enjoyed by everyone. Those not involved formed a circle around the two opponents. Time was allowed for jackets or jumpers to be removed. This was called 'stacking the drapery'. Then it was on! There were no holds barred and fighting did not cease until one threw in the towel or both quit due to exhaustion. Re-matches were permitted if desired so it was not always sudden death to the loser. I managed to win more fights than I lost but often ended up with a black eye or blood nose. Many of my bouts were with Les, both at school and on the farm. Still, we remained the best of friends.

Each year, one of the older boys took his place as leader. Les loved brawling and eventually worked his way to the top but two years later when my turn to reign arrived, I came up against a boy called Bill Davidson. He was a year older than me but I was stronger. We agreed that top position would have to be decided after school. I can't remember exactly who won the first bout but whichever it was, the other won the second. Rematch after rematch took place until it reached a stage where we both realised neither one was going to get the upper hand. The only way we could rectify the situation was to split the school. Democratically, we used a ballot system. Bill chose a boy for his side, then I chose one for mine. On we went until all the boys belonged to one side or the other. I named my band "Robin Hood and his Merry Men" with me, of course, as Robin Hood. We all remained good mates but from then on, both groups matched each other in everything. If two boys from opposing sides wanted a fight, then Bill and I, as leaders, made the arrangements. Lots of encouragement and tactical advice was given as a defeat meant black marks against the loser's gang.

    In one corner near the school where two roads met, thick creeper grew over the ground. By tunneling our way through it, we made excellent headquarters for my gang. Bows and arrows were constructed and stored there. Sometimes, during a cowboy and Indian war, a boy would find himself with an arrow hanging from his leg. Many times this happened and although the wounds were not serious, it is amazing how we all escaped with such minor injuries. It could so easily have been an eye that was taken out by one of the flying missiles. One lunchtime, my band and I were gathered in our headquarters when we saw a boy we knew coming along the road on his horse. His name was Len Sutton and he had not long left school. He pulled up as we rushed onto the road and started chatting and answering the numerous questions being aimed at him by the boys. While the gang kept him occupied, I quietly loosened the buckles connecting the reins to the bridle. At my signal, we suddenly started a ruckus and shot a few arrows in the direction of the horse, all of which missed by miles as the noise had already set the animal into a gallop. When Len tried to pull back on the reins, they came away from the bridle as planned. Len stuck to the saddle like glue. The last we saw of him was as he disappeared down the road, clinging to the horse's mane. We got a good laugh out of that episode and returned to camp to concoct our next prank.

Eventually, Mr Jones was replaced by Mr Turner and school for most of us became a living hell. Turner was single, around twenty three years old and a sadist. He enjoyed using the cane and six of the best became a daily routine for many of the boys. I remember so well his arrival. We formed two lines outside in the yard and marched into the classroom before seating ourselves. Turner sat facing us from behind his desk. Not a word was spoken. Finally, the silence got to a boy named Lawrence (`Skinny') Trinidad. He saw the funny side of the situation and broke into giggles. At this, Turner looked up, pointed a finger at Skinny's smiling face and said, "*Take that idiotic grin off your face or I'll take it off for you!*" They were the first words he had uttered since setting foot in the school. I was eleven and had the job of milking eight or nine cows every morning. Inevitably, this made me late and no matter how fast I ran the three miles to school, I found it impossible to reach there on time. I howled as I milked and cried, "*Look at the sun, look at the sun, I'm going to be late.*" Les had left school that year and he and Bill laughed and thought it was a great joke. The moment I finished, I grabbed my bag and took off along the road. No excuses were accepted by Turner. Automatically, my hand went out for the cuts. Luckily, through working hard on the farm, my hands had toughened and the cane became bearable. Turner took a particular dislike to a boy called Harry Jones. Harry was not especially talented when it came to school work and for this he was constantly abused and hit. Although it meant little to us at the time, looking back now, I realise how Harry must have dreaded every day of those two years under Turner. It never occurred to me to tell my parents what was happening. I just accepted it as part of life. But there were a few kids who did report to their parents. One lady, Mrs Anderson, having been shown cane welts by her son Frank, fronted at the school. She flew at Turner and yelled, "*If you ever put a finger on him again, I'll be over in a flash and by God, you'll really know I'm here.*" Turner never touched Frank again but he continued to vent his spleen on others. Unluckily for me, Turner remained at the school for the longer part of the years I had yet to finish. Arriving after Mr Jones had already been there a while, I only had him for a year, then Turner came and stayed three years — although it seemed more like ten. Following his departure, a Mr Greep took over. He was fantastic. He courted and eventually married our foreman's daughter, Eileen Ford. I idolised him as I did my father and soon became his favourite.

Mr Greep was responsible for starting the local Boy Scouts Club. I was lucky enough to be a member of the scouts and proudly wore my uniform, hat and badges. One weekend, Mr Greep took a group of about fifteen boys to Flinders Bay for a bivouac. He owned one of the first T-model Ford cars in the district and had to ferry us in groups of five to the camping site where we set up camp for the two night stay. The next day he decided to take us for our first look at the Leeuwin Lighthouse.

Again we went in shifts. I remember the trip vividly. The thoroughfare was a crude bush track cut roughly into the side of a steep hill which fell to the ocean below. We arrived safely and climbed to the top of the lighthouse. On the return journey however, Mr Greep skidded the car so that the front end was hanging over the edge of the drop. Unperturbed we all dismounted and between us lifted the lightweight vehicle back onto the road.

If I had not been so turned off school by Turner I think I would have continued under Mr Greep's tuition but the rot had set in and I couldn't wait to escape. I ended up lying about my age and said I was fourteen. As no records were kept, my word was taken and I was permitted to leave. Ironically, the teacher that followed Mr Greep was a chap called Steve Wallis. He taught Winnie, Harry and David but years later when I entered the army camp at Northam, he was there as my instructor. We went to the Middle East together and became great mates.

My father was thrilled to bits to have me home. He was always telling my mother that I was his top worker, so it benefited him when I became a full time labourer on the farm. By the time I left school I had gained the nickname of "Pud". In England, I had been "Dumpling" because I was fairly plump. This became "Pudding" in Australia and finally "Pud". Most people today know me by this name and some have to think twice if asked about George Challis.

...Chapter 4

Quite a while after we got **Kate** we started taking Sunday excursions to Flinders Bay, a small settlement on the ocean front. It was a weekly ritual for many families and a day for showing off the horses. Kate was spruced up with a curry comb till she shone, then harnessed to the cart. As we jogged along, other families joined us and sometimes there was quite a long line of horses and carts along the bush track. We felt very superior if dad touched up Kate and overtook another family. No one glanced sideways or showed any acknowledgement of the other's presence. The same happened if we were passed. But as soon as we reached our destination, everyone greeted each other in a friendly way. The kids headed for the beach while the women found shady spots to sit and chat. The horses were watered at a small creek, then fed from nosebags. While they ate, the men gathered together to discuss the merits of their animals. Dad was quite an expert at telling the age of a horse by examining its teeth, so he was often asked to do so by some of the men. Most times he was accurate to within a year. Kate came to a sad end years later. After we left the farm, new owners took over and they must have eventually turned Kate out into the bush because she was getting old. Neighbours informed me one day that Kate was caught up in their fence and in a bad way, so I took my rifle, found her and put her out of her misery. It saddened me greatly to see such a faithful worker come to this but I was grateful that she had not been left to a slow, lingering death.

With all the settlers being on the same level, which was poor and struggling, no class system or snobbery existed. Everyone attended any social events that took place or rallied to help anyone who was in trouble. Alcohol on many of the farms was non-existent in the early days. Most people could not afford to buy it though this did not curb our social life. Sometimes, either mum or dad took us elder four to a neighbouring farm for the evening or we played host to several families ourselves. We participated in all sorts of games and tricks and if anyone played an instrument, we had a sing-a-long. Supper was always provided by the host family and often these shows lasted till three or four in the morning. Everyone went to bed sober. There was, however, one chap who more than made up for the lack of business we gave the hotel. His name was Bill Hitchmough . He was a bachelor and a bosom buddy of my father. Bill was a Gallipoli veteran who had been shell shocked in the war. This in no way reduced his capacity for hard work and we all thought he was a top bloke. Once a month, Bill went into Augusta for supplies. Included was a case of beer which held five dozen bottles. After a lengthy session in the pub, he would start for home in the horse and cart. Never once did he miss turning in at our road. Each visit took the same format but one, when I was thirteen, stands out clearly as an event that brought me even closer to my dad. As soon as Bill arrived this day, dad and he settled down with a beer for a chat. Dad smoked a pipe whereas Bill, while drinking, preferred a rolled cigarette or "twirly" as it came to be known. I hung around because eventually Bill would ask the question I wanted to hear. *"Fred, do you think one of your boys could come over and milk my cows tonight?"* Straight away I volunteered and more often than not got the job. I sat in the back of the cart while dad and Bill yarned together up front. On arrival we helped unload the supplies, then I went to milk the cows. Being well practised it did not take long as there were only about nine milkers. I separated the milk, cleaned up and fed the calves, then returned to the house. By now there was a roaring log fire burning in the hearth in front of which sat a very convivial twosome, sipping from their bottles and happily puffing away while they chatted. As I entered the room, Bill said, "*You better have a bit of tea boy.*" "*Yes Mr Hitchmough ,*" I replied, "*I am pretty hungry.*" "*Well, just help yourself then.*" On the table was stacked a month's supply of food and in it, my favourite treat - tinned crab. This was the main reason for my eagerness in volunteering my services for milking - the wonderful reward that followed. I was allowed a whole tin to myself and savoured every morsel. After I finished eating, Bill asked me to roll some twirlies for him. This done, I handed them to him and said, "*Here's your cigarettes Mr Hitchmough - they're all made.*" "*Have one yourself boy,*" announced Bill. "*No, I'm not allowed to smoke Mr Hitchmough .*" I replied. "*Well, who said you can't smoke?" "*My mum and dad,*" I answered. "*They don't allow me to smoke.*" He stalled for a minute and my heart started to beat a little faster. I had suspected dad knew I had the occasional puff, but up until now, nothing had been said. Then Bill looked over at dad and asked, "*You wouldn't mind if he had a smoke, would you Fred?*" Dad's face turned to me and on it, a grin slowly appeared. "*Oh,*" he drawled casually, "*You can have a smoke I suppose boy.*" Well, that was one of the big moments of my life. I was so excited that when I got home at around two in the morning, I woke Les to tell him the news. Somewhere along the line I managed to acquire a cigarette holder. From then on, if I was lucky enough to be given a cigarette by Bill, I could smoke it openly in front of him and dad, but I was eighteen before I ventured to do the same in the presence of my mother, even though Bill had done so at an earlier age.

To earn extra money for mum, Bill and I took up possum snaring. The bush was full of these beautiful animals and I could get one pound for a dozen pelts from buyers that toured the area. The snares hardly ever strangled the possums. They just tangled in the bushes rendering the animals immobile. I then had to kill them with a waddy which I secretly hated doing but times were hard and money was scarce. Once I found a mother snared with a large joey clinging to her back. As I approached the baby took off up a tree, stopping every few feet to see if mum was following. The mother looked from her joey to me with almost pleading eyes till I caved in and released her. Normally I killed the mothers and kept the smaller joeys to raise in a cage at home. They would have certainly died if left in the bush and they were too cute to kill. Most times I was raising around ten or eleven babies. Every evening I let them out of the cage for a run. They followed me everywhere and climbed over me as though I was their mother. It sounds silly now that on one hand I kept them alive to release back into the bush while on the other, I most probably snared a lot of them later as fully grown animals. I learned to peg the pelts correctly for drying and the art of skinning and inverting the tails with a piece of wire so that no moisture would be trapped inside causing the pelts to rot. On a good night I caught perhaps six or seven possums from the hundred or more snares set.

Another fur that was very valuable was that of the water rat. As far as I know I was the only one in the district who trapped them. They were quite large vicious animals with very soft pelts and the buyers paid up to ten shillings per skin. I caught them in rabbit traps set on the foreshore of the river. It was easy to know when a trap was occupied by the rat's loud screeching and gnashing of teeth. Often when we were fishing rats swam out to the nets after a feed of fish. Today they still exist in their thousands round the river and continue to filch fish from my nets, neatly removing all meat from the body and leaving the backbone, head and the mesh of the net intact.

I suppose the next biggest thrill of my life after being allowed to smoke was when I was given a pony which I named Fill. She was a filly, (hence the name), about eighteen months old and belonged to a chap called Freddie Tomlinson who worked on a farm nearby and courted the owner's daughter. They decided to move to Melbourne and dad was approached about taking the pony. I showed the keenest interest in her and so she became mine. She was of racing stock and ran like the wind. Together we covered a lot of territory. I was now normally the one sent for the stores. Placed in sugar bags which tied at the neck they could be hung from the saddle for easy carrying. As at school there was always someone among the young bucks ready to challenge for position of top dog. Sometimes if I was riding to Flinders Bay and met one or more of the local boys, we would ultimately end up racing for the finish line. One day a boy named Ernie Gale happened to be travelling the road from Augusta to Kudardup, a distance of about four and a half miles. I met him just outside Augusta and agreed to race to Kudardup. He rode a massive horse, so big in fact that Fill could almost walk under it. Undeterred, I sidled up beside him and away we went. With both horses at full stretch I managed to stick with Ernie to within a quarter of a mile from Kudardup, but the size and length of stride of his horse was just too much for Fill. We were pipped at the post. Still, I was proud of her effort and took the loss in good spirits.

One day when I was cantering out of Augusta with stores, a truck startled Fill and she shied slightly to the side of the road. I saw that the vehicle was being driven by a local bully boy called Tiny Maxwell but I took no notice and continued on my way. About a week or so later, on leaving the town after purchasing more supplies, I was confronted by Tiny and four or five of his mates straddling the road. They were all around eighteen years of age, whereas I was only ten or eleven. As I walked my pony past them, Tiny came across and blocked my path. I pulled up, thinking he wanted to ask me something but terrified nevertheless. He grabbed Fill's reins close to her chin, looked up at me and said, "*What did you think you were doing the other day?*" I did not have a clue what he was talking about and questioned what he meant. 'He continued, "*I was coming along in my truck and this* (indicating Fill) *reared right up in front of me!*" By now I was really scared but managed to say, "*I think she was just a bit frightened by the truck and shied to the side of the road.*" "*So it was her fault was it?*" he smirked. "*I don't know,*" I said, "*That is just what happened*" Next thing, he laid off and kicked poor Fill squarely in the belly with his boot. I burst into tears and rode home, vowing to one day get even with the coward. My wish was granted years later after I married. I was running a local dance and had the job of announcing each dance. To my right and slightly behind me sat Tiny Maxwell. As I called one of the dances, he shouted sneeringly, "*Why don't you make a bloody row?*" This was the opening I needed. I swung round furiously and proceeded to remind him of the time he had kicked my pony. I continued, "*You had better keep a button on your lip from now on Tiny because it'll only take one word from you to make me pay you back for that incident - with interest!*" He sheepishly lowered his eyes and never uttered a sound. At last I felt as though I had justified my inability to protect Fill from this lowlife bully. I was very particular about who rode my pony and never lent her to anyone outside the family. Bill had no interest in riding but Les borrowed her from time to time, especially after he started a job.

By now we were selling fish around the area and Fill proved invaluable for carrying them. People placed orders with me as I travelled round from farm to farm. We sold them for one shilling and sixpence a dozen. Most took a shilling's worth and these became standing orders. Though not always able to guarantee delivery we usually managed during the week to catch enough to fill the requirements. Mum wrapped and tied the orders in parcels which were labelled and put into sugar bags. There were groupies (as we called them), that became favourites with me. They would not let me leave without staying for a cup of tea and something to eat. A few were not as generous and so were dealt with politely but swiftly. Clothes never worried me at all and in all weathers I mostly wore just shorts and a singlet. I became known as the local weathercock by my customers because I developed a talent for predicting the weather up to three days in advance. Wherever I visited, the occupants would say, "*And what's the weather going to be like Pud?* Rarely was I wrong but in those days it was a lot easier than it is today. I suppose pollution and interference with the atmosphere has made forecasting a lot more difficult for those of us who like to do it without the aid of technology.

I had Fill up until the time I left the district which was when I was in my nineteenth year. She had a new foal with her then. A chap called Millstone asked if he could take her. I agreed to let him have Fill, the foal, saddle and bridle on one condition - he was to give them a good home, always take care of them and never show any cruelty towards them whatsoever. He agreed to the conditions and made me a promise to do as I had asked. With regret, I said goodbye to my faithful filly and handed her to her new owner. I never saw Fill again but when I returned to the district after World War II, a lapse of about fifteen years, Ernie Gale told me if I'd arrived six months earlier I would have seen her. She had stayed with Mr Millstone until he left the district, had two or three foals in the meantime and when no one wanted her, had been turned out with the brumbies. She lived the rest of her life in the hills, roaming free with her mates - a fitting end, I thought, for a beautiful animal.

...Chapter 5

As I have already briefly mentioned, we had started fishing on the Blackwood. Before that we bought fish from a chap called Wall who was the first group settler to net the river. About twelve months after arriving on the block we were given a small boat by the owner of the farm from which Fill came. The boat was eight to nine feet long, narrow and called "Bluebell". We bought sixty yards of net and proceeded through trial and error to catch a feed of fish. I remember the first time we put our net in the water. It was about four in the afternoon. Bill was on the oars and dad was feeding the net out from the back of the boat. The rest of us were watching from the shore. As the net hit the water, so the fish hit the net. We all jumped and screamed with excitement at the spectacle of water splashing and fish jumping and flashing in the sunlight.

Most of the fishing in the early stages was done by setting the net in the evening and then pulling it the next morning. As we improved we bought a longer hauling net. It was made of cotton and came in a bundle complete with corks, leads, ropes and twine. Firstly the ropes had to be stretched to get all the kinks out of them. Then the net was hung. The ropes, with corks or leads threaded at regular intervals, were attached to the top and bottom of the net with the twine. There was an art to this process which we perfected as time went by. My mother, always ready to try anything, often hung the nets for us. To prevent the cotton rotting in the water, we tanned the nets in forty four gallon drums. Gum was collected from the redgum trees by cutting wedges into the sides of them and placing tins under the cuts. Often the gum would spurt out into the tins but most times it was congealed in lumps on the bark and this could be collected in bags. It was a hard job as a lot of gum was needed to fill the drums. The next step was to light fires under the forty fours, boil the gum, then drop the nets into it. Once tanned, the nets were spread over rails to dry.

Bill, Les, dad and I worked all day on the farm, hauling logs and clearing land. Often we were still firing and stoking fires till one in the morning but weather permitting, we sometimes decided to go fishing instead and would start well after sundown. Les usually stayed behind and with mum, took care of the milking. We took some milk, sugar, tea, a billy and a bit of tucker to sustain us through the night. Now and then, Bill or I grilled some fish on the banks of the river if we had time. Generally we hauled nets from around midnight till two o'clock in the morning. If during that period we found ourselves near the spot where we normally camped for a sleep, we put dad off at the landing, then continued fishing while he prepared a fire. He always carried a hurricane lamp and piece of cloth in his pocket. After gathering wood, he poured a drop of kerosene from the lamp onto the rag, lit it and set it beneath the wood. Some nights were pretty rough where it would have been difficult to start a fire with matches so the rag always assured success on the first attempt.

On one occasion Les and I set off in the Bluebell to try our luck with our net. As we headed for the channel we saw a boat about twenty feet long anchored there with another smaller boat operating nearby. Being very curious about anything different happening in our neighbourhood, we rowed over towards the smaller boat where all the action seemed to be taking place. Two young fellows stood in the water at the rear of the boat, hauling aboard a net full of mullet and pilchard. As they worked we saw them tossing quite a lot of fish back into the water. Watching them from the other end were two other chaps, one a massive man called Alby Smith and the other, his partner Clanes. We learnt they were from Busselton and that they towed the boats down occasionally to fish the river. We had only been there a few minutes when Alby said, *"Would you like some fish lads?"* Would we! This was manna from heaven. We pulled our boat alongside theirs and they proceeded to throw a bundle of beautiful fish into our boat. Having hauled all their gear there wasn't a great deal of room left in their boat so Alby said, *"You could take me back to the other boat, couldn't you lads?"* "Oh, yes, definitely," we enthusiastically replied, never doubting for one minute that poor little Bluebell would cope with the extra weight. Alby sat at the rear while Les and I handled the oars. Somehow we managed - with very little freeboard

– to make our way across to the mother boat. Our eyes widened with delight at the sight that greeted us. The whole length of the boat up to the height of the seats was covered in huge salmon trout. As Alby climbed aboard he said, "*Hold your boat there a second and I'll give you a feed of these.*" He then popped two or three dozen on top of his previous donation. We thanked him profusely and made our way home, feeling on top of the world. I never forgot his generosity and have always tried to follow his example. Over the years I have given thousands of pounds of fish away and still, to this day, supply friends and family whenever I can.

Around this time we acquired another boat. Bill and I set the net one night across the river at a spot we called simply the "Duck Peg". Next morning we were up and on our way well before daybreak so it was still dark when we hauled the net containing a few fish onto the Bluebell. Rowing home, Bill caught an oar in something. He said "*I think there's a net here Pud.*" Sitting at the rear of the boat, I leaned over and felt around in the water. Sure enough it was a net and hanging from it were quite a lot of large bream and mullet. Deciding it might be a good idea to swell our supplies a little I busily started plucking. With about a dozen fish in the boat, Bill suddenly whispered, "*Here comes somebody.*" Quickly I let the net go as Bill pulled away and headed homeward. Next moment, a boat loomed out of the half light. It seemed to move like lightning, sleek and beautiful in the water. On the oars was a chap (we learned later) called Nick Soulas and sitting at the back was his father-in-law. Nick gave a yell and we answered. He drew his boat alongside ours and said, "*Haf you seen a net?*" in a strong foreign accent. "*No, no,*" we replied innocently. "*We haven't seen a net.*"

"*Oh,*" he exclaimed, "*Ve come from Bunbury last night to Vest Bay Creek. Ve arrive late but I vant to put a bit of net in vater, so I come and set, but not sure vere.*" We later discovered that the "bit" of net stretched from one side of the river to the other, more gear than we had ever seen. He pulled out a packet of tailor made Capstan cigarettes, offered us one and introduced himself and the old chap. We thought it was Christmas sitting there puffing contentedly as we talked for a while. Weeks later they came again and found out from where we were operating. Making contact, Nick asked if we'd mind them using our landing and also if we'd cart their fish to the siding. "*No worries,*" we said, "*We'll do that for you.*" The father-in-law was quite old but strong as an ox. He carted sixty to eighty pound boxes, one at a time, on his shoulder from river to the house, no mean feat for a man half his age. On each of their visits, we examined and admired their boat. It was solid, superbly crafted and fast Several weeks passed. During half time at a soccer match, a truck drove up with Nick and his father-in-law in front. By this stage I had become very close to Nick and was very pleased to see him. He drew me aside and said, "*Listen, vould you like to look after my boaty?*" "*Oh yes,*" I replied. "*I'd love to look after it.*" "*Ve are going back today and I don't vish to take the boaty with me. Ve'll be back next year. You can use it till then.*" I could not believe it. It was like winning charities. We became the pride of the Blackwood.

As the time drew nearer to Nick's return we all felt rather sad at the thought of making do with the little Bluebell once more. He arrived and I asked him when he wanted to pick up his boat. "*Oh,*" he said, "*I brought another boaty down. You can keep that vun.*" It's hard to describe how we felt at that moment. A new world had opened up, and to be given such a wonderful craft without any cost gave us a head start straight away. To show our appreciation, we named her "Nicky". The first big haul we caught in her occurred when I was thirteen and was probably the point at which we considered ourselves professionals. Dad, Bill and I hauled nets till about four in the morning. Our efforts had only produced under a box of fish when we pulled into the shore for a sleep. Dad lit a fire and boiled the billy. We ate our grub, drank a mug of steaming tea, then collapsed into a dead sleep. It was sunup when we woke. We decided to put a shot in at Rocky Point - always a sure fire place to catch a feed. But not this morning. One flounder was the grand total of the catch. By now Bill was completely fed up. He announced that he wanted to give up and go home. I, on the other hand, hated the thought of stopping after such little reward. "*How about we cruise over to Piggy Island?*" I suggested. "*We might just see something there.*" Bill flew straight into me and shouted, "*No way! We're going home. I've had enough! We've worked all night and got nothing to show for it.*" Then a voice came from behind me. "*I think it might be a good idea boy!*" My father, as always, backed me up. Bill said sulkily, "*Well, you can bloody well row because there's no way I'm going to!*" I set off for the island while Bill and dad sat fore and aft of the boat. Immediately they were asleep. We were usually so tired that we slept whenever we had the chance. I could tell when dad dropped off because his pipe would fall from his mouth and hit the floor of the boat. As I rowed past the bank near Piggy Island, I saw two big pilchard lift out of the water. The moment I saw them, I quickly woke dad and said, "*Hop out dad and grab the peg.*" Dad was out of the boat like a rocket while Bill slept blissfully on, still sitting erect on the seat. I had about a quarter of the net run when Bill woke. *"What the hell are you shooting here for?"* All I replied was, *"You'll see in a minute."* The next thing the pilchard hit the net and Bill came alive. The water boiled as we closed the net round the catch. We realised we could not unmesh them all where we were, so we hauled the net, fish and all onto "Nicky" and awkwardly rowed home. As it was we filled the boat and we could easily have filled a second one if we'd had double the amount of net. Arriving at the landing the word quickly went around and we soon had some helpers. Three chaps who owned a small cockleshell of a boat and thought the fishing game was easy had tried all night with little result. Actually they were pretty hopeless fishermen but nice blokes and willing to lend a hand. Mum and Les joined them and together we stripped the net and carted the fish in bags to the house, an uphill trek of about four hundred yards. There they were washed and boxed ready for market. Shortly after I'd started school, a train service began linking Busselton to Augusta, which enabled us to send fish to the Perth markets by rail. We rewarded our three helpers with a couple of boxes of fish for which they were very grateful. That haul netted us just twenty quid and with pilchard at about sixpence a pound, the catch must have been approximately eight hundred pounds in weight.

...Chapter 6

As with the fishing, learning by trial and error, we managed to build a hay shed and stockyards. We weren't satisfied with anything less than perfection. Les, Bill and I often walked miles through the bush searching for the perfect tree to provide a railing or post. Each one was free of knot holes and when stripped of bark looked flawless. Many had to be carried by the three of us back to the house. We were very proud of our efforts but decided to enlist the help of contractors to erect a cowshed and dairy. We watched with great interest as the cement floor was laid, the first time we had ever seen the process. Carpenters followed and soon we owned two sturdy buildings. With the installation of a separator, we gathered cream which was sent by rail to the butter factory. Years later, a truck travelled from farm to farm collecting the cream cans, thus saving us the effort of delivering them to the railway siding.

Sometimes stray cattle wandered onto the farm.

They had been left to fatten up in the bush before being rounded up and sold. One steer I remember well had rickets from eating a certain type of palm. Consequently its rear quarters had a mind of their own and swayed crookedly as it moved. Another manifestation of the disease is horns that drop over the eyes of the cattle. This steer had one droopy horn and one that was long, sharp and perfect. Anyway, dad said to me, "*Listen boy, you better get that steer off the property*". Pasture was pretty limited and we couldn't afford to feed extra mouths. I set off on an angle across the paddock and gave the steer a scare to get it moving. Despite the lack of coordination in its back legs, it could still really move. As I gained on it is stopped suddenly, swung its rear quarters round and headed straight for me. I left the ground and took off like a rocket. By the time I reached the house I was quite distressed and shaken. Dad asked, "*What's the matter boy? Have you got that steer out yet?*" "*No fear I haven't,*" I replied. "*What's wrong then?*" he asked. "*It'll go for you!*" I exclaimed. With that dad burst into laughter and said, "*Good God! I've never heard the likes. Fancy being frightened of a damned old rickety steer like that.*" "*I'll bet you're not game to go and get it out,*" I said indignantly. Laughing, he wandered towards the paddock. Knowing a drama was about to unfold, I followed apprehensively. Stopping near a ring barked tree, dad picked up a bit of a stick, more for something to hold than use, and headed towards the steer. He was about ten feet from it when it let out a bellow and charged. Luckily there was a fairly big tree nearby to which dad headed at about ninety miles an hour. As he ran round the base the steer followed, throwing its back legs out and keeping its good horn about six inches from dad's behind. In the meantime I'm panicking because I'd positioned Dave and Harry at one of the gates leading to the bush. I'd told them to make sure the steer went through the correct gate and not let it into our bush paddock. Knowing that at any time the steer might head in their direction, I took off to warn them. This saved the day for dad because when the steer spotted me racing past, it stopped chasing dad and gave him a breather. Having made sure Dave and Harry were safe I returned to find dad in the house yard. He had managed to sneak away and duck from tree to tree back to the house. He was pretty exhausted and not half as happy as he'd been before. I was still upset at the thought that something might have happened to my father. As we stood there panting, brother Bill strolled out. *"What's going on?"* he asked. By now the steer had wandered to the yards. *"That rickety steer,"* said dad, indicating the beast, *"By God, it'll go you."* *"That old thing,"* smirked Bill, *"What a joke! Don't tell me you're frightened of that?"* *"I'll bet you're not game to go and drive it out of there!"* said dad. The steer had made its way through the solid railed yards and into a little chute at one end. Casually Bill grabbed a home made hockey stick lying nearby. We made them from peppermint trees. This one was well seasoned and hard as a rock. Off he strolled, straight into the chute. The steer obediently turned and staggered past him without so much as a glance and went to a corner of the yard near the haystack where it was once again trapped. This time, it decided the boy had to go. Letting out a roar, it charged. To his credit Bill stood his ground. As the animal neared him Bill laid off with the stick and hit the steer fair on the side of its head, almost lifting if from the ground. Bill jumped through the rails to safety as the steer landed on its feet and proceeded to charge the rails over and over again. One more defeated foe retreated to the house yard. We decided to let it find its own way out. Eventually it wandered into another paddock. Dad said the only thing to do was shoot it. We owned a .44 rifle but only one bullet. Bill was a crack shot so he was given the job. Together he and I made our way across the paddock using the trees for cover. I stayed well back as he crept within range. His nerves must have been shaken because he missed the mark. With no more bullets and none of us game to front the sod, we closed off the gates to the homestead leaving only the one to the bush open. Next day it was gone. I saw it several times after that when I was on my pony. It had joined up with a few mates and seemed quite healthy and content. I made sure I stayed right out of its way, even with the security of Fill beneath me.

There was an old sow we had, called Dora. She had farrowed many times in the yard but on one occasion when she was nearly due, we let her out for a ramble not realising just how close to farrowing she was. Next morning when she didn't turn up at the yard we went for the big search and Les and I found her in the swamp surrounded by piglets. When we tried to approach her she charged us so we thought better of it and went back to the house to report our find. I said to dad, *"She's not very happy if you go near. She's got a lot of pigs with her. We tried to count them but couldn't sort them out."* In fact it turned out she had sixteen. Dad seemed unconcerned and said he'd go down and see what he could do. He put on a big pair of hob nailed boots which he always wore whenever he went outside but he never bothered to tie the laces. We trailed along behind him as he headed for the swamp. When he reached it he casually bowled up to old Dora with the intention of collecting the piglets and driving them and Dora back to the yard. But Dora was having none of it. She sprang to her feet and charged straight at dad. Dad started to run but as she gained on him he decided to turn and front her. As her jaws opened dad let fly with a kick. His boot went in her mouth and stayed there. Having always worn shoes, his feet were very tender and the swamp was fill of stakes and dry rough ground. The sight of dad hopping about yelping each time he took a step on his bare foot should have made us collapse laughing but we always felt concerned when he was in trouble - such was our love for him. He made his way safely out of the swamp and hobbled home. The boot was retrieved later. We waited till Dora had suckled her young, then took her a feed. Luring her with the food we grabbed the piglets and carried them home. Dora followed as meekly as a lamb. The pig yard was covered in sleepers to keep it clean. Often they were overturned by the pigs rooting around with their noses. The sad part of this story is that silly old Dora killed eight of her young by crushing them under a sleeper.

With the farm ticking along nicely we spent more time on the river. Sometimes we fished all day and most of the night. Whenever we took a break we literally fell with bags held in front of us onto the rushes and immediately were asleep. During winter the water was so cold we almost froze and it took ages beside a fire for us to thaw out. Sleeping soaked to the skin, we were oblivious to everything until the time came to rise and head back onto the river. We loved it despite the cold, the tiredness and our aching backs. As time passed we grew to know the river well, giving names such as Hungry Basin, Turnwood, Turner's Point, Scott Basin and Rocky

Point to our favourite spots for catching fish. By standing on a seat in the boat and watching the water closely we learned the different movements that fish make in the water and became very adept at spotting schools of whiting, mullet, bream and pilchard.

For recreation, Bill, Les and I joined the local soccer team in Kudardup. There were several other teams from as far away as Margaret River and the rivalry was great. Bill played right full back, Les outside right and I played right half back so the Challis brothers covered most of the right side of the field. Unlike today, body contact was allowed and it was a very rough and tumble game, a cross between rugby and Australian rules with a bit of soccer thrown in. Shoulders were used freely to flatten opponents.

I remember three brothers who played for Augusta - Morty, Des and Walter Ewing. They were all big men and formidable on the field. Being hit by one of them was like running into a brick wall but you either learnt to take it or otherwise not play. Admittedly, I gave as good as I got and at fifteen made it into the top team. Actual fighting during a match was rare. Instead any differences were sorted out after the game was over. These bouts were popular and drew a big following - women included. Once all was settled, the ladies served tea, sandwiches and cakes as though nothing had happened.

Two men, Bert and Frank Flanagan belonged to our team. They were like chalk and cheese. Frank was a gentleman player whereas "Dirty Berty", as we called him, was a completely different kettle of fish. Both were valued team members. Somewhere along the line they palled up with the Ewing boys who just happened to have a couple of attractive sisters, and were eventually kidded into playing for Augusta. This news almost caused a riot in our camp and we threatened to do all sorts of things when next we met them on the field. The first few encounters ended with them hammering the daylights out of us. Dirty Berty loved taunting the opposition. He'd clap his hands when we were penalised and niggle us with snide comments. It had been okay when he was on our side but now it was like a red rag to a bull. This particular day, Augusta came to play us at Kudardup. Our coach, "Squeaky" Hall, an ex-professional soccer player, had held a meeting during the week and drummed into us the importance of winning this match. We were fired up and ready to give it our best shot. When their team arrived in an old bus, we watched as they took to the field for a warm up. To us they looked smug and confident, ready to thrash us once again. The game started. Everything went right for us and by half time we were two goals to nil. Mr Hall gave us a pep talk. He said, *"Now lads, make certain your defence is solid. You've got two goals on the board and all you've got to do is stop them breaking through your defence."* Although we still doubted our ability to win, we entered the arena with renewed vigour. The dream run continued. We managed to kick another two goals in the second half and kept Augusta scoreless. More than the thrill of winning was the satisfaction of seeing Dirty Berty and the Ewing boys leaving the field with their tails between their legs. We made certain they did not hear the last of it for weeks to come.

...Chapter 7

Work on the farm still took priority over fishing and as the years passed, our property became something of a model farm. We were all sticklers for doing jobs properly. One hundred and seventy five fruit trees planted in the orchard stood in straight, evenly spaced rows. Every type of vegetable grew in well laid out plots. Fences were constantly maintained and new ones erected as more land was cleared. I often took my two younger brothers, Harry and David, with me when I slashed new undergrowth. Their job consisted of picking up bark and sticks. David was never a problem and happily plodded along but it took a lot for me to keep Harry going. He was very cunning and used the need to go to the toilet often as an excuse to shirk his work. One time when he was about eight or nine, he tried my patience once too often. In front of our house, towards the river, we had paddocks we called the "flats". Tall clover grew on them and it was

Bill's job to drive the horses behind which was dragged a mower. Dad kept an eye on the mower whilst the rest of us walked ahead looking for sticks or anything that might catch in the blades. Harry as usual was trying a disappearing act. I stormed over and started in on him. He moaned that he was crook - his stomach hurt. I yelled at him, "*Yeah, I'll bet you're crook.*" Just then dad strolled over and asked. "*What's wrong with Harry?*" "*He reckons he's crook,*" I replied, "*But I know how sick he is. He doesn't want to pick up any bark and sticks. I know what's wrong with him.*" I left dad bent over Harry who must have put on a very convincing show because the next thing dad picked him up and proceeded to carry him home, an uphill walk of several hundred yards. I watched in disbelief. When he returned he said to me, "*There's no doubt about it. That boy was crook alright,*" I said, "*Look, you'll see how sick he is when we go home for lunch.*" "*Oh!*" answered dad quickly, "*He went straight to bed. He really is ill.*"

Time came for lunch. Bill unhitched the horses while dad and I wandered up the hill. When we got to within thirty or forty yards of the house I said, "*Listen a minute.*" From the yard came the screams and yells of the younger kids at play and loudest of all were Harry's. Dad was absolutely shocked. He recovered enough to say, "*Well, he must have put one over me.*" And that was an end to it. Such was my father. We nicknamed Harry "Springs" because he seemed to bounce from one disaster to another. Once he fell down a well, another time he fell out of a window onto the side of a crosscut saw. He seemed to be always in trouble of some kind. Luckily, mum was very good at first aid and any injuries were dealt with utmost efficiency.

75 QUID AND AN AXE

In the evenings if we weren't too dog tired, we sometimes played whist or other card games. My mother had acquired a melodeon from somewhere. It was like a small accordion and I took great interest in it. By now Bill and Les were allowed to attend the local dances. I did not worry until I reached the age where it should have been my turn to go. For some reason unknown to me I was overlooked and Winnie was taken instead. This caused me a great deal of grief and I cried on the night she went with her brothers and mother. My dear old dad quietly said to me, "*Don't you worry boy, don't you worry. You'll be alright. Let them go. We'll be okay.*" Together we occupied the evening checking the possum snares and setting the net.

From then on I looked forward to having my father to myself. On blustery cold nights we lit the open fire, had a treat of boiled eggs or suchlike and then I picked out tunes on the melodeon. My first effort was a song called "Now The Day Is Over". I played it so many times it was a wonder my dad didn't announce, "*And now the tune is over - I hope!*" But he was very patient and gave me lots of encouragement saying, "*By gee, that was good boy!*" He suggested other songs for me to try which I eventually managed to play with some degree of fluency. I will always be grateful to my father for the start he gave me on that instrument. Years later I progressed to the button accordion and still derive a great deal of pleasure from entertaining anyone who cares to listen. Occasionally dad serenaded the whole family with a large repertoire of songs. He had a good voice and we enjoyed listening without interruption in front of the fire, lying on a big rag rug that mum had made. One song I remember well was "The Miner's Dream of Home". At every New Year's

Eve dance for years and years, dad was requested to sing the old year out and the new one in.

Not long after Winnie started attending dances I was finally allowed to go. I think a word from dad on how upset I had been may have softened my mother. She bought me some pants and a shirt but no shoes so I happily went barefoot. I learned to dance by following the steps of any girl or lady who asked me. The "band" consisted of a piano, sometimes accompanied by accordions and later on a set of drums. More often than not we walked the three miles to the dance, but now and then we took the horse and cart. It was always a wonderful night out. Everyone mixed and danced with each other and the atmosphere was one of friendship and camaraderie. Wherever I went, I always wore a hat and took great pride in it. Everyone, women and men alike, wore them as part of their dress.

When I was fourteen, I saw an advertisement for hats in the newspaper. They were very reasonably priced and so I decided to save for one. I gathered wood for Mrs Fisher at threepence a time, did odd jobs for others and slowly my cache grew. Soon I had gathered enough pennies together to pay for a money order, stamp and envelope. Anxiously I waited as the days passed. On the big day I went to collect the mail, I was so excited I nearly fell out of my saddle. Sure enough a box was there at the post office. I knew without checking that it was my hat but decided to wait till I got home to open it so I could skite a bit in front of the others. Arriving home I unsaddled the horse, then clutching my precious parcel I marched proudly into the house. Everyone gathered round to watch the unveiling. As I opened the lid I gazed in shock at the contents. There sat a little Charlie

Chaplin bowler. Reluctantly I placed it on my head. It looked like a pimple on a pumpkin. My sympathetic siblings cried with laughter, rolling around on the floor in hysterics. Me - I stood, hat on head, with tears rolling down my cheeks. It was the first and last time the bowler was worn and definitely the last time I answered any advertisements.

Any money I earned from snaring and trapping went to my mother. It wasn't until I started going to the local dances, held about once a month, that I was allowed the entrance fee of one shilling. The Kudardup store, owned by Mr Hillier, was always open as he lived on the premises. It was like a magnet to the youngsters attending the dance just up the road. P.K. chewing gum - very popular in those days - could be purchased for a penny and a packet of cigarettes cost sixpence. One night temptation got the better of me and I spent threepence of my shilling. When I reached the door of the school I made up some elaborate excuse about losing the coin in the bush but it did not wash with the doorman and I was refused entry. Outside I ran into a chap called Jack Beard. He was a humorous sort of bloke and when I approached him for the loan of threepence he generously gave me a shilling. I promised to return the ninepence change inside the hall but he told me not to worry until I had the full amount. Time ambled on and I found it impossible to raise the money. Several dances later I made the fatal mistake of repeating my previous escapade and again spent threepence from my entrance fee. There was no way I could request another loan from Jack Beard, being already deeply in his debt, so I asked a chap named Bill Pratt. To my surprise he handed over two shillings with the same conditions of payment as Jack. Now I owed three shillings. That debt stood for many years. Unfortunately I was never able to pay Bill as he was killed during the war but one day in the fifties when I was bulldozing my property, a chap came walking across the paddock towards me. I sat there trying to figure out who he was. It turned out to be Jack Beard. Climbing down from the dozer I shook his hand and invited him home for a cup of tea. As we sat reminiscing I said, "*Jack, I'm in your debt mate.*" "*How do you mean, in my debt?*" he asked. "*Well,*" I replied, "*I owe you a shilling.*" He had no idea what I was talking about and even after I explained the whole story he still couldn't recall the incident. "*I'm quite willing to pay you back,*" I said, "*And there should be a bit of interest on it by now.*" He laughed and assured me the debt was clear.

...Chapter 8

The biggest handicap in fishing was the lack of ice. There were no freezers or fridges on the farm, so block ice was sent from Perth packed in bags, then straw. It came from Langfords who owned the markets. Each blocked weighed about a hundred weight which is the equivalent of one hundred and twelve pounds. On hot days, when we needed it most, the blocks arrived up to half their size. As soon as we got them home, we hung them in the well where the air was much cooler. This kept them reasonably intact until we washed and boxed our catch. After breaking the ice over the fish, hessian was tacked over the top and the boxes taken to the siding. The trip to Perth took nineteen hours which meant the product was not altogether fresh when it reached its destination. Winter was better but weather often prevented us from dropping a net for a week or more at a time. On Sunday ice was not available. Fish caught on those days went to market regardless. Fish prices were very low. Good fish like whiting and mullet fetched around sixpence a pound. Pilchard dropped at one point to twopence a pound. After taking out freight charges and commission we were left with very little at the end. Sleep was a treasured commodity when fishing and we snatched every opportunity to close our eyes. Sometimes if we were lucky, we completed two or three hauls by midnight, leaving us three or four hours to bed down by a campfire. If when we returned home mum did not have breakfast ready, I would race onto the verandah, strip off my wet clothes and hit the cot for another half hour. I usually got a serve from my mother for not being ready for breakfast but it was worth it just to lie on that warm, sun soaked mattress. After eating it was back to work on the farm.

...Chapter 9

There were now nine children in the family. The eighth was Harold. He was born in Karridale on Centenary Day. The matron wanted to name him Centenary but mum decided on Harold, even though we already had a Harry in the family! She allowed the matron to use Centenary for his middle name but the matron went all the way and wrote in Harold Centenary Day Challis. As a toddler, he was a funny little chap. Where I hated wearing shoes, he hated wearing pants and usually got around with a singlet and bare bottom. There was a big passionfruit vine growing up the side of the house and Harold loved picking the ripe fruit. He climbed onto a cage, in which we grew seedlings, to reach the vine. Several times I caught him and each time the same thing happened. I sneaked up and said, *"What are you doing there?"* With a start, he jumped down, turned and pointing up said, *"Pashy, pashy, pashy."* As soon as I looked up at the vine he dashed off and the last thing I saw was a bare bottom disappearing around the tank at the corner of the house. I always played along with him just to watch his exit. Margaret was born two years later, also at Karridale. Not long after, my parents were dealt a crushing blow.

The farm looked a picture. Of the one hundred and sixty five acres we had been allotted, one hundred and five were under pasture with the rest well on the way to being cleared. We owed about seventy five pounds in interest on our repayments but had set aside eight heifers which, when sold, we thought would cover that amount. One day, Bill Hitchmough visited and said to dad, "*I believe you're pulling out Fred?*" "*What do you mean, Bill?*" asked dad. *It's in the paper,*" he said, "*It says you're being evicted.*" Dad was absolutely shocked to hear this news and had no idea what was meant by it. Sure enough, we got the notice to move out. Although devastated and wondering how this could happen after nine years of hard slog, my parents took it on the chin and within a fortnight left on the train for Perth.

The new owners, Mr Logan, his wife and son Dick moved in. Les, Bill and I stayed to find work. Bill moved into an abandoned house on the block next door. It had originally been erected in Augusta, but when the owners moved to the bush, they had had the house dismantled and shifted. The walls were lined with hessian. Bill was a hopeless bachelor. Anything he opened or used for eating was piled on the table and sometimes it was difficult to see him over the debris. He earned a few bob trapping possums.

Les jumped the rattlers (trains) and spent seven months moving around the state, working wherever he could find it. I was offered a job by Dick at seventeen and sixpence a week plus keep. It was from him, a few weeks later, I heard the story of why we lost the farm. Dick and his parents occasionally visited Flinders Bay for holidays. He was a carpenter who one day told his father he'd like to have a go at pulling teats instead of knocking nails. Mr Logan said, "*Well what's to stop you? If you want to give it a try we'll see about buying a farm.*" They saw the local supervisor and made it quite clear they wanted to see a really good property. Immediately the supervisor said he knew one of the show pieces from Busselton down. I recall plainly the day Dick and his father arrived. Following introductions and the reason for the visit, dad, being extremely proud of his holding, was only too happy to show them around. I remember watching them leave in an almost brand new brown A Ford car. According to Dick, the moment they began to move off, the supervisor said to him, "*Well, what did you think of that place?*" Dick replied, "*I don't want to see any more if I can get that property.*" To which the supervisor answered, "*There's nothing stopping you. All you have to do is pay the outstanding interest and three hundred pounds off the principal and its all yours.*" This was done in due course and the farm changed hands. The Logans bought a few odds and ends from my father before he left but never a word was mentioned about the changeover. Dad just put it down to the interest being in arrears and held no grudge towards the new owners. When my mother went to see Mr Pullen who was the top man in the agricultural bank in Perth and explained about the interest he was very sympathetic and said if the farm was vacant and hadn't been purchased privately, he would have us back there immediately. He said it was too late for that now but if my parents wanted to choose a farm anywhere else he would make sure they got it. They remained in Perth for about twelve months before moving to Northcliffe but the heart had gone out of my father. The block was covered in big karri trees and was very run down and he just did not have the incentive to start again.

Meanwhile, I was quite happy that I had been offered a job with such good pay. The Logans knew nothing about farming so it was up to me to show them the ropes. Old Mrs Logan was a darling woman. We thought the world of each other and she treated me like a son. Food was plentiful and delicious. A new family called the Cosgroves set up camp near where Bill lived. I met and liked them very much. Being fully employed on the farm I had little time for fishing so I gave the boat and nets to the Cosgroves on condition I could use them if ever I found a spare moment. Dick Logan had a girlfriend called Nora who visited now and then. She was very pretty and a lovely girl with it. I was a bit envious and thought how lucky he was. They married later and eventually had four sons.

Time passed - perhaps six to eight months. Les returned and moved in with Bill. He was like me - meticulously neat. In one day he had the shack looking like a palace. One night the three of us went fishing. It was freezing and by the time we came in we were saturated and chilled to the bone: Reaching the house I said, "*I don't know about you, but I'm having a cuppa before I hit the sack.*" "*I'll be in that,*" said Les. We lit the open fire and stacked it well to get the water boiling. Bill said, "*I'm not waiting up,*" and retired to his bed. Les and I stripped off our trousers and settled into canvas deck chairs near the fire to get warm. Almost immediately we dropped off to sleep. Through sheer luck of having undressed, the heat of the roaring fire on my bare skin woke me. I opened my eyes to the sight of the whole wall of the house going up in flames. The old timber was like tinder and the hessian highly inflammable. I yelled, "*Look out, the house is on fire!*" Les, confronted by the wall of flames, froze in his chair. All he could do was scream. Bill came out of the bedroom like a rocket. The only thing we had to hand was a forty four gallon drum of tan, (a mixture of gum and water), which stood just inside the door. Quickly we filled buckets and threw the contents on the fire. We eventually managed to douse the flames but oh what a mess was left. Sticky gum and brown water covered the floor and wall. Throughout the ordeal Les sat glued to his chair unable to move, completely paralysed with fear. It took a while for him to recover from the shock and a lot longer to restore some semblance of order to the house. Not long after the fire Bill and Les left the district to find work.

Back at the Logans, all was fine. Dick and I got along well together. Then one night I sat down to dinner with the family. As the meal progressed I related a true account of some incident on the river. When the story finished Mr Logan made it quite clear that he did not believe a word I had spoken. I, naturally, got a bit hot under the collar and said, "*But this is absolutely true.*" I don't think he was too impressed at being addressed like that by a farmhand. It was normal practice for me to help Mrs Logan with the washing up but this night when the time came, I said to Mr Logan, "*You can do the washing up tonight because I'm not going to!*" Somehow, I feel that was the reason for my subsequent sacking. Only days later I was given a fortnight's notice by Dick, who had already arranged for a mate of mine, Bill Dunn, to take my place. I think the fact that Bill took the job upset me more than the sacking.

...Chapter 10

The day I was given notice, I walked over to the Cosgroves' after work. Mrs Cosgrove said on seeing me, *"Hello! What are you doing here this time of the day?"* "I've got the sack," I replied. *"Well,"* she asked, *"What are you going to do. Have you got another job to go to?"* "No," I answered, *"I've got nowhere to go."* *"Oh! Well,"* she replied matter of factly, *"Don't worry. You can eat here and we'll soon set up a bed for you."* I was very grateful to be offered shelter and readily accepted. Their property was still virgin bush as they had not long arrived. Originally they had been given a block north of Karridale but were, I believe, unable to make a living from it. They decided to move to Kudardup where they thought their sons might make a new start. The sons, Ted and Mick, had helped erect a humpy made from saplings and poles cut from the bush. Then Ted left to work in Kalgoorlie, a mining town nearly four hundred miles east of Perth.

Most of the Cosgroves' income came from the catering Mrs Cosgrove did for the dances. She was a phenomenal cook. How she managed to produce such delicious food under those conditions never ceased to amaze me. After rolling out pastry, she got me to place it on the roof for the night. I suppose this was to keep it cool as there were no refrigerators. A job I relished was helping make lamingtons. She cut large sponges into squares and I had to dunk the cakes into chocolate sauce then roll them in coconut. For every dozen I completed I was allowed one to eat. I thought I would never refuse the chance to consume these delicacies but after coating six or seven dozen, I sometimes had to leave the last couple allotted to me.

Normally at the dances, a cup of tea, sandwich, tart and cake sold for sixpence and it was on the takings from these nights that the Cosgroves existed. They had no idea about fishing so a proposition was put to me. If I fished, with the help of Mick, they would give me part of what I earned. The money meant little to me really. I was happy if I got a smoke, bed, good feed and time on my beloved river. Together, Mick and I and sometimes Mr Cosgrove hauled and set nets to gain a little extra income. One night, having worked from sundown to sunup, we rowed ashore with only three quarters of a box of fish. Sitting over breakfast Mick and I started talking. I said, "*Gee, I wish we had got enough to fill the box,*" which would have amounted to sixty pounds in weight. "Well, how about we go out again." said Mick. "A good idea," I replied. "*We may see nothing but then again, we might pick up enough.*" I rowed the boat towards the front of the old homestead. Along the way, Mick saw fish moving in the shallows and went crook at me for not putting in a shot. Being completely inexperienced at spotting fish, he didn't realise they were tiddlers - far too small to catch with a net. I ignored his mutterings and continued rowing. Suddenly I saw a school of big pilchard. With the excitement I always feel at these moments I said to Mick, "*Now get a peg and be ready to jump out the boat when I say go.*" Sure enough, as soon as I gave the word, Mick hopped into the water and I rowed around the fish. Imagine our delight when we hauled in the net and filled about ten boxes to the brim. The train for Perth left at 1:00 p.m. We had to get the fish to the siding before then. The only way to the house from the river was through muddy, rush filled swamp. Mick and I jogged through the mire carrying the boxes one at a time on our shoulders. Mr Cosgrove owned a sulky - suitable for carrying perhaps one or two boxes but not ten or more. He went over to the Logans' and borrowed their horse and cart. While he was away Mrs Cosgrove rode to the store and purchased thirteen kerosene boxes for seven shillings and sixpence. We didn't have any ice so we just washed the fish and packed them. With time running out I suggested we leave the sealing of the boxes till we reach the siding. If the train was there it would wait for us. Many times before the driver had backed the train if he saw us coming along the track. Billy was the horse attached to the cart and with a bit of encouragement, he took off at a cracking pace. As we reached the last corner before the siding we saw the smoke from the engine in the distance and knew we had failed to make it. Undeterred we swung the horse round and raced back to the Kudardup store. The owner, Bill Hillier, owned a Chevrolet truck. I dashed in and said, "*Look Bill, we've got a load of fish out here and we've just* missed the train. Could you run them to Karridale for us please?" "Well," he replied, "*I'd do it willingly, but go and have a look at my truck.*" Outside round the side of the store stood the vehicle, full to overflowing with goods he had unloaded from the train the night before. There were bags of sugar, flour, wheat, pollard and all manner of things. Quickly I summed up the situation, went back to Mick and said, "*Look, we've got to do something fast.*" Back into the shop I went. "*Bill, if we unload the truck for you, would you run the fish through for us?*" "Sure," replied Bill. "*You get them on and I'll be ready and waiting.*" The bags weighed between fifty and seventy pounds but we, being very fit, tossed them around like feathers. With the truck cleared, we loaded the fish. I rode on the back so that I could nail the bags on the boxes and label them while we travelled. With Bill driving like a madman over a very bumpy road, I bounced around trying to secure the bags with tacks. Luckily the wood was soft, making the job easier. Finally as we pulled into the Karridale siding, we saw the train coming along the line. We had managed to beat it after all we had been through. With a sigh of relief, we loaded our catch and headed for home. I was as happy as a sandboy, looking forward to my pay so that I could buy a suit and a few pieces of clothing - badly needed at this point in time. We were already down twelve and sixpence, what with the price of the boxes and Bill's delivery fee of five shillings, but this did not unduly worry us. We knew we'd cover the overheads and more. Cheques always arrived on the Monday train and we looked forward to it with great excitement.

On the Monday, Mick and I went to Rocky Point to put the nets on the boat. We hung them on railings when not in use, otherwise, if left wet, they tended to rot. We were standing one either side of the boat folding the nets onto a board at the rear when out of the bush emerged Mrs Cosgrove with a huge grin on her face. We immediately stopped working and with joyful anticipation went to meet her. "*Well Pud, how much do you think we made from the fish?*" she asked. Wanting to be conservative and underestimate the amount so that the eventual outcome would be an even greater surprise, I said, "*I reckon, the top end would be about seven or eight quid.*" "*What do you think Mick?*" she questioned. Being a dry witted character he responded cockily, "*Ah... nothing less than a tenner!*" At this Mrs Cosgrove burst into laughter, increasing our hopes to a higher level. "*Well,*" she said, "*You're both wrong. I've had a cheque for five shillings and twopence.*" I felt like I'd been hit by a ton weight. My stomach dropped as I stood there dumbfounded. She continued that on the docket had been written "Fish arrived unfirm". Where we had gone into debt over the sale, someone in Perth was making a healthy profit. But, as was the way, we soon got over it and put it down to experience. I gave up fishing for a while after that episode and managed to make a few bob doing jobs around the district.

 Ted, the son who worked in Kalgoorlie, came home for a visit. Mick was away at his girlfriend's in Forrest Grove. I can't recall ever seeing the two boys together at one time. I don't think there was a lot of love lost between them. Neither of the boys had ever smoked or drank as far as I knew. One night Ted and I decided to go to a dance at Kudardup. I had managed to buy a new pair of trousers of which I was very proud. Dressed to the nines we harnessed the horse, "Lady Offa", to the sulky, hung a hurricane lamp on the axle and away we went. We'd been at the dance for a while when the booze truck arrived. It was the usual practice for the men to congregate outside between dances to have a few drinks. In those days, whenever I got a chance which wasn't very often, I loved to drink port and hardly ever touched beer. The price of a bottle was either two or four shillings. Pooling our resources, a few of us bought one then retired to the shelter of nearby pine trees to demolish it. Ted was still in the hall and even though I knew he didn't drink, I thought it only right to at least ask him to join us. Entering the hall, I singled him out and asked, "*Would you like a drink Ted?*" To my surprise he readily accepted and followed me outside. When his turn came for a swig he certainly made sure he got his share. Once the bottle emptied a collection was again taken and another purchased and so on till, by the end of the evening, three or four had been consumed.

A short distance from the pines stood a huge gum tree. As Ted put his hand out for the last bottle, he started to back pedal. I have never seen anyone reverse so quickly. He travelled all the way to the gum tree before falling over, where he lay, blissfully unconscious. I must have followed his example and collapsed also because I don't remember anything until after we reached home. Apparently our mates had laid Ted on the seat of the sulky with me flat out on the footboard. They lit the lamp, tied the reins back and sent the horse home. My first glimmer of awareness came when Ted said, "*Come on Pud, come on. We're home.*" Staggering out of the sulky we managed between us to unhitch the horse, feed her and reel off to bed. Waking early as usual, I nursed a thumping head - port always had that effect on me. But I put on a great front as I entered the kitchen where Ma

75 QUID AND AN AXE

Cosgrove was preparing breakfast. She asked me about the evening and whether I had enjoyed it. Responding brightly I tucked into my meal, still feeling very much the worse for wear. *"Give Teddy a call, will you Pud? His breakfast will be cold if he doesn't hurry."* I went to where Ted slept and shook him several times without success. Returning to the kitchen, Ma asked, *"Where is Teddy?"* *"Don't know,"* I replied, *"He's a bit lazy getting up this morning. I'll go see again."* This time I shook him awake and whispered, *"Hey listen, your mum is getting pretty concerned about you. You'll let the cat out of the bag if you're not careful. Now you better do something. You've got to get up!"* Slowly he raised himself from the bed, looking very green round the gills. Unable to face breakfast, he wandered off to Rocky Point. I returned once more to the kitchen and on being asked yet again where her boy was I replied, *"Well, he's up. He must have gone for a walk or something."* Accepting this explanation Mrs Cosgrove carried on with her routine and I went to work. During the afternoon, Mr and Mrs Cosgrove left to attend a cricket match at Karridale. It was a Sunday and Ted and I intended fishing that night. Feeling much better, we walked to Rocky Point and started loading the nets. Next thing, through the bush came Mrs Cosgrove, but unlike the time before she did not have a smile on her face. In fact, it was more like a snarl. Pausing, we wondered what was wrong. *"Teddy!"* she commanded. *"Why, what's the matter?"* he asked. *"You were drinking last night!"* In a flash, Ted, being a fiery little customer, raced up and stood almost nose to nose with his mother and demanded, *"Who told you?"* Mrs Cosgrove looked him squarely in the eye and said, *"I'm not telling you Teddy."* *"Well,"* responded Ted, *"If it's a man, I'll knock his block *off and if it's a woman, I'll yank her tongue out!"* This remark really tickled me. I was having a quiet chuckle to myself when the attention shifted in my direction and I received a sobering serve from Ma. Later I realised she held me fully responsible for Ted's drinking even though he was three years older than me. She told me that if ever there was a repeat performance, I would have to leave. Greatly upset by this statement, mainly because I thought the world of the old couple, I resolved to behave myself and not rock the boat. I never let on that Ted had been a willing participant and he, being unaware of the ultimatum placed on me, did not realise he could have set the record straight. So the episode passed, unresolved, into history.

    I was approached by a Mr Pratt who owned a farm near the siding. He said he would give me three pounds a month to erect a fence, a distance of approximately half a mile. I accepted. The walk I took each day to work was a round trip of about eight miles. Firstly I had to clear the fence line which in those days was all done by axe. I followed the railway line for some distance then turned at right angles directly into the path of a large swamp. It was like entering a jungle. I hacked my way through it, heading I hoped in the right direction, until I emerged on the other side onto open plain. Making the final turn at the far corner I found myself heading back into the swamp but this time it was a little easier as some clearing had already been done. With the line ready for fencing my next job was to chop suitable trees for the posts and struts. Once felled, I cut these trees into lengths with a crosscut saw. The same applied to the corner strainer posts but they were of course a lot bigger. Each post was then stripped of bark and holes bored for the wires with a brace and bit. Using the Pratts' horse and snig chain, I laid all the posts along the fence line, then dug all the holes. After burying the posts, I ran the wires and tightened them. Where the fence went nearest the house I constructed a wire gate and installed it between two strainer posts. At Mr Pratt's request, I dug a six foot well in the swamp and built him a woodhouse. I completed all this in two days under a month. Mr Pratt came to me and said, "*Well Pud, you've done a good job. I'll pay you the full three quid as agreed.*"

Occasionally, for a bit of entertainment, the locals corralled some wild brumbies and organised a rodeo. A funnel shaped fence was built leading to a yard into which the horses were driven. Usually an animal was blindfolded to keep it quiet before being let into the paddock with rider on board. Many a time my nether regions hit the ground as I was bounced around and tossed off those fiery animals, but a lot of fun was had and the get togethers were a welcome break from work.

With work becoming scarcer to find I was prepared to take anything offered. Word went around that caretakers were needed on farms that had been abandoned. Life and making a livelihood was so difficult then that some people gave up and walked off their properties, leaving cattle unattended. The pay was three pounds a month and for this the cows had to be milked twice a day, calves fed and the cream taken to the siding. I accepted a job on a farm opposite the school, but boarded with the Berrymans next door. Each morning I walked to my farm, milked, tended the calves and cleaned up, then returned to work for George Berryman to cover the expense of my food and lodging. This way I cleared the three quid a month. A mate, Jack Hitchmough and I liked nothing better than to have a few drinks together. One day he proudly announced that he had a brand new Malvern Star bicycle. We had transport to get to the hotel in Augusta!! Pooling our resources, we came up with about two quid. While I perched on the cross bar, Jack pedalled along the gravel road. When he tired I took over from him and so, by switching places now and then, we eventually reached town. Entering the bar, we glanced over the 'crowd'. Behind the bar stood the proprietor, Harry Staines, drinking with his only customer Scotty Kerr. Both looked like they had consumed quite a few. Scotty was a mechanic and a whiskey drinker. The money he made on the former, he spent on the latter. He beckoned us to join him and offered to buy us a drink. *"Try some whiskey,"* he said jovially. Having never tasted it before we were quite happy to give it a go. One followed another and another till the time ticked round to eleven o'clock - closing time. Scotty worked and lived in a repair shop a short distance from the hotel. He said, *"You boys, come to my place. I've got some tinned sausages. You can have something to eat before you head off home."* By now, we were both pretty weak in the legs, but nevertheless managed to stagger to Scotty's place, wheeling the bike between us. Having eaten the meal, which reacted adversely with my stomach full of whiskey, I left Jack talking to Scotty and went outside where I curled up and went to sleep in the gutter. A short while later Jack shook me awake and said, *"Come on Pud, we've got to get home."* Reluctantly I rose to my feet and took my place on the crossbar. I can honestly say that in the length of about a mile we fell off the bike at least twenty to thirty times. First Jack had a go at pedalling, then me, then him and so on. Each attempt ended with us and the bike flat on the ground. Covered in gravel dust, Jack finally declared, *"Well, what I think is - it's the bloody bike's fault!"* With that, he lifted the bike and thumped it up and down on the ground for several minutes. Again we mounted and tried to make some headway but there was no improvement and again we fell in a heap on the ground. Staggering to his feet, Jack announced, *"There's only one thing wrong. We haven't got the light on."* The lamp on the bike was a lovely chrome carbide one but missing from it was the carbide. Jack reckoned he could get it going with matches and made several futile attempts. When these failed he pulled the lamp from its bracket and smashed it on the road. After riding and crashing a few more times we gave up and started walking, taking turns to wheel the bike. By now, a few hours had passed and gradually we sobered up. Daylight broke as we reached Cosgroves' turnoff. I decided to pay them a visit so I said to Jack, *"You'll be okay now mate. You can ride your bike home on your own."* He agreed and straddled the bike. I looked down at the wheel and said *"Gawd, Jack! The bike's out of shape."* Sure enough, when we lined it up, one wheel stuck out about six inches to the side making it practically impossible to ride. I left Jack to his fate and as I walked away I recalled the initial trip to the hotel and the comment Jack had made several times on the way. We had felt very important as we rode that new bike and every now and then Jack had proudly announced, *"Well, there ain't nothing like having a bloody Malvern Star. Ten bob down and five bob weekly."* The payments stopped abruptly after that outing and the Malvern Star went back to Perth on the train.

...Chapter 11

During his time away my brother Bill found work in the wheat belt but an accident brought him back to the old homestead which the Logans had vacated after they went broke. He lost an eye when a piece of wire pierced it. He was compensated with over three hundred pounds, part of which he used to buy a Don Bradman Chevi Coupe. It was a lovely little car with a dickie seat at the back. Bill asked me to work for him for ten bob a week so I left Berrymans and the caretaking job and shifted back into familiar surroundings. Before actually starting work I took my first break in years and travelled to Northcliffe to see the family. It was my second time on a train since entering Australia. Luckily a chap I know, Ernie Gale, boarded with me at Kudardup and helped me quite a bit. I had to stay overnight in Busselton, catch a train north to Boyanup then another south to Pemberton.

Ernie knew a Scots family in Busselton who

accommodated lodgers. He introduced me to the lovely, jolly lady who ran the place and she took me under her wing. I was very unused to meeting strangers and felt awkward and out of place but after a while I relaxed in the comfortable, friendly atmosphere and started to enjoy myself. Next morning after a hearty breakfast, I boarded the train for Boyanup. My night in Busselton had cost two shillings and sixpence. Arriving in Boyanup I waited for the connection to Pemberton. From the station tea rooms I purchased a pie and a cup of tea. By now I was down to six shillings. My journey continued, eventually terminating in Pemberton at eleven p.m. - the trains were not noted for speed. It had taken about fifteen hours to cover a distance of one hundred and thirty miles. The night was freezing. I had been alone in the carriage for the whole journey and I was chilled to the bone. Outside the countryside was covered in frost. Alighting from the train I asked a couple of other passengers if there was anywhere I could get a bed for the night. The only place they could suggest was the hotel. Pemberton was blacked out by this time so I also asked them for directions. Arriving at the door of the hotel which was dimly lit by a single light, I sat down on the cement steps and wondered what to do. The door was open but I was too scared to venture inside. About an hour passed. I was numb with the cold. Then I saw a chap cross the passage. Like a rocket I ran after him. "*Is there any chance of me getting a bed?*" I inquired. "*Yes,*" he replied. "*I'll fix you up.*" He led me to a room and left. All I'd had since breakfast was a pie. Hungry and freezing I tried to warm myself under the blankets but by morning I was still cold.

The passengers the night before had informed me

that my only chance of transport to Northcliffe would be on a truck that might come from there to pick up goods from the train. I was so worried I'd miss it I left the hotel before breakfast. My suitcase contained a few bits of clothing and an orange. Outside the hotel, I saw a chap and asked, "*Can you tell me how much it costs for a bed?*" He said that he thought it was two shillings and sixpence. Explaining I was in a hurry, I asked if I could leave the money with him, which he accepted. Rushing to the station, I inquired about the truck. "*Well,*" said one bloke, "*Many days there are none from Northcliffe. They only come if there is something for them on the train.*" "*Then how far is it to Northcliffe?*" I asked. "*A little over twenty miles,*" another replied. "*Which road do I take and are there any turnoffs?*" Pointing the way, one said, "*Just keep on that road and it'll lead you straight there.*"

My footwear, a pair of flimsy dancing pumps, were completely unsuitable for long walks but they were all I had. I set off on the gravel road hoping to hitch a ride somewhere along the way. The suitcase was light but awkward to carry so I constantly switched it from shoulder to shoulder, front to back to side, trying to relieve the ache in my arms. Knowing I still had a few bob I resolved to stop at the first building I came to and buy myself a meal. Not far out of Pemberton I saw a farmhouse quite a distance from the road but I decided to pass by as it would only add distance to my walk. On I trudged. The shoes afforded little protection from the gravel and were wearing thinner by the mile. Eventually I reached a bridge beside which stood a house. It was one of the original old homesteads and to me, being aware of class distinction from living in England, I felt it might be too posh for someone of my standing. Instead

75 QUID AND AN AXE

I climbed down by the bridge, had a drink from the river and ate my orange. Continuing, I plodded on to within two miles of Northcliffe without seeing another house or a living soul. By this time it was mid afternoon and I was getting very weary and hungry, having only eaten an orange since the day before. Suddenly I heard the sound of an engine behind me. It was music to my ears. Along the road came a lovely car with one occupant. He pulled up and said, "*Would you like a lift?*" Gratefully, I climbed in next to him. As we motored on, he asked, "*Where have you come from?*" When I said Pemberton, he gasped and said, "*Good God, have you walked all the way? What time did you start?*" "*Pretty early,*" I replied. "*But where did you come from in town?*" he persisted. When I told him about the hotel, he realised who I was and said, "*I'm the proprietor of the hotel. You gave the money for your room to a chap, didn't you? Well, it was really three and sixpence for the bed and if you'd stuck around, you could have had breakfast and a lift all the way with me.*" I offered to pay the extra shilling but he refused to accept it.

We reached Northcliffe and pulled up at a store owned by Ernie Weston. The driver related my story to him and when they discovered I had hardly eaten anything for two days, Ernie immediately took me to the kitchen when a lovely lady called Phyllis Jones made me sandwiches and tea. I savoured every bite. Ernie kindly drove me the remaining five miles to my parent's home, a gesture for which I was very appreciative as my shoes were in tatters.

My arrival and adventure caused little concern to my family. It was just one of those things. My brother Les was at home again and it was good to catch up with him. While separated we had kept in touch by letter. Les had sent me a photo of his latest girlfriend. A couple of times before I had sort of pinched girls from him unintentionally. Being close, Les and I hung around together. If he and his girlfriend of the time had an argument, the girl used me to get back at him. I really had no interest in girls at this stage so they didn't stick around long. When he sent me this particular photo, he wrote that this was the girl of his dreams and that no way would I get her away from him. I wasn't in Northcliffe long when I met Rosina Coe, the girl in question. She lived with her parents on a block nearby. My first impression was of a very pretty girl with lovely dark brown eyes. She was sixteen at the time and I, nineteen. She told me years later that her first impression of me was that I was the ugliest boy she'd ever seen.

...Chapter 12

Les and I got jobs on sustenance which is like working for the dole. We worked two and a half days a week for thirty shillings. Every Sunday we travelled to a tent camp where we remained till Wednesday lunchtime. It was hard manual labour clearing vacant blocks with axes, mattocks and crosscut saws. We bought an old motorbike for fifteen quid to use as transport for work. Naturally we were both keen to ride it and took turns, but for some reason Les just could not get the knack of balancing and like the Malvern Star, we spent most of the time on the ground whenever he was in "control". After several spills and a lot of gravel rash I demanded that I be the only driver in future and Les agreed.

One Wednesday we knocked off work at midday as usual, but hung around for a while having a smoke and chat with the other men. It was about four o'clock when we mounted the bike and headed for home. The boss of sustenance, Mr McKern, drove a type of ute. He was a maniac behind the wheel and hurtled everywhere at top speed. Every day he picked up his little girl from school. This Wednesday we left the camp and reached a part of the road that sloped steeply down a culvert over a creek then turned sharply on the other side round a blind corner. As we neared the creek Mr McKern came flying round the bend and over the culvert. He was on my side of the road. Instantly I knew it was impossible for him to swing his vehicle to the other side of the road without rolling it so I took to the bush. Down the hill we went. The bike cleared the narrow creek, ploughed up the bank and came to rest on the road with both Les and I still seated and completely amazed that we had escaped unscathed. Mr McKern's little girl on the other hand was thrown from the ute when he braked suddenly, but luckily was unhurt. When we walked back to them, Mr McKern was in shock and could hardly speak. He knew that if we had collided both Les and I would have almost certainly been killed. The following Monday at breakfast, all the talk was about our close shave. A few blokes rubbished us and said, "*The boss will have a ticket waiting for you boys!*", meaning we would get the sack. After eating we went to McKerns' house and stood outside waiting for job assignments. The weather was cold and wet. Mr McKern came out of his office and began allotting different tasks. Some men were given ring barking, others sawing or grubbing and so on. As their names were called, the men ambled off to begin work. Finally there were only two left in front of the house - Les and me. We felt like shags on a rock. The last few men to leave turned, grinned and waved goodbye. We stood there waiting for the inevitable. When everyone had disappeared, Mr McKern said seriously, "*Come into *my office."* My stomach churned. Without sustenance, we would be in dire straits. On entering, he sat in his chair and said, *"Well boys, we were very lucky the other day, weren't we!" "Yes, we were,"* we replied in unison. He continued talking about the episode, marvelling at the way I had made the split second decision to go off the road, knowing he could do nothing but stay on the wrong side. Then he said, *"Look, there's a whole lot of produce in the shed that needs sorting out. Would you take care of it?"* Absolutely delighted with such an easy task and one under cover, we readily accepted. That afternoon we were again rubbished by the blokes but this time they called us crawlers and softies. Well satisfied with ourselves, we gave them as good as we got.

Another week we returned to the camp on the Monday morning instead of the usual Sunday afternoon. We were a little over half way when the bike stopped. Knowing nothing about the mechanical side of it, we fiddled around for a while and got it started. On we went, then again it stopped. This happened several times till it gave out completely. Leaving it beside the road, we walked the rest of the way. After work on Wednesday we returned and managed to get the bike going for a short time but finally it died. Between us we pushed the bike home, a distance of about four miles. I took it to a mechanic called Crawford who said he'd take a look at it. He discovered that the engine was completely devoid of oil causing the piston to become so hot it had welded to the rings. I should have known better but in those days such things were new to us and as long as an engine ran, we were happy. He fixed it though and it ran like a bird. We sold it later for three quid.

Les and I joined the local soccer team and gymnasium

that had been set up in an old group house. Included were darts, quoits and other activities. Often Les and I boxed with each other and there was no quarter spared on either side. Usually we joined Rose and her brother Sid to walk to the club. One night on the way home from the gym Sid and I were wandering along yarning ahead of Rose and Les. Suddenly I felt a hand slip under my arm. There was Rose, walking beside me. I didn't say anything to her and continued talking to Sid. As we neared the turn off Sid left us and went on his way. I saw Rose to her gate, said goodnight and departed, thinking nothing more about the incident. Reaching home I went to the verandah where Les and I slept. There I was confronted by my brother. He was furious and in a fighting mood. Although we didn't come to blows I knew that one wrong move from me would have given him the excuse he needed. He tongue lashed me, accusing me of taking his girl. This angered me and I shouted, "*I didn't take your girl. I want nothing to do with her. She came and pinned herself on my arm and I felt I had to walk her home. That's all!*" Satisfied with my explanation, the air cooled and we both settled down. That night saw the end of the relationship between Rose and Les. Whatever happened on the way home must have been more serious than I thought. Rose took up with another chap called Tom Crawford (no relation to the mechanic) who was a sleeper cutter. I really liked Tom to the point that one night he, having fallen into disfavour with Rose and feeling pretty low, I tried to reconcile them. We were at a dance. Rose looked beautiful in a shiny dark green dress. Tom looked glum, sadly watching her from a distance. He and I had a drink together and he asked me to dance with Rose and put in a good word for him. Wanting to oblige I requested the pleasure of her company on the floor. While executing some fancy foot work, I spieled on about Tom's attributes but there was no way I could convince her to resume the romance. I believe she did see him casually for a little while but there was definitely no future for them as a couple. Meanwhile I took up with a girl called Gladys Pratt who was fifteen years old.

Les and I managed between us to buy a van. It was a Stevens of which little is known today. It had two separate seats in the front and an enormous engine. We bought it for about thirty quid. One night, after completing the milking I decided to visit Gladys. The van needed at least five to ten minutes of idling to warm the engine but me, being like a bull at a gate, hopped in it and started backing out of the lean-to we had erected as a cover. The engine coughed a few times whilst in reverse so before heading off, I chose to sit for a minute and rev the engine to warm it. As I planted my foot on the accelerator, a loud bang erupted from under the bonnet. My father who was in a shed nearby separating milk with a very noisy machine heard the explosion quite plainly. When I lifted the bonnet I discovered to my dismay that one of the cam rods had been driven straight through the side of the block. What a mess - and all because I hadn't warmed the engine. I approached Mr Crawford with my problem. He said he thought he could fix it. Feeling fairly skeptical, I left him to it. Amazingly he adapted that engine to run on five cylinders and it performed almost as well as it had before.

The nearest beach to Northcliffe was at Windy Harbour. Jones, the chap who owned the garage in Northcliffe kept a boat at the coast. Through the grapevine I heard he was going to Sandy Island, twelve miles out from Windy for a day's fishing with five or six others. I asked if I could join them and was pleased to be accepted as part of the crowd. Reaching Windy Harbour we all piled into the boat and set off for the island. On the way someone asked Mr Jones if he had enough petrol for the journey. Dryly he replied that he had about a mouthful. When we arrived on the island, Mr Jones proceeded to show us how to fish. He rolled his pants up, walked out in the surf and threw his line over the waves. It was a completely foreign way of fishing to the rest of us and we did not hold much hope of him catching anything but sure enough, he soon pulled in a big groper. Straight away we all prepared our lines and joined him. Several small fish were hooked during the next few hours but nothing as large as Mr Jones' which would have been about thirty or forty pounds in weight. We thoroughly enjoyed the outing and the mouthful of petrol got us safely back to shore.

 Les and I took one trip to Perth while I was in Northcliffe. By now the train ran right through the town. The line had increased but not the speed of the engine. We had heard you could get off the train while it was moving, pick flowers and return to the carriage at a walking pace. Of course Les had to try this even though it was not allowed. While he was off the train I glanced out the window and saw the guard jump down from his van and walk quickly towards Les. I yelled a warning and Les scrambled back into the carriage but the guard knew where we were and followed him in. He sat down and started giving Les a lecture, then took out his book to record Les's name. I felt rather frightened by all this because in those days, not being used to the ways of the world, I never knew what might result from these type of situations. Luckily an old chap in the same carriage had a quiet word with the guard and he let Les off with a warning.

The train reached Perth around nine p.m. Never having seen neon lights and hardly any electric ones for that matter, I felt, when I saw the station lit up, that I was entering fairyland. Terrified that I might become lost I followed Les like a fox terrier, almost sitting inside his back pocket. He had been to Perth before so was very confident. He led me up some steps onto the Horseshoe Bridge, crossed the road and stood at the kerbside. I asked, "*What are we going to do? What are we waiting here for?*" "Oh, we're going to catch the tram," he answered. "*A tram!*" I exclaimed, "*Well, how do you know when it's going to come?*" Don't worry ",he said, "*There'll be a tram along directly.*" Sure enough, round the bridge trundled a tram. "*How do you know which is the right one?*" I asked. "*You tell by the numbers,*" he answered, "*The fifteen or sixteen are the two we can catch.*" We climbed aboard and took a seat. I was fascinated by the flashing neon signs outside and the adverts that lined the walls of the tram. Every so often the tram stopped, taking on and dropping off passengers. Eventually, Les stood up and said, "*Come On, we get off here.*" Stepping down, I asked, "*What are we going to do now?*" "Oh, we're going up to Ferns' place where we're going to stay." "*How do you know where it is?*" I inquired. "*Just follow me.*" he said. Over the road and up the street he went with me in close pursuit. When he entered a gate and said we were there, I could have believed he was God. It stunned me that he was able to find one particular house amongst the multitude of others that lined the street.

The Ferns were a wonderful family and made us feel

very welcome. A bed was made up on the floor and for the first time I got to listen to a wireless. Next morning when I went outside, I could not believe the hundreds and hundreds of houses that confronted me. I was used to the bush and open spaces and to look over the roofs spread like a blanket down the hill left me speechless. I still could not credit that anyone could possibly find their way round the city and said as much to the Ferns. For a little joke they asked me to walk to the corner shop for some things but there was no way I would venture further than the gate. Les said, laughing, "*You haven't seen the city yet Pud!*" It was so hard to imagine that any town could be so big. That day Mr Fern, Les and I caught the tram to the city centre. I did not see much on the way because my eyes never left the others. I was petrified of getting lost. Dismounting in William street we wandered round looking in the shop windows. In Caris Bros Jewellers, the glass was so clear, I felt I could reach out and touch the display items.

   One highlight was the Ambassador theatre. The ceiling was painted to represent the open sky. We watched a silent picture accompanied by wonderful music played by a chap on a huge organ that rose from beneath the stage. The only pictures I had seen were hand turned ones in Augusta, a far cry from this modern wonder. Following the movie, we made our way to an underground pub call the Allambra Bar. The beer was sixpence a pot. We enjoyed a few and it didn't take long before we became a little unsteady on our feet. The more we consumed the more afraid I got of losing my two companions. My trips to the toilet included Les. No amount of talking could coax me to spread my wings and go anywhere alone.We remained in Perth for about two weeks, the most exciting and terrifying experience of my life.

...Chapter 13

I spent about a year in Northcliffe before returning to Kudardup to work for Bill. For the first couple of weeks I got paid as stipulated, but after that wages were not readily forthcoming and I worked on for nothing except my food. Bill, on the other hand, was having a ball, living the life of Riley. He tootled round in his car socialising while I slogged away on the farm and managed all the household chores as well. Bill bought a young Jersey bull, which I still think today, along with the Guernsey, are the most aggressive, unpredictable bulls alive. New people - the Halls - had moved onto Pratts' property next door. There was Les, an extremely artistic man, his wife Joan and son Dennis who became a musician and later formed a couple of bands. They sometimes paid us a visit and we enjoyed their company very much. One beautiful moonlit evening they wandered over taking the shortest route through the paddocks. Following a pleasantly entertaining few hours, they departed for home. Bill retired to bed immediately. I was mucking about doing a couple of chores when I heard the bull roaring. The moment the sound reached me I knew what was happening. Walking quickly to Bill's room I said, "*That bull has bailed up Len and Joan for sure.*" Bill's reaction was to ignore my remark and stay put under the blankets Worried for their safety I bolted outside, grabbed a bit of wood and headed across the paddock. Sure enough the bull had them cornered. There was no way the Halls were game to turn their backs on him to climb the fence. Not feeling all that brave myself but knowing I had to do something, I stepped between them and the bull. Brandishing my wood and yelling loudly, I slowly drove that stubborn beast backwards all the way across the home paddock. He defied me till the very last moment, when he finally turned. I gave him a couple of belts on the rump and sent him on his way. Nerves, plus the energy I had expended waving and screaming, left me shaken and totally exhausted. Taking a few minutes to recover my composure I went back to escort the Hall's the rest of the way to their block. Bill was still awake when I returned home so I fronted him. *"Listen," I* said, "That bulls got to have his horns off .*He's going to get somebody. It could be you or me or someone that comes on the property.*" "Don't worry about it," replied Bill, "*He's all bluff.*" "Look, I'm telling you he's got to be dehorned." I countered. "*No way!*" said Bill. "*He's not losing his horns.*"

A few days later Bill left on one of his jaunts; I think to Busselton this time. He informed me he would not be back for at least two or three days. Seizing the opportunity created by his absence, I made plans to dehorn the bull. Every day after milking, it was the bull's habit to push through a swinging rail, open a gate and enter the mangers where I fed him some pollard. He'd wander from stall to stall cleaning up the remains of the feed left by the cows then depart through a side gate. I had a strong hemp rope from which I fashioned a running noose. Armed with my "snare" I set a trap in a spot where I knew the bull was sure to put his big head. Night was falling by the time I finished milking and my prey entered the arena. Like clockwork, the plan worked. With the bull bucking and pulling on the rope I had to act quickly and get another rope round his horns so that I could loosen the noose before it choked him. Manoeuvring the now very discontented animal to a strainer post, I secured him tightly and added another rope through the ring in his nose. I made sure he had enough freedom to lay down if he wanted as it was too late that night to complete the job.

Next morning I rose early and went straight over to see how he was. Apart from being in a foul mood, he had almost succeeded in burying himself. The only tools I possessed for the operation were a small saw and hatchet. Unfortunately, dehorning is a very painful experience for an animal and I tried to finish the job as quickly as possible. With one horn almost sawn through, the bull went berserk. Grabbing the hatchet, I knocked the horn off completely. The pain and shock caused the bull to drop half conscious to the ground. Immediately I jumped over his back and started sawing the other horn. When I again reached half way, I used the hatchet to sever the remaining horn. Packing tar over the raw wounds, I made sure that flies would not be able to get to them. When I eventually released the poor beast, the sting had really gone out of him. Slowly he wandered away and joined the cows in the paddock. He did not venture near the shed again and stayed as far from it as the paddock would allow. I walked over and checked on him a few times during the next couple of days, but left him alone as much as possible.

Bill arrived home! When milking time came around I went and brought the cows in, minus the bull. Bill helped with a few jobs and was doing something when he finally noticed the absence of his pride and joy. He said, "*The bull's not here Pud. Where is he?*" "Oh," I replied matter of factly, "*he's out in the paddock somewhere. I wouldn't know.*", and left it at that. The next day Bill became more interested as to the whereabouts of his animal and decided to go look for him. Normally Jerseys are very pretty cattle, but with matted blood and black tar covering his face and horns, the bull looked far from attractive. Bill went crazy. He really performed, yelling and abusing me like there was no tomorrow. I countered the attack by shouting back. "*Look mate, the two horns are over there by the strainer post. If you want the bloody things on then you put them on, because there's no way in the world you can do much about it now.*" The air was rather chilly for a while, but eventually things got back to normal.

It wasn't long after that episode that I decided to leave and try to join the navy. Old Mr Wall was an ex-navy man and I enjoyed listening to his reminiscences of his days in the force. One day, I must have mentioned I'd like to be a sailor. He urged and encouraged me to follow through with my dream. "*You want to go,*" he said, "*It's a wonderful, clean life. You get good food and a chance to see the world and you won't have any trouble getting in. They'll grab you as soon as they see you.*" Feeling cocksure and heartened by his words I thought all I'd need was five quid to get to Perth and enrol, then everything would be supplied and taken care of. I wrote to my mother for the money and she sent it. This time I travelled to Perth alone on the midnight train. The trip took nineteen hours. I'd watched the tram routine very closely from the previous trip with Les so knew which one to catch and how to reach the Ferns'. They obligingly drew me a mud map of the city from which I was able to find my way around. The recruiting office for the navy was in Fremantle, the port at which we'd landed ten years before. By asking directions I found the building okay and went into the office thinking that in a few minutes I'd be a navy man. The chap behind the desk asked what he could do for me. I said I wanted to join the navy. He looked me up and down for a moment then said, *"Well, I'm sorry but we've just completed our quota of recruits. If you'd been a week earlier you would have been accepted."* He displayed interest in my enthusiasm for joining the force but there was nothing he could do till the next enrolment in three months time. I was shattered. With no money or job prospects, I made my way back to the Ferns feeling very dejected. After discussing the problem with them, they suggested I go to the labour bureau in the city. Next day, I travelled in and after making inquiries was offered a job at Lake Brown as a teamster for twenty five bob a week plus keep. Lake Brown lies about one hundred and eighty miles Northeast of Perth in the wheatbelt. Although I knew nothing of that area I decided any job was better than being unemployed.

...Chapter 14

I left Perth the following day at 5:00 p.m. The bureau had paid my fare which would come out of my first pay. On the train I bought a pie and a cup of tea at the first stop. This left me with three and sixpence. Apart from an occasional drink of water from the water bag hung on the side of the coach, that was all the sustenance I had till the following night. The train pulled into the town of Mukinbudin at about 11:00 am. Loathe to spend my last few shillings I resisted the temptation to buy any food or beverage. It was an extremely hot day so I made sure I slaked my thirst from the train's water bag before making inquiries about Lake Brown. The train did not go there so I had to find some transport. Fortunately I got a lift on a truck almost immediately. The journey was about twenty five miles over a gravel road. Pulling in to Lake Brown, the truck dropped me in front of the only building that constituted the "town". It was a combined store, post office and house, owned and run by a Mr Smith. I alighted from the truck and as no-one seemed to be around, I parked myself on a bench outside the store to wait for my new boss who had been, I hoped, contacted by the bureau. Time passed. I watched a few cars arrive, each time hoping that the nice looking families were coming to collect me, but all left after visiting the shop. Someone must have mentioned my presence to Mr Smith because he ambled out after the customers departed. He had St Vitus Dance which caused his head to move constantly. He asked, "*Who have you come up to work for?*" "*A Mr Pearce.*" I replied. He went quiet, his head shook a little more quickly and he muttered, "*You've got my sympathy son.*" With that, he turned and entered the store. Not being sure what was meant by the comment, I felt quite happy that I had the sympathy of the shop keeper as a friend perhaps. I learned later that in the end the labour bureau refused to send anyone to the Pearces'. Most took one look at the property and left before commencing work. I was not so fortunate.

Shortly my transport arrived - or what there was of it. The truck consisted of an open engine, topless cab, bench seat, windscreen and a tray back with several planks missing from it. There were no mudguards. Behind the wheel sat a woman wearing a straw hat and beside her an unshaven ginger haired man. My heart stopped. I thought, "*God, please don't let these be the ones.*" The chap climbed out and walked towards me. I prayed. He walked straight past me and into the shop. My heart started beating again. A few minutes later he reappeared and addressed me. "*Who have you come to work for boy?*" "*Mr Pearce.*" I replied. "*Well, that's me.*" he announced. "*I'll find room on the truck for you in a moment.*" He walked over and spoke to his wife then whistled me like he would a dog, indicating I should climb aboard. I tried to find a spot where I could sit without falling through the floor. Thinking we would head straight for the farm I was dismayed to discover we had to go to Mukinbudin from whence I had just come. The old truck bounced over the corrugation throwing red dust up through the floor and all over me. By the time we reached our destination I was unrecognisable. Neither had spoken to me on the trip and I had yet to hear Mrs Pearce say one word. In the town they left me on the truck, again without a word or offer of something to eat or drink. I hadn't eaten since the day before and the dust had made me terribly thirsty but I dared not leave the truck. Having completed their errands the Pearces returned to the vehicle and set off for home. Still no words had been addressed to me. I was beginning to feel like the invisible man It was dark by the time we passed the shop at Lake Brown. On we went. I had no idea where we were going or when we would get there. Next thing we pull up at a water scheme. The Pearces dismount, beckon me to follow them and commence watering the sheep. By now the time must have been about ten or eleven at night and I was feeling very peckish. Once the sheep had been taken care of, we climbed aboard the truck and drove away into the night. I discovered later that the Pearces owned three properties. The one we had just visited was purely for grazing sheep. Now we were headed for the homestead, or so I thought. Several miles further on we reached Benolly farm named after their two children, Ben and Olly. The house was just a rough shack. Inside I was greeted by the offspring who were both around my age. At last someone had spoken to me. I glanced round the room. The table was constructed from undressed planks with a couple of benches for seats. Apart from a stove and a couple of makeshift cupboards, the room was devoid of furniture. Mr Pearce barked at his daughter, "*You got anything to eat?*" She replied, "*Yes, there's a leg of mutton in the oven*". He removed the meat and dumped it on the so-called table. Using a knife and fork he carved a couple of slices from the leg and tossed them to me. Feeling like I had entered a prison, my appetite disappeared and I only managed to swallow a few bites. Ben, the son, went outside and I followed him. "*Is this the place I've got to work?*" I asked. "*No,*" he replied, "*You'll be working at Springfield. It's about three miles from here.*" Returning to the kitchen I was given a mug of tea.

In no time, we were on the road again. Luckily it was moonlit because the truck had no headlights and Mrs Pearce, I discovered, had only one eye. We followed a little track that wound between the salmon gums. Suddenly the truck came to a halt. Mrs Pearce had fainted. In the dim light I saw Mr Pearce massaging her back and neck. Somehow he brought her round. She took a moment to regain her balance, started the truck and continued the journey. It was after midnight when we arrived at Springfield. The first thing Mr Pearce said to me was, "*Come with me. We'll go and feed the horses.*" Over to the stables we went. After humping bales of chaff for the animals, Pearce said, "*I'll show you where you're going to doss down.*" No offer of a cup of tea or anything! When I saw where I was to live I almost cried. It was a tent like structure made from hessian bags. Inside, the decor consisted of two beds - one a bare iron spring and the other constructed by threading poles through bags which rested on a frame. The floor was littered with rubbish and dirty bags. Dust filled the air. There were no blankets, pillows or mattresses. Placing the lamp he was carrying on the floor, Pearce passed one final comment before departing. "*Tomorrow I'll give you an alarm clock so you can get up on time in the mornings.*" I looked around. Not knowing where to start, I decided sleep was my main priority. Shaking the dust from several bags, I placed some over the iron spring, folded a couple to form a pillow and used the rest as blankets. The night was freezing as were most of the ones I spent there. Like an idiot I undressed from my red dust covered clothes and slipped into my pyjamas. Fatigue enabled me to sleep for a couple of hours but the cold eventually woke me. Somewhere along the line I had acquired a blue serge overcoat. It was a Godsend. I slept the rest of the night in my coat with my feet inside a bag and others covering my torso.

Dawn broke and with it a yell from Mr Pearce. He instructed me to dress and join him at the huller, a machine used for removing the husks from wheat which was then fed to the pigs. He did not suggest I wash or show me where I could. I was still covered in dust when I donned my working clothes. I think the only use for water they knew was to give to the animals or drink themselves. We worked for a while using the huller and bagging the wheat. Then we fed the pigs. A shout from the house called us to breakfast. This would be the one and only time I ate this meal inside. Two boiled eggs and two slices of toast plus the mutton from the night before constituted the only food I had had in thirty seven hours. Still no words passed Mrs Pearce's lips. Hardly waiting till I finished eating Mr Pearce led me outside and started showing me all the jobs I would have to do. He asked me if I had any experience with horses and I assured him I was well acquainted with them. The morning passed as I did odd jobs and familiarised myself with the layout of the farm.

Dinner time arrived. We entered the weather board shack and sat down to a plate of greasy mutton stew which was to become my staple diet. Hardly ever during my stay did I see fresh fruit or vegetables. There was only one bench seat for us to sit on. I sat one end, Mrs Pearce took the centre position and Mr Pearce the other end. He oversaw the distribution of the bread and having cut it, slung it down the table to me. My ration was two slices. When, one day, I asked for a third, he got quite upset and said, "*You got worms or something?*" That was the last time I requested more than my share. The evening meal was mostly a repetition of dinner. I recall getting steak one night, a welcome relief from the muck we normally ate.

Next day I rose at four in the morning, dressed and went to work, again without washing. I felt filthy but was too afraid to ask for a bowl of water. An old pair of sandshoes was the only footwear I possessed for work. The first task was to feed the ten Clydesdale horses that made up my team plus seventeen brood mares and their foals plus the stallion that serviced the mares. The stallion was the biggest horse I had ever seen. With my arm raised above my head, my hand could just touch his withers which is the highest part of a horse's back, below his neck. At night he stood inside a narrow bower shed. I had to carry his feed along between him and the wall to his bin. Once there, I was trapped. The only way cut was by the way I'd entered. All the stallion had to do was move sideways and he would have crushed me or stood on my feet. If he decided to savage me at any time, which can often happen, I would have been at his mercy. Several times over the next few months he played up and made life very uncomfortable for me. It was a scary operation, even with all my experience of these beautiful animals. While the team fed, I harnessed them. This involved putting on collars, hames and blinkers. I left the bits out till they finished eating. With the horses organised I went to see about breakfast. In the yard a small fire burned. On a frame over it a billy hung. Mr Pearce sat on a kerosene box and another had been placed for me. I was given two boiled eggs and two slices of toast, a diet that did not alter during my entire stay. Hardly a word was spoken during breakfast. In fact, talking was definitely not their strong point and seldom was I addressed.

After breakfast I connected the ten Clydesdales together in one line abreast and set off for the paddocks. The sun was just peeping over the horizon when I started work. The harrow was already in the field and it was just a matter of connecting the horses to it before commencing the long arduous task of driving the team round and round the paddock. Tines ripped into the hard earth, turning the soil over and unearthing the softer clods beneath. I sat on the machine as it jumped and vibrated along. Some days it was so cold I almost froze. Not possessing any jumpers I cut holes in a corn sack and wore that over my clothes. It was surprising how much body heat was kept in by those sacks. The horses were well behaved and docile except for one mare who didn't mind lashing out at anyone who walked behind her. I was extra careful when grooming her but the rest were completely harmless. I worked till dinner, ate, fed and watered the horses, then continued till sundown where the process was repeated.

After two or three days of freezing in bed I got up the courage to ask Mr Pearce to purchase a blanket for me at the store. Unable to pay for it, I asked that it be deducted from my pay. The first Sunday that came along I prepared a bath for myself in a tin tub. It was wonderful to remove the grime of the trip and several days work. From then on Sundays became bath days, the only washes I had for the weeks I was there. I also shaved once a week. Looking at myself in the small mirror during this operation gave me a feeling of having company. Sometimes I talked to myself, just to hear the sound of my voice. My mother wrote to me occasionally, telling me of the struggle they were having and requesting financial help. I discovered much later that the struggle was not quite as bad as made out but being used to giving my money over to her, I regularly sent most of my pay to Northcliffe, keeping back just enough for tobacco and a few toiletries. Hunger was always uppermost in my mine. Often I fed the pigs so I knew where the wheat was stored. I filled my pockets with grain before going to work and munched on it to stave off the pangs in my stomach.

Sundays were supposed to be my days off but I still had to feed all the animals in the morning and again at night. There was no where to go and no-one to see so I spent the day cleaning up my tent, having a bath and shave, doing my washing and perhaps writing a letter. I had nothing to read, no radio, no company. I was never invited into the house except for dinner and tea, then it was back to the loneliness of my quarters. I had no knowledge of the outside world. It could have disappeared for all I knew. Ben and Olly never visited once in the time I was on Springfield. As the Pearces had to pass Benolly on the way to town, they used those occasions to see their children. My friends were the animals and birds. Whenever I could snatch a break from work, which was not often, I wandered among the trees watching the antics of the many varieties of birds that lived in the area. This occupation of my mind kept me, for a few brief moments, from dwelling on the predicament I was in. The best way to describe my stay at the Pearces' would be one of solitary confinement. It was as if I was being punished for something but what I did not know.

Weeks and months rolled by. The routine was always the same; feed and harness the animals, breakfast, work all day, greasy stew, loneliness - silence. I would not know how long I was there. What I did know was that I was becoming desperate and felt I would go mad if I stayed. Day after day I constantly sought ideas for escape. Without money and knowing no-one, running away was an impractical plan. Putting in my notice would leave me in the same boat - no transport, friends or money to get home. My naive mind could not comprehend that perhaps Mr Smith at the shop may have helped me. It was not in my nature to ask strangers for assistance. One day an idea came to me. The only way off the farm would be if I was injured to the point where I needed medical help. Thinking of a suitable injury that would look feasible but not damage me too much took many hours of deliberation. In hindsight, I think I might have been slightly crazy at the time to even contemplate what I was about to do. I had decided to lose a finger. I chose my left forefinger as the one I could most easily do without. One morning as I ate breakfast in the yard, Pearce informed me that he was going to Perth that day and his wife was going to Benolly. This meant I would be completely alone on the farm. I was seeding at the time. The wheat and superphosphate had been carted by truck to the paddock and put in dumps at regular intervals. As the bins on the combine emptied, I replenished them from the dumps. Behind the combine was pulled a small set of harrows which flattened the ground over the seed. To fill the bins I had to lift a two hundred pound sack onto my shoulder, step over the harrows and on to a running board behind the bins. By standing on the board I could then empty the bag into the bin. The cogs of the combine operated the machinery that controlled the distribution of the super and seed. My plan was to put my finger in the cogs of the combine. I could say that the skittish mare had started the team moving while I was loading the bin and I had grabbed the nearest thing to keep my balance; namely the cogs.

It was about nine in the morning as I remember. I could tell the time approximately by the position of the sun. I stood on the board, set the team moving, then thrust my finger into the cogs. Instantly the top half was crushed. I pulled it out to discover the flesh had been ground off but the bone was still intact though splintered and flattened. Quickly I put the finger back in again. Seconds later the job was done. I had made sure I carried a clean cloth with me and tightly wrapped my hand in it. Leaving the team, I walked three miles to Benolly. Informing Olly and her mother of what had happened they demanded I show them the injury but I said there was no way I was going to remove the dressing as the bleeding was so bad and I did not want to aggravate it.

They gave me some more cloth to bind round my hand, then loaded me in the truck. Mrs Pearce had run Mr Pearce to the station earlier, so had transport. This time I was given a front seat. Arriving at the store Mrs Pearce related the accident to Mr Smith and asked if he would take me to the Kununoppin hospital sixty five miles away. Mr Smith said he already had his own problems with his dying father and was unable to help. Mrs Pearce climbed back in the truck and took me to Mukinbudin. She entered a shop there, returning a few minutes later to inform me that I could have a lift to Kununoppin with a commercial traveller, but not until 4.00 p.m. With that she and Olly departed. Luckily I was physically very strong and was holding up well. I had not eaten or drunk anything since 4.00 am on top of which I had lost quite a lot of blood, but I sat it out till the salesman drove me in his lovely comfortable car to the surgery. By the time we got there it was around 6.00 p.m. The doctor's name was Finklestein, a short stocky chap. He asked, *"Now what have you done to yourself lad?"* I explained what had occurred, whereupon he asked the salesman to drive me round to the hospital and said he'd be along shortly. When I got there, I thanked the salesman very much and we parted company.. An orderly took me to have a bath. Dressed in hospital pyjamas, I was led to a bed in a closed verandah. A few patients occupied other beds. Hardly had my head hit the pillow when Finklestein arrived and walked me to the theatre. I had never been inside one before but I knew about chloroform and how it was used to render patients unconscious. Pleased that I would not have to endure any more pain I confidently climbed onto the table. A pretty little matron pulled a trolley laden with instruments alongside the table. I'm not sure why but it was then I started to tremble and was unable to control it. The doctor said, "*Are you cold lad?*" "*No, not really,*" I replied. "*Are you frightened then?*" "*No,*" I answered. "*I'm not at all frightened.*" "*What are you shaking for then?*" he asked. "*I don't know,*" I said, "*I couldn't tell you why.*" He looked at me and inquired, "*When did you eat last?*" "*Oh about four o'clock this morning,*" I answered. "*What did you have?*" he persisted. "*Two boiled eggs and two pieces of toast.*" "*What have you had since then?*" "*Nothing.*" I replied. He hesitated for a moment, then said, "*You sure deserve to be shaking. Well just put your hand over here and turn your head and look the other way.*" It went through my mind at that moment that he had forgotten to give me the chloroform. I wasn't too worried as I reckoned he had to know what he was doing. With that, he gave me a couple of local anesthetic injections, trimmed the flesh and bone neatly round the stump and stitched the wound. By the time he finished all the pain had gone and I felt like I was in seventh heaven. I did not realise till then just how much pain I had been in all day. A message had been sent to the cook to fix me a meal. Back in bed, I struck up a conversation with a young chap next to me. It was wonderful to be clean, out of pain and have company. My appetite had returned with a vengeance. I said, "*By golly, I'm hungry. I could eat a horse.*" "*You'll get plenty of good food here, no worries.*" answered my new companion. Being an out of routine order, the cook had to start from scratch preparing the meal. In the meantime, the anaesthetic wore off and with each heart beat, my finger throbbed. It was relentless - the pain incredible. The meal went back to the kitchen almost untouched.

As the days passed the throbbing eased and I started

to enjoy my stay. I discovered through the doctor that I was entitled to workers' compensation, something of which I was completely unaware. Young Ben Pearce visited, bringing my belongings and some pay owing. It happened that his football team was playing in Mukinbudin, enabling him to see me. Apart from my hand, I felt perfectly well. For the first week or so I remained confined to the hospital. The matron often sat on my bed late at night chatting and smoking with me. I can't describe how wonderful it felt to converse with a human being and even more than that, one of her standing. I felt very important and special to be receiving the attention. Little did I realise that perhaps the matron felt more than a passing interest in me. My affections lay with the cook, a lovely girl called Mary. We started taking strolls around the town in the evenings. With money in my pocket I was able to treat us to some sweets or tea and sandwiches.

Curfew for patients was 10:00 p.m. but being unaware of the rules, I sometimes stayed out till nearly midnight. One morning a nurse came to me and said, *"You're in big trouble."* "Me in trouble?" I answered. "What have I done?" *"What time did you get in last night?"* she asked. *"It might have been eleven o'clock or thereabouts,"* I said. *"I'm not really sure. Why?"* *"You know you're supposed to be in by 10.00 p.m. don't you?!"* she announced. "Well, I didn't know," I replied. *"With what I've got I don't see that it matters what time I go to bed."* *"I'm afraid it's the hospital rule and everyone has to abide by it."* she continued. *"I think the matron's told the doctor!"* Not understanding why my friend would dob me in and concerned that my compo might be stopped through breaking hospital rules, I looked forward with trepidation to the doctor's next visit. His practice was to dress my hand every day but before he arrived the matron used to prepare me - unwrapping the bandages and making sure all was in readiness for the redressing. Next day, the matron failed to appear at my bedside. I thought it rather strange. Then Dr Finklestein arrived. "*Here it comes,*" I thought. "*How are you going Tiger?*" (His nickname for me.) "*Good doctor, read good.*" I replied. We chatted on amiably as he dressed my hand and just as I started to relax, out of the blue, he said, "*Keeping a few late hours, I believe Tiger?*" "*I don't know really,*" I replied. "*I've been out till eleven or twelve a couple of times.*" "*Oh yeah?*" he said. I waited apprehensively while he packed his gear away, then he looked at me and said, "*Now are you having a good time Tiger?*" "*Yes doctor,*" I replied. "*I couldn't wish for better.*" "*Well that's all that matters.*" he responded. I heard later that the matron was none too pleased to learn I had not been hauled over the coals. From then on her attitude cooled towards me. Still it had not occurred to me that jealousy may have been the reason for her behaviour and I felt rather sad that the friendship had ended. Mary and I continued to enjoy each others company.

 Not long after I entered hospital I palled up with a chap called Archie Grossman. We took to each other like ducks to water. He owned a farm at Yelbeni, situated about twenty miles south west of Kununoppin. Archie had a severe back complaint which was the cause for several visits to Perth doctors. In his cupboard he kept an accordion and delighted us all by playing it whilst lying in bed. Much later I purchased the instrument for one pound. Archie's name for me was Hunky. A saying had originated around this time that "everything was hunky dory", meaning all was fine. It had become one of my favourite phrases. Archie had not heard it till I met him, thus the tag was given to me. Many times he said, *"By golly Hunky, I'd like you to come and work for me." "Well, what's to stop me working for you?" I* asked. *"I can't pay you,"* he replied. The cockies (farmers) were going through a bad patch and money was hard to find. When the time came for me to leave hospital Archie was still there, so working for him was impossible at the time. For some reason I felt obligated to return to the Pearces'. Whether it was guilt or the fact I had left them in the lurch I will never know, but I returned to Springfield with my hand still heavily bandaged and very tender. Pearce inquired after my injury. When I told him it was very sore, he said, *"You won't be much good for work the way it is now."* Immediately I took my cue and replied, *"No, I don't think I can do much with it yet." "Well it's no good you hanging around here then,"* he stated. With my heart in my throat I asked, *"Would it be alright if I returned to Kununoppin?" "I think that would be the best idea,"* he replied. Hearing those words was like music to my ears. Before he could change his mind I hurriedly took my leave. I can't recall how I got to or from Lake Brown but however I did it, the leaving was certainly a lot more enjoyable than the returning.

...Chapter 15

Archie was pleased to see me, as was Mary. Talking with Archie I suggested that if he could provide me with tobacco, toiletries, a bed and food, I would work for him. "*Oh,*" he replied, "*I can give you a quid a week.*" "*That'll do me,*" I said. On the day of his discharge Archie's wife Phyllis and son Lawrence arrived to collect him and I was driven by Archie in a lovely Buick car out to his farm. What a difference his place was compared to the Pearces'. I was allotted a comfortable bedroom adjoining the house before being given a delicious meal in a warm kitchen with talkative people. This was heaven to the hell I had been in. Instead of horses Archie owned a tractor which made life a lot easier. He did have two ponies, Flossy and Peggy, but they were more pets than workhorses. I settled in easily to the new routine. In all my life I have never had a boss that showed me so much affection as Archie. He idolised me and the feeling was reciprocated. He delighted in telling visitors of the work

I had done and the feats of strength I displayed. I must admit I was a workaholic, but it pleased me to do extra things for Archie and he repaid me with kindness. One thing I loved about the man was his complete trust in me. If ever he had to go away for any length of time he left me in charge without instructions knowing I could handle everything efficiently. This helped build my self confidence again after the beating it had suffered at the hands of Pearce.

My romance with Mary continued by letter. One day I approached Archie and asked if I could borrow his Chev truck to go to Kununoppin. "*Of course you can Hunky. You go whenever you like.*" The truck was unlicensed so I had to drive on a bush track that followed the telephone line parallel to the main road. Mary was thrilled to see me and we spent a lovely evening together. Next day, having treated myself to a night at the hotel, I trundled back to the farm. Not long after, Mary left Kununoppin and went to cook for sleeper-cutters in Manjimup, one hundred and eighty miles south of Perth - too far for short visits.

About five or six months had passed since I joined Archie and I was feeling very homesick. Over a year had elapsed since I'd set eyes on my family. I explained to Archie that I needed a break and although distraught at losing me he agreed it was time I had a holiday. Arriving in Perth I went to collect my compensation and was astounded when I was handed a cheque for one hundred and ten pounds. Cashing it at the bank and feeling like a millionaire, I went to see my sister Winnie who was working in the city. After lunch I offered to buy her anything within reason. "*I've got a few bob at the moment so now's the time to speak up,*" I said. Not being one to take from anybody she had to be persuaded to accept a pig skin handbag and a few other little items. "*How are you off for stockings?*" I asked. "*Well I could do with a couple of pairs,*" she replied. What occurred next turned me off shopping for life. We entered a store where rows and rows of stockings were displayed. There must have been a thousand pairs. Winnie looked at all of them. Then the salesman brought boxes of hose from the storeroom and she went through that lot. I stood waiting, amazed that so much palaver had to be gone through for such a simple purchase. Feeling really browned off and running out of patience I watched unbelievingly as she returned to the racks and chose two pairs from those examined earlier. I said to myself, "*I'll never go shopping with a woman again.*" Rarely in my eighty years have I broken that promise.

Before leaving Perth I spent a couple of days treating myself to a few luxuries like clothes, shoes, records and suchlike. On the way to Northcliffe I called in at Manjimup and booked into a small boarding house. Mary of course was out in the bush at the sleeper cutters' camp but she knew from my last letter of my arrival and had agreed to travel to Northcliffe with me. Next day she joined me and we caught the train home. Everyone was pleased to see me again and all took to Mary, especially my mother who thought she was wonderful. We attended a few dances at which I ran into Rose Coe again. She had a boyfriend and didn't give me the time of day but many years later she gave me curry over the fact that I did not invite her to my twenty first birthday party, held shortly after arriving home. Although she pretended it did not matter, I don't think she liked seeing me with anyone.

My mother received ten pounds from my depleted

wad, Mary scored a watch and I bought all the stores during our stay. On my birthday I got a lift on a motorbike to Manjimup where I bought a cake. Mum made a potent home brew and together she and Mary prepared a delicious spread. Quite a crowd gathered and soon the party was in full swing. An old chap called Smithers who lived over the road turned up. We called him the old soldier. He had a large bald head and used any excuse to visit and sample mum's brew. His favourite saying after downing a glass was, *"A very nice drop Mrs Challis,"* whereupon his supply was replenished. He drank that night till he finally collapsed on the floor and blissfully went to sleep. My brothers Harry, Dave and Harold, who were seventeen, fifteen and seven respectively, amused everyone by drawing cartoons on his head. A great deal of alcohol was imbibed during the night and many had very sore heads the next day.

Soon the time came for Mary to leave. She went to Three Springs north of Perth where her family lived. From there, in a letter, she broke the news to me that she had a child who lived with her parents. She hoped we could marry and become a family. I'm afraid in those days, the stigma of divorce or having children out of wedlock, was strong. My mother went berserk when I told her and would not believe it till she read the letter. Then she absolutely disowned the girl she had thought so highly of. As for me, I felt I was too young to settle down and did not relish taking on the responsibility of someone else's child so I replied by mail that I thought it best if our relationship finished. My next romance was with a local girl called Gladys Pratt. I'm afraid I was no Casanova and treated my girlfriends more like mates than dates. Whatever their intentions I managed to remain fairly casual, though polite and attentive.

Seeking work I travelled to Perth and roamed around, putting my name down for employment wherever jobs might arise. One morning while walking along Milligan Street I ran into my friend Archie Grossman. He was over the moon that we had met again and straight away offered me a job. Of course I accepted without hesitation. Handing me ten shillings, he said, "*When can you start?*" "*I'll go this afternoon if there's a train,*" I replied. "*Righto,*" he said. "*Come on, I'll buy your ticket. I can't go back yet but you know what to do.*" Several hours later I was on the train heading back to a job I relished. A few days later Archie returned and life went on as though I hadn't been away. Old Mrs Grossman, Archie's mother, was staying with him and Phyllis for a while. She owned the original family farm nearby. A chap called Bill Ramsay looked after her property and occasionally helped Archie on his farm. I remember a funny incident occurred over there. It revolved around a stocky little horse named 'Tom Thumb'. Apparently when it was born it was allowed in the house like a pet dog because of its tiny size. One day Archie said that he was going to get some chap to come and break in the little animal. "*I'll do it for you if you like,*" I offered. "*Can you do it Hunky?*" he asked. "*Oh sure,*" I replied, "*I'm an old hand at that game.*" *Well if you can handle it, that'll be beaut,*" he said. Over dinner that night discussion turned to Tom Thumb. Phyllis scoffed and said, "*Tom Thumb! He won't even raise a buck. He's as tame as anything.*" In answer to this statement I said, "*I've seen a few of these ones. They're often very docile at the start but it's a different cup of tea when you try to ride them.*" "*No, no, no!*" Phyllis replied. "*He'll be perfectly tame, you wait and see.*"

Arrangements were made to do the job the following Sunday. On the day, we all drove across together. Reaching the farm you could have been forgiven for thinking there was a grand final football match about to take place. Cars were lined up in rows in a paddock. People and children thronged the area. Turning to Archie I asked, *"What's going on? Is there something on here today?"* *"Yeah,"* he replied nonchalantly. *"What?"* I responded. *"You!"* he declared. *"They've all come to see you break in Tom Thumb."* *"Good God,"* I said, *"I can't believe it!"* *"You've got to remember,"* said Archie, *"There wouldn't be one of these people who've ever seen a horse broken before."* Well all right then, that's fair enough," I answered. Ceremoniously Tom Thumb was led into a paddock, recently fired and covered in black dust. It was not my practise to use a saddle for breaking horses, just reins, bridle and a surcingle of rope. Archie and Bill Ramsay helped me prepare the horse for the big event. Admittedly I was feeling pretty cocky and important by this time and determined to give the crowd a good show. I instructed my two offsiders. *"Just stand one either side of his head and hold the reins. With your free hands shade his eyes. When I give the word, let go!"* Placing my hand on his withers I leapt into the air and landed on his back. Immediately the two men dropped the reins. As my backside lodged into position Tom Thumb sat back on his haunches, came forward and threw me through the air. Executing a few somersaults during flight I landed flat on my back in the dirt. Up went a cheer from the spectators. My ego shattered, I wished I could crawl under a rock. Picking myself up I walked to where Tom Thumb was being held by my helpers. I flew into them and said, *"Now look, that was your fault. I told you to hold* him till I gave the word to let go! I didn't have time to grab the surcingle* or get myself set. [*Strap made of leather.]

One thing's for sure, he won't be doing that again!" This time I slipped my hand under the rope before leaping on. Obediently Archie and Bill held the reins. "*Right! Let him go,*" I shouted.

To this day I have never seen a horse buck like this little fellow. We went up and down and round and round that paddock with me holding on for dear life. Tom Thumb was covered in lather. I was covered in sweat. He did not let up for an instant. Heaven knows how long the ride lasted but to me it seemed like days. I knew I had to stay on till he gave in or the job would not be a success but I felt my time was running out. Finally he came to a quivering standstill.

Another minute or two and I think he would have beaten me. Totally exhausted I sat for awhile, patting and soothing him, then slid to the ground amid thunderous applause.

Later I decided to ride him back to the house. As I climbed on his back, the game little devil gave a few half hearted jumps before admitting defeat. This did not stop him trying to rub me off as we passed through gates and by trees. Physically he may have been broken but his spirit was alive and well. Back at the homestead I made sure he was well fed and groomed before leaving him to rest. From then on he was beautifully behaved and for a while I became the local hero.

The morning after the ride I really knew I had been on a horse. Stiff and sore I managed to work all day as usual but the following morning I could hardly raise myself from the bed. Somehow I got through another day's work. By Wednesday morning I could not stand up.

Crawling on all fours to the kitchen to make the morning cuppa I dragged myself around, groaning in pain with every tortuous movement. Meanwhile Archie had risen and when he entered the kitchen and saw me he asked in a surprised voice, "*What's wrong Hunky?*" When I told him he said, "*You can't work in that state.*" "*No way,*" I replied, "*I couldn't even if I wanted to.*" Archie said, "*Now you go and hop in the double bed in the spare bedroom and we'll fix you up.*" Gratefully I crawled between the covers feeling very sore and sorry for myself. In the kitchen Archie gathered up some small flour bags. He filled two thirds of each bag with bran and placed them in the oven. Not knowing what he was doing out there I waited expectantly for the relief he had promised. Soon Archie came in with two bags and said, "*Now, I want you to place these on your thighs and leave them there.*" The bags were pretty hot but I put them on as ordered. As the bags cooled they were replaced with two more from the oven. This process was repeated many times during the morning. By three in the afternoon I was running around like a two year old. Archie had been as good as his word and I was eternally grateful.

Time came to harvest the wheat. A new tractor had been purchased. It was a beautiful machine - a McCormick Deering with big rubber tyres. I was quite excited about using it as the old Holt I'd been driving was very hard work. Archie informed me that he planned to get another chap in to help take off the crop. I said, "*What do you have to get another bloke in for? Why can't I do the job?*" My pride was dented and I felt a bit hurt that he thought I couldn't manage on my own. "*Well Hunky,*" he replied, "*You've got to have two blokes to take off a crop. Every year, for as long as we've had the farm, we've* always had two men for the job." Stubbornly I persisted, "*I can't see why! I haven't done it before but there's only one tractor to drive.*" "*Yes,*" replied Archie, "*But the other chap handles the bags on the harvester and a few other things that need doing.*" Like a dog with a bone, I refused to let go of the matter and kept niggling him. At the finish he said, "*Do you reckon you could take the crop off Hunky?*" "*Yeah,*" I answered, "*No worries. I'll do it for you.*"

Crops were classed by the amount of bags filled in an acre. Archie's was usually a five bag crop which was considered average. Some were eight to ten bags if the growth was really good. Among the wheat grew wild turnips. A watch had to be constantly maintained to ensure they did not block the combs of the harvester. Another job was to keep an eye on the flow of wheat into the bag which was hung on hooks below a chute. As the bags filled they had to be left in dumps around the paddock to be collected later. Archie showed me the ins and outs of the operation after which I announced I was ready to begin. For the first round Archie came with me to make sure I knew and understood everything, then I was left alone. By the end of the day I had ninety six bags to show for my effort. When I entered the kitchen that night Archie asked, "*Well how did you go Hunky?*" "*Good,*" I replied, "*Really good!*" "*How many bags did you get?*" he asked. "*Ninety six,*" I replied. Pausing for a moment, he said, "*You couldn't get ninety six - no way.*" "*Why?*" I questioned. "*Golly alive,*" he answered, "*The best I've had on a five bag crop with two men is ninety four!*" "*Well, there's ninety six,*" I replied. "*No, you must have counted wrong Hunky.*" Stubbornly I stated, "*There's ninety six in the paddock anyway.*" Next morning Archie counted the bags for himself and proved my tally correct. He was astounded. I worked on, my best total for a day being one hundred and eight bags. Archie was beside himself. He broadcast my feats to anyone he cornered. To me it was just another job. Once organised and in a routine, all that was needed was stamina and muscle, both of which I had plenty. On completion, the bags had to be loaded on a truck for transportation to the silo. Archie approached me and said, "*Look Hunky, you've done a great job with the crop but you'll have to have somebody to help with the carting.*" "*Why?*" I asked obstinately. "*There's no way in the world you'll be able to lift the bags up on the truck on your own. You have to have someone there with the hooks to haul them on.*" "*I don't think so,*" I replied. "*But you've got to.*" he insisted. "*No,*" I said. "*If I get a couple of planks and make a bit of a slide up onto the truck, I can pull the bags up myself.*" With confidence in my ability but with some reservations, Archie replied, "*Alright Hunky, we'll see how you go but I'll tell you what mate - you'll be battling.*" I must admit he wasn't far wrong. It was backbreaking work. Firstly I shifted a one hundred and eighty pound bag to the base of the planks. Hooking the top of the open bag I dead lifted the weight up the planks onto the truck. This I repeated thirty times till I had a full load. Then it was off to the silo where the bags were unloaded and emptied.

    I was on my third or fourth trip when a chap called Ted Perkins pulled in to the silo with his load. He was a big strong rangy chap, standing around six foot four inches. At one time he had held the heavyweight boxing championship of W.A.. Actually I had seen his last fight at the Unity Theatre in Perth. He said to me, "*Who's helping you to cart your wheat?*" "*Nobody Ted*", I replied. "*You're not loading it on your own, are you?*" he asked.

"*Yes,*" I said "*I'm doing it on my own.*" "*Well,*" he replied, "*You're a better man than I am Gunga Din because there's no way I could do it.*" I realised that being tall he would have had great difficulty bending down to hook the bags but I still felt quite elated by his compliment. A few days later the job was finished and Archie was thrilled with the results.

    Not long after I decided to move on again. Archie was so desperate for me to stay he offered to sign half the farm over to me. "*Look Hunky,*" he said, "*I'll tell you what I'll do. You can have the Buick. Go back to Northcliffe, get married if you want, then come back here; you can move into this house, complete with furnishings. I'm getting a new house built so you can have this one and half the farm!*" For a chap in his position this was a most generous offer and I would have been a fool to turn it down — I was a fool! Somehow I reasoned that as yet I hadn't seen much of the world and the thought of marrying and settling down in one spot did not really appeal to me. Feeling very sorry for this dear friend of mine I reluctantly refused his proposal. When he saw me off at the station the tears flowed freely down his face, making my departure a sad one.

...Chapter 16

Walking around Perth a day or so later I ran into a chap called Alan Cooper who had just finished working at the Norseman mines, four hundred and forty miles east of Perth. I knew Alan from my days in Northcliffe where his family were group settlers. He was a big happy man with a hearty laugh. Together we had a fine time in the city - namely talking, drinking and eating.

Yarning over a beer one afternoon, we decided to have a go at sleeper-cutting. Although we were both quite good axe-men and knew how to use crosscut saws, we had never handled broadaxes. This did not deter us one bit. We thought if other guys could learn then so could we. Back to Northcliffe we travelled. From there we went to Manjimup and contacted a contractor by the name of Don Plechich. He was a Slav and had several leases in the area. He said, *"You cutta da sleeper before?"* *"No,"* we replied, *"We've never cut sleepers before."* *"Ah well, you soon learn,"* he answered.

Being contractors now, we had to supply our own tools. Broadaxes, wedges, hammers, and saws were purchased from a local store. On top of these items we needed food and living requirements. Our resources dropped drastically to the point where, instead of a tent, we could only afford a tent fly. This was normally used as a covering for a tent as extra protection against rain, but slung over a pole and pegged out, it served our purposes well. Don gave us a lift to the lease we would be working. It was called Deeside, situated about twenty five miles from the town. Already established in a neat row of tents were five Slavs. We pitched our fly on the end of the line and set up our little outfit, complete with cooking facilities. The other blokes were terrific people. They took us under their wings and knowing we knew nothing of the work involved, donated, in turns, two hours a day to show us the ropes, especially the art of using a broadaxe.

Cutting sleepers is a fairly involved operation. The first and perhaps hardest part is choosing a suitable jarrah tree. Diameters range between two feet six inches up to five or six feet. Felling is done with an axe, then the branches end is cut off with a crosscut saw. Next the trunk is measured into sleeper lengths and sawn through. The lengths are rolled out and stripped of bark. Using a piece of chalk, the cutter works out how many sleepers can be fashioned from the sections. Wedges are driven in on the marks and the billets or potential sleepers are split from the main log. Each billet is placed on skids made from two small saplings. A string which has been wet and rubbed in ash or against a dead tree provides the means to make the straight lines on the wood. This is done by attaching the string to one end of the billet, pulling it to the other end, then flicking it which leaves a black line clearly visible along the length of the billet. An ordinary axe removes all the wood on the edges of the billet to within an inch or so of the line, then a broadaxe finishes the job, smoothly and evenly. The four sides of the billet are treated in the same manner before the finished product is stacked alongside the skids. Each sleeper is branded on the end with the cutter's initials by hitting the branding iron onto the wood. There is no way anyone can remove the brand by cutting it off because the sap carries the bruise right through the full length of the wood. Everything depends on the choice of timber. Sometimes we would be at the broadaxe stage, having done all the other preparations, only to find small bore holes in the wood which had been made by some insect. If noticed by the inspectors at the sidings these sleepers were condemned so there wasn't much point in sending them in. All that work was subsequently a waste of time. Many cutters, including us, found a way of overcoming the problem when there were only a few holes. We filled them with pieces of matches, tapped them into place and rubbed dirt over the ends. An inspector had to be very observant to discover this rort and luckily we always got away with it.

In previous years the bush on the lease had been cut out about five times so good trees were scarce and hard to find. The going rate for a nine feet by ten inch by five inch sleeper was two shillings and sixpence which was very poor considering the work that went into each. Still, we enjoyed the work and the company and had no complaints. Most nights around the campfire I entertained everyone with my accordion which went over well with our new friends. Alan bought a Calthorpe motorbike which was our transport to Manjimup on occasional weekends. He was a fantastic rider and sped through the bush on the rough track as though he was in a rally. In town we did not frequent the pub. Instead we went to a wine saloon and drank vermouth cocktails. How we discovered them I really can't recall. I don't even remember what constituted the mix but we certainly enjoyed the taste. Usually we stayed overnight at a boarding house. It wasn't long before we met up with two young ladies and sometimes squired them around town or went to their house for a few drinks.

It was in Manjimup that I crossed paths with Rose Coe again. She was working as a housekeeper for a family called Muir. Alan and I had made three or four trips to town before someone mentioned a girl from Northcliffe called Rose was working there. I was very surprised and asked of her whereabouts. The next time I went to town I looked her up. Both of us were pleased to see each other and over the next few weeks we went out regularly together. Every time we reached her house after a date, she always kept me talking for ages, saying, "*You don't need to go yet George. Stay a bit longer.*" One night after I mentioned that I ought to be going she pleaded with me to stay and chat. I must admit I didn't need much persuasion so sat and talked for a while longer. When I eventually got back to the boarding house it was locked. Realising there was no hope of entry I wandered down the street, round the corner and over the railway line into the bush. Gathering some wood I lit a fire, laid back and went to sleep. Suddenly I woke to the sound of something crashing through the scrub accompanied by a fair amount of mumbling. Into the firelight came

Alan. He said, "*The bloody boarding house was locked!*" I replied, "*I know, that's why I'm here. But how the blazes did you find me?*" "*Find you!*" exclaimed Alan, "*As soon as I got back on the street and was wondering what to do, I heard you snoring!!*" Before I got my tonsils out I had a reputation for being a very loud snorer but this comment certainly made me realise just how bad I was! Alan settled down near the fire and we both slipped contentedly into dreamland. Next morning we washed at a tap near the garage then went to the boarding house for breakfast before returning to work. For the next month or so life followed a regular pattern. Sleeper-cutting from Monday to Friday followed by a good weekend in town. Rosie and I were going 'steady' and I was extremely happy. Then the supply of trees ran out. Don did not have any other leases for us to work so we were forced to move to another area. Again Rose and I parted company.

A chap named Alf Fry had a lease at Quininup which wasn't that far from Manjimup but in completely virgin bush. Alf's property was the only one for a radius of maybe ten miles and the road to it was just a rough track. The lease started approximately three miles from his property. No one had cut there before which pleased us no end as we were the only two on it and could have the pick of the trees. A track had to be forged through the scrub and with only a motorbike for transport we decided to return to Northcliffe and get the old Stevens van. Mum and dad were happy to let us have it as it only ran on five cylinders and was hard to start. Making a new track to the lease was quite simple I just drove wherever there was a space between the trees. Our main concern was finding water so we continued travelling till we found a swamp where we set up camp. We erected the fly and set up our beds with a box in between on which to stand a candle. The van had an overhead light in it which came in handy at night. We unbolted the two seats from the front of the vehicle and used them, together with a table, as our dining facilities. Before long we had made ourselves quite comfortable.

Work began in earnest. During the week the only person we saw was Alf when he came to collect our sleepers and bring supplies. He was a terrific chap who kept us up to date with the news and told us different things about his life. One story that fascinated me was of when he was a soldier in the First World War. Apparently he was a bugler and a sniper and on one particular occasion took aim at one of the enemy. He was just about to squeeze the trigger when he received a big jolt to his shoulder. Not knowing what had happened he went for cover straight away. Puzzled, he tried to figure out the cause of the recoil. On examination he discovered that a bullet had been fired, presumably by an opposing sniper who had Alf in his sights, directly down the barrel of his gun. The odds of this happening would be millions to one, but he had the bullet to prove it. I believe the story went to air either state or Australia wide on a radio broadcast at some time as one of the amazing flukes of wartime. Many times over the years I related the tale to friends, some finding it hard to believe. Then one day I saw Alf's photo in the Post magazine, complete with bugle and an account of the sniper story. It made me feel good that any doubts people might have had on hearing my tale were now put to rest.

Both Alan and I looked forward to Alf's visits and always used them as a smoko break and a chance for a yarn. To me this was one of the best periods of my life. Alan and I got along marvellously together. We were free and easy, living in beautiful surroundings. The mornings were magical. With the sun streaming through the trees, the dawn chorus began. Many species of birds lived in the area and all their different calls made up the orchestra. Evenings were spent beside the fire, talking and playing the accordion. There were no arguments over who had cut how many sleepers. All money was divided equally between the two of us. I loved the work and the way of life.

One evening, a few weeks after settling in, I offered to go to the creek for water while Alan started the fire. Yodelling was in vogue at the time and as I wandered along, I tried to master it. My efforts resulted in loud answering howls from several dingoes which must have been in the bush on the other side of the swamp. I thought it most humorous and gave out another yodel to which I received the same response. I was laughing my head off when I returned to camp and said to Alan, "*Listen to this.*" Abruptly my attempt to yodel again was stopped by Alan saying, "*No Pud, don't you dare.*" I realised that he was terrified. Finding it hard to understand in a man who spent most of his time in the bush I nevertheless let the matter drop.

For a while on weekends we used the motorbike to go to Northcliffe but because we never seemed to get our return times synchronised, I ended up riding dad's pushbike. One particular Sunday, instead of returning to camp, some circumstances forced me to stay in town till the Monday. Alan, I presumed, had gone back on Sunday so when I arrived Monday afternoon I expected to see him. The camp was deserted but after looking around I felt someone had been there. I didn't worry too much and busied myself cooking a stew. After the meal I sat for a while in the stillness, contentedly smoking and contemplating life. Feeling drowsy I rolled myself a twirly and smoked it while lying in bed. As I stubbed it out and rolled on to my side I coughed sharply. Immediately a howl went up from some dingoes very close to the tent. I'd been told that they have one of the most bloodcurdling howls of any animal and at this close proximity I did not doubt it for a second. They were so close I could hear them draw breath for a further rendition. Initially I'd almost jumped out of my skin with fright, then fright turned to concern because the tent fly was open on all sides, leaving me completely exposed. The thought crossed my mind there was a slight chance I could be attacked if I slept. Rising, I lit a candle and went outside. Unable to see the animals but still gauge their nearness by their howls, I grabbed a kerosene tin and banged it loudly with an axe. The noise in the night air was deafening and achieved its purpose. The howls became more distant. Thinking it might be wise not to take any chances, I put my mattress in the back of the Stevens. With the rear curtains closed I felt completely safe and slept like a log for the rest of the night.

Next morning I had breakfast and went to work. Lunch time arrived and still no sign of Alan. I wasn't unduly concerned and reasoned that he'd turn up when he was ready. Around three in the afternoon the big fellow appeared through the bush, a grin splitting his face from ear to ear. He was in an excited mood and couldn't get his words out quick enough. *"How did the dingoes go last night?"* "Ah," I replied casually, *"They kept me interested."* "Well," he said, *"I came here Sunday night and I'll tell you what - I didn't get a wink of sleep. As soon as day broke, I took off. There was no way I was staying out here alone."* And he never did. He always made sure I was heading back to camp before leaving town himself.

Not many people would probably know about the phenomenon of the king and queen jarrah. I think the story originated from the early jarrah cutters who came upon them on very rare occasions. Usually found within a short distance of each other, these two trees outgrew all others in their area. For some unknown reason they were always perfectly formed, the wood of the highest quality and they appeared unaffected by bushfires. I first learned about them whilst living in Kudardup. Mr Fisher had a pair on his property which he and Bill Hitchmough chopped down to make fenceposts. From the two trees they produced hundreds of posts in beautiful straight grained timber. Alf Fry's lease was fenced and any cutting beyond its perimeters meant big trouble for the contractors. One day while working near the fence I spotted, on the other side, a big jarrah. Straight away I said to Al, *"I'll bet you all the tea in China that's a king or queen jarrah."* Unaware of what I was on about, Alan asked, *"What do you mean?"* *"Well look,"* I said pointing, *"That tree is exceptional. For some reason, there'll be another one nearby. They call them the king and queen jarrah."* I explained the rest of the story, after which Alan said, *"Wouldn't it be nice if the other one was on the lease."* *"You're telling me it would."* I replied, then continued, *"Listen, we'll just have a walk round to see if I'm right."* Within a distance of fifty yards or so we found the partner but unfortunately it too was outside the fence. Both trees were magnificent and almost identical. Nothing growing in the vicinity matched them for size and perfection. We looked at them longingly and said, *"If only they were inside the fence."* While we talked, a plan started taking shape inside my head. I said, *"Now Al, if we took the risk and felled these two, the big problem would be getting them on to the lease without anyone knowing."* Where they were situated was the other side of the swamp from our camp. To avoid Alf's truck bogging in the creek, we had often carted sleepers on our shoulders from one side of the swamp to the other. An idea occurred to me. *"How about I ask Alf if we can borrow his horse and snig chain? Then we could cart the sleepers across the swamp and Alf won't need to come out to where we are working."* *"Do you think it'll work?"* asked Al. *"Well, it's worth a try,"* I replied. The next time Alf came to collect sleepers, I mentioned my plan. *"There's a lot of good timber on the other side of the swamp,"* I said, *"And it would be a lot better for you if we could get the sleepers back over here."* *"You're telling me!"* replied Alf. *"That creek will take a bit of crossing,"* I continued, *"so do you think we could borrow your horse and snig chain?"* *"No worries,"* said Alf, *"Come and get the horse whenever you want.* Grinning like Cheshire cats, Alan and I returned to camp for tea and discussed our plan of attack. Next day, together, we felled the trees, then worked on one each. I can't begin to describe how beautiful the timber was to work with. The grain was so straight the wood split like a carrot and much of the time the use of the broadaxe was unnecessary. Looking back it was a crying shame that these giants of the forest were felled. I doubt whether there are any pairs in existence today. Anyway we eventually turned them into sleepers and with the horse and snig chains dragged them a few at a time to the dump where other sleepers were already stacked. It's not hard to imagine the track that was worn by the horse dragging all that timber through the scrub.

75 QUID AND AN AXE

When Alf arrived we greeted him as usual and over a smoke chatted about all manner of things. He looked at the dump and said, "*By golly, they're a nice lot of sleepers you've got there. You must have got among some nice timber.*" "*Yes,*" I replied casually, "*We struck a couple of good trees Alf.*" Not saying much, Alf's eyes moved slowly across the bush. "*Whereabouts did you bring the sleepers across the creek?*" he asked. Knowing the crossing was almost in the opposite direction to our normal one we realised the game would be up if we showed him the track so decided to lay the cards on the table. "*Look Alf,*" I said "*I'll come clean with you. Whatever happens - if we have to be punished then that's fair enough. You'll know best.*" With that I explained the whole story to him about the king and queen jarrah. After listening to my account he said, "*Do you know, if you can find a couple more of them, the horse is always at your disposal.*" "*Good Alf,*" I replied with a grin, "*That's lovely - thanks very much.*" Regrettably, we never found any more royal couples and to this day I have not come across one pair or heard of anyone who has.

The lease took about six months to cut out. Alf and I decided not to continue sleeper cutting after that so we packed up our gear to leave. The old Stevens had not moved or been started the whole time we were at the camp. A few attempts at turning the engine over proved fruitless so the only alternative was to ask Alf if he would tow it out to the road to where I knew there was a steep slope. Obligingly Alf complied with my request and hauled the van through the scrub and to the crest of the hill. With an encouraging push from Alan and Alf I engaged the gears and trundled off down the road. The noises that came from that vehicle were like those made on Guy Fawkes night. There were bangs and splutters and backfires, coughs and smoke. Towards the bottom of the gradient the five cylinders fired and the old girl came to life. With fond farewells to Alf, we headed for Northcliffe. All went well till about a mile from the town where the Stevens stopped, never to go again. We walked the distance to the garage and told the owner if he wanted to collect the van he could have her. That was the last I saw of the old Stevens, a vehicle that had served me faithfully and well. Al and I parted company in Northcliffe. We saw little of each other after that. He paid me a visit years later having married and produced two children in the interim.

...Chapter 17

Shortly after returning to **Northcliffe** my parents decided to leave and move to the city. Dad had lost all enthusiasm for farming and the property was almost non productive. Out of nine children, seven happened to be at home at the time. The only two missing were Les and Bill. I was delegated to drive the family in an old Pontiac through to the city. The vehicle has been cut down from a sedan to a ute. I did not possess a driving licence because they were not enforced much in those days but the car itself was licensed. Together with some belongings, into the ute piled mum, dad, Harry, Dave, Win, Harold, Margaret, Joan, me and a big adopted stray Alsatian Collie cross dog called Blossom. Only dad, Win and myself rode in front. Mum travelled on the back to keep an eye on the rest of the brood. We must have looked really comical with all the little heads poking up among the luggage and the big boof head of the dog hanging over the side.

It was thought best that I get a licence in Pemberton if I was going to drive in the city where rules were stricter. Reaching Pemberton I pulled up in front of the police station and went inside. The copper glanced outside and seeing the spectacle of the crowded ute, did not even bat an eyelid. When asked to issue me with a licence, he completed and handed one over as though I had asked for a packet of cigarettes. He asked, "*How's the bus? Is it all in order?*" "*Yes,*" I replied, "*It's good, really good.*" "*How are the brakes?*" he questioned. "*Oh, they're good too.*" I responded. Actually there were no brakes at all in the Pontiac but I was not about to admit that to the policeman. Accepting my word he bid me farewell and away I drove. The car had a beautiful engine and we purred along at a cracking pace of thirty five miles an hour.

Having never driven in the city before I knew only the tram route to the Ferns' house. I worked out that if I crossed the river on the causeway and drove along St. George's Terrace, I could turn into William Street and follow the tram lines out to Mount Hawthorn. But this had to be achieved without brakes. It was around five in the afternoon when we reached Perth and I entered St. George's Terrace without incident. All intersections along the streets were controlled by policemen on point duty. With much gear shifting I managed to negotiate the first couple of stops and starts even though my nerves were rather on edge. As we neared William Street, I said to Win, who had worked in the city. "*Now, when I turn up here, I have to go round the policeman don't I?*" "*Keep to your right!*" said Win. "*But,*" I exclaimed, "*I've got to go round...*" "*Just keep to your right,*" she interrupted. Several times I tried to verify the correct way to turn the corner but all she insisted on saying was, "*You've got to keep to your right!*" At this point, with nerves shattered, dad decided he'd had enough and at the next stop he deserted us and made his way home on a tram. Still arguing the point with Win I finally reached the intersection. Not only was a copper at work in the middle directing operations, but a tram was stopped at its terminus in front of me. Taking Win's word as correct I swung right and found myself in the narrow gap between the tram and the oncoming traffic. Knowing immediately I was in trouble, I glanced around for a means of escape. A chap who had pulled up quite close behind the tram realised my predicament and backed far enough for me to squeeze in behind the tram then pull out into the next lane. How I didn't hit anything I'll never know. The policeman had watched the whole episode. When he saw the circus on the back as I rounded him he took pity and decided to let me off. On we went. I thought I was going really well when suddenly ahead of me, a tram came to a halt. Crashing gears furiously and pumping a pedal that was useless I rolled to a stop, the bumper of the car a finger width away from the rear of the tram. The conductor looked down as if to say, "*By God, you've run it fine there mate!*" Eventually we made it to Ferns'. As I alighted from behind the wheel I announced, "*Well, as far as I'm concerned, that's where that bus stays. You'll never get me to drive it again.*" Les, at this stage, was delivering ice for Cartwrights in Mt Hawthorn. He knew the city well and in his spare time drove me all over the place in the Pontiac without any trouble at all. It amazed me the way he handled that ute and I felt completely relaxed when he was in control.

Shortly after, Les left Perth and went to work at Wubin in the wheatbelt, about one hundred and seventy miles north east of Perth. My family stayed with the Ferns' for a few days. They were marvellous people to take in such a crowd but that was how people were then. I can't recall whether or not my parents rented a house for a short period but in the meantime mum took me to see a brand new house, recently completed, at 91 Egina Street, Mt Hawthorn. The asking price, complete with block, was seven hundred and fifty pounds. I could tell mum was rapt but she said there was no way they could afford to buy it. I asked what was needed as a deposit and she told me it was thirty five pounds. It so happened that dad had recently sold the Pontiac for exactly that amount so I said, "*Look, take the house, pay the deposit and I'll make the payments till the rest get jobs.*" This was rather a bold statement as I had yet to find work but mum took me at my word and went ahead with the purchase.

Now my worries really started. Jobs were like hens' teeth to find. I had my name down everywhere, from building sites to factories and shops. I attended any interviews going and walked the town from morning till night. The thought of not carrying out my promise distressed me a great deal and as the days passed I became more and more desperate. Win, who had been on holiday, resumed work as a cleaner at Parmelia Court but she only earned ten shillings a week. Les was earning two pounds a week in Wubin but that barely kept him. Bill was sacked from his job of carting wood in the hills outside Perth when the brakes failed on a steep slope and he deserted the truck, leaving it to run off the road and be smashed beyond repair. Things were looking very bleak.

One day, just before Easter I was job searching as usual when I met up with a chap called Bill Edwards who was originally from Northcliffe. With only one shilling and sixpence on me, but plenty enough for a few beers, I joined him for a drink. Bill was quite a character and I would have thoroughly enjoyed his company if it hadn't been for the constant worry I felt at not being employed. During the conversation I mentioned that I was thinking of having a go at hod carrying which is carting bricks on a portable trough to bricklayers on building sites. As soon as I mentioned the idea Bill tapped me on the shoulder and said, "*Whatever you do, don't be tempted to have a go at that!*" "*Why?*" I asked."*Well, I'll tell you a story,*" he said. "*I went for a job at a building site recently. When I asked the foreman if there was anything going, he said to me, 'Sure there's a job, but can you carry a hod?' Now I'd never seen a hod let along use one but I told him I was a gun at it. He instructed me to buy a hod and a larry [a sort of hoe used for stirring the mortar in the lime boxes]. Anyway, I went and bought my equipment and back to the site I went. First of all, I didn't have a clue how to load the hod. There's a real art to it. It takes twelve bricks which have to be stacked in the trough to form a perfect diamond shape. I watched other carriers until I finally got it loaded, then I put my shoulder under it to lift it up. Good God, I thought I had an elephant on my back. The hod and bricks weigh about one hundred and twenty five pounds. I managed to stagger to a ladder and put my foot on the first rung. With one hand clutching the ladder and the other trying to balance the hod, I got to about the sixth rung before I fell head over turtle down onto the ground. I'm lying there surrounded by bricks when the foreman appeared. He must have been watching me for a while because he said, 'Look mate, I don't think you've carried a hod before, have you?' I looked up at him and said, And you can take it from me I bloody* won't be carrying one in the future - ever!" So I'd advise you under no circumstances to have a shot at it. You know," he added as an afterthought, "*The sad part about the story was I took my hod and larry straight back to the shop and lost five bob on the refund.*"

The story amused me greatly but did not deter me from my original idea. I didn't care what I did as long as I could earn enough to make the payments on the house. There were a mob of brickies working in Roe Street. I'm not sure but I think it was the same place as in Bill's story. On entering the site I spoke to a 'hoddy' called George Dean. "*Do you think there's any chance of me getting a job here?*" "*I think you'll be battling,*" he said, "*And even if you do, the job won't last long. Have you done any hod carrying before?*" "*No,*" I replied, "*But I'm always ready to accept a challenge and I really need work.*" "*Have you felt the weight of a hod?*" he enquired. "*No,*" I answered. He filled his hod and handed it to me. "*Feel that,*" he said. "*That's okay,*" I replied, "*It doesn't worry me at all.*" "*Well look,*" he said, "*I've got a job coming up in Hay Street at Mortlocks after Easter. If you like I'll try and get you a start.*" I really appreciated this offer and thanked him profusely. It so happened he lived two streets away from me in Mt Hawthorn and visited me a day or so later to say I could start work with him. Being almost broke, I scraped together enough to buy a second-hand larry and a hod which was old and much heavier than the newer models. George offered to pick me up on the Monday morning on his motorbike and sidecar. About three weeks had passed since last I worked which meant I was a bit out of condition but of course I didn't realise that at the time. Sure enough George arrived as promised. His brother-in-law was seated in the side-car and obligingly held my hod and larry while I positioned myself on the pillion.

Arriving at the site we went to the rear of Mortlocks where a pit had been dug in preparation for an extension to the main showroom. The day was hot and being enclosed on all sides by buildings, the site became stuffy and airless. Wanting to create a good impression I attacked my job with enthusiasm. Luckily there were no ladders to climb as yet but still the work was fast and furious. As the heat rose I stripped to my singlet. The sweat poured off me and I developed a raging thirst which I frequently quenched from a hose. This was the worst thing I could have done. By crib time I was a spent force. Too exhausted to eat my lunch, I found a bit of shade and laid down. When the time came to start again I reluctantly rose to my feet and battled on. I would have to say it was the hardest day's work I have ever done in my life. Three o'clock rolled round. I was like a drunk, staggering shakily back and forth with the hod. Finally I went to George and said, "*George, I'm sorry but I just can't make it mate. If I keep going I'll fall over.*" "*Well look,*" he replied, "*There's only a couple of hours to go. Larry up some lime and just fill in the time but hold out if you can.*" Feeling boosted by the support he was giving and not wanting to let the job beat me, I plodded on till five o'clock. I was such a mess that George insisted I ride in the side-car for fear I would fall off the pillion. On the way home he stopped opposite the Oxford Hotel. "*Would you like a beer Pud?*" "*No thanks,*" I replied. The thought of walking across the road was enough to deter me. Thinking I was refusing through lack of funds, he offered to buy me one. Still I declined to leave the side-car. I waited while he and his brother-in-law had a couple of drinks, then we all headed for Egina St. My dad was standing on the front verandah as I dragged myself through the gate. With a concerned look on his face he said, "*By golly boy, you look buggered.*" "*That would be the understatement of the year,*" I replied tiredly. Inside the house mum wanted to feed me but I said, "*I don't want anything to eat. All I want you to do is run me a bath of cold water and then leave me - I'll be alright.*" Stripping off, I climbed into the water and slowly washed all the grime and sweat from my body. Unable to find the energy to eat I fell into bed and a deep sleep. Next morning, feeling a little better, I ate a good breakfast. George arrived and asked, "*How are you feeling today?*" "*Oh, a lot better,*" I responded. "*You were really shattered last night weren't you?*" he laughed. "*You can say that again,*" I answered.

At work I kicked off again and managed to make it through till about four o'clock before I again got the staggers. With only an hour or so to go I stuck it out till finishing time which pleased George who seemed determined to help me keep the job. The third day saw me whistling while I worked and from then on I had no problems whatsoever. A week passed at the end of which came the long awaited payday. Mr Brooks, who was the boss and a brickie, hardly knew me apart from an occasional greeting, but as he handed me my pay he said, "*By God, you were pretty game, weren't you?*" "*What do you mean I was game?*" I asked. "*You did it very hard the first couple of days, didn't you!!*" "*You're definitely right there!*" I agreed with a grin.

That job lasted for about six weeks. With no prospects of further employment I scanned the papers and found a vacancy for a hod carrier on the Oxford Theatre in Leederville. Classing myself now as an experienced hoddy I immediately rode my bike to the site. As I pulled up so did a lovely big Hudson Terraplane sedan. I discovered it belonged to the boss, Jack Hawkins. He and two brothers and their father owned the large company of Hawkins and Son which employed several hundred men. Approaching him I inquired after the job only to be informed another bloke had beaten me to it. My spirits fell. Noticing the distressed expression I must have been displaying, Jack said, "*Look, if you really want a job, go to the Repat. in Adelaide Tce and you can start straight away.*" "*Just give me time to collect my larry and hod and I'll be there,*" I replied. The joy and relief I felt at that moment was incredible. Racing home I grabbed my equipment and headed for the city. The job involved building additions on to the Repatriation Centre. I was given the task of mixing mortar and supplying bricks to two brickies. There were several types of mortar needed and each was mixed by hand on a platform. Added to this I was required to erect scaffolding which was made from wooden poles lashed together with rope. Not being skilled in this area, the brickies helped me out and I soon mastered the art of the job. Racing up and down ladders with loads of bricks and mortar and mixing in between kept me very busy but I handled it and the brickies were never kept waiting. Then a plasterer arrived on the scene - without a labourer. The room he had to render was a long way from my platform but I was expected to supply him with 'mud' also. The pace quickened. I was trotting from one to the next to the next with hods of bricks and hods of mud. Not for a second did I get a break. My brother Les who was home from the wheatbelt came to see me and apparently went to my parents and said, "*He won't last. It'll kill him. He was like a grease ball. Just a lather of sweat."* The news left my mother unimpressed - I think she thought I was too tough to kill. Anyway the brickies and plasterer must have put their heads together during the afternoon and decided I had to have help, even though I had not complained or asked for it. Unbeknown to me, Jack Hawkins was approached when next he visited the site and in no time a second labourer joined the outfit. With the two of us working, the job became a breeze and a lot more enjoyable.

From there I moved around from site to site for eleven months with Jack's company. Never once in that period of time did I open a pay packet. Each one was dropped on the table for my mother to do with as she wished. The going rate for hod carrying was four pounds twelve shillings a week, being the highest wage paid for any unskilled labour in the city. I earned quite a lot more in overtime, sometimes bringing home the grand amount of nine pounds. From my pay mum gave me fourteen shillings a week as spending money. It was a struggle to manage on this pittance, for apart from buying tobacco and odds and ends I was once again courting Rose who had moved to Perth. Sometimes I had to borrow from my mother to take Rose to the pictures and even though it was my money I was borrowing I was obliged to pay back the loans. Several times my mother mentioned that Les was sending her money and that she was banking it in a savings account for him. I shrugged it off but it hurt me a bit. One Saturday she bragged about how much she had put away for Leslie. Feeling tired and perhaps sick of hearing about the subject I shouted, *"And how much is in my bank account?"* Immediately my mother flew at me, accusing me of not appreciating her and all sorts of things until I dissolved in tears. Later, realising she was wrong, she did an about face and said to me, "*What I'm going to do from now on is take only a pound from Les's wages and one from yours and bank them in your own accounts.*" "*No mum,*" I declared, "*Whatever you do, don't use any of Les's money for housekeeping. Anything he sends down, I want you to bank.*" She ignored my advice and opened an account for me but this was not revealed till I left the company.

It was difficult for dad to find work because of his age. Les was back in Wubin and Bill, being out of work, came to live at home for seven or eight weeks. He did not bother looking for a job and accepted money from mum which annoyed me a little as it was coming out of my wages. On top of that he broke my beloved accordion so I was glad to see the back of him when he eventually departed. Most of the overtime work I got involved putting in engine beds. After working all day I'd come home for tea then ride my bike back to the site and continue toiling till eleven at night. One day a job involved working on the steeple of Wesley Church in the city centre. An independent scaffold was erected around the steeple and instead of carrying the hod, I used buckets and pulleys to raise the mortar to the top. A brass cockerel on top of the steeple was removed during the work then replaced later. It went back bearing the initials of the two plasterers and myself.

Relations between myself and Jack's brother Neil Hawkins soured slightly after an incident that occurred when I worked at the Perpetual Trustees building. Neil was crippled and worked in the office of Hawkins and Co. He was also the paymaster. While working at Perpetual I used the lift to transport the bricks and mortar. It was a weekend job warranting overtime and my presence was acknowledged by a visit from Jack and Neil who shared the lift with me. When pay-day arrived my envelope was given by Neil to a plasterer called Williams to pass on to me. Immediately I saw it I said, "*Where's the other envelope?* " "*What do you mean?*" asked Williams. "*My overtime!!*" I exclaimed ."*Did you have overtime?*" he inquired. "*Overtime!!*" I declared. "*Did you get yours?*" " *Yes.*" he answered. "*Well golly alive,*" I replied, "*I was labouring for you on the weekend you just got paid for!*" "*Oh yes, of course,*" he answered. "*You should have got overtime.*" The next place Neil had to go with the pay packets was in the Terrace so I jumped on my bike and followed him. When I arrived I went up to him and said, "*Neil, I didn't get my overtime pay.*" "*What overtime?*" he asked. "*My overtime for the weekend,*" I said. "*You and Jack came to the job and went in the lift with me!*" By his reaction I felt I had committed a crime for questioning his authority. He snapped, "*Come down tomorrow morning and get it.*" Climbing into his car he drove off, leaving me feeling bewildered and rather put out because the office was a long way from home and the trip one I should not have been made to make. From then on Neil seemed to have it in for me.

On the last job I had with Hawkings and Co. I was assigned the task of mixing mortars for thirteen brickies. To do this I started half an hour before everyone else. Once organised I managed easily to handle the pace. One Friday a terrible accident claimed the life of one of the carpenters. It could nearly have been me as I was quite close and saw it all as though it was on a movie screen. To one side of me two carpenters were working. Behind them in the yard was a load of timber. Jack Hawkins stood on a scaffold, surveying the site. The first thing I knew was when I heard Jack yell loudly, an uncommon occurrence as he was usually a very quiet man. I looked up and saw a huge girder which was being hauled aloft, come loose at one end and start to swing in an arc towards the two men. Both raced for a doorway in the building. The first shot through and was safe. The second, if he had followed, would have been okay too, but for some reason he stopped, looked round and started back-pedalling. As he ran, so the girder followed him. Suddenly he fell back on to the stack of timber and at the same time the girder hit him. His right leg was flattened above the knee and his right arm severed above the elbow. It almost seemed unreal. He hardly murmured as we gathered round him and tried to stem the bleeding. Still conscious, the poor devil was taken by ambulance to hospital where he died on the Sunday. I hardly knew him but it still had a profound effect on me. We were all allowed a half day off for the funeral.

Work continued. By now I had palled up with a chap who was labouring for the plasterers. As we worked in close proximity we often talked across to one another. Near the end of the day we were able to relax a little as we had enough mortar mixed to see the time out. This particular pay-day, around 4.40 p.m., Neil arrived on site. I was standing, larry in hand, talking to my mate. Neil handed me my envelope and continued on to the rest of the men. When he returned I was still not doing a lot as I had everything up to date and it was near five o'clock. As it was, I was doing the work of two men all day so felt completely justified in taking a breather when I could. Neil passed by without a word and left the site. We were preparing to knock when the foreman, a nice chap called Alf Watters, approached me. "*Now look Pud,*" he said, "*I've got to do this but I want it to go in one ear and out the other. Water under the bridge. Just forget I ever said it.*" Wondering what on earth he was talking about, I said, "*Righto Alf. Whatever you've got to say - say it.*" "*Well,*" he said quietly, "*What were you doing when Neil came through with the pays?*" Flabbergasted I replied, "*I don't know really. Larrying or something. I'm not sure, but something anyway. Why?*" Alf said, "*When he came up to pay us he asked me who was in charge of the bloke doing the mixing. Naturally, I told him I was. Then he said he had been through the building twice and it looked like nothing was being done. He told me I had to do something about it.*" The moment he said this, I said, "*Look, has Neil left the building?*" "*Yes he's gone,*" replied Alf. "*Then I want my time,*" I stated. Alf tried everything to get me to stay. When the gong went at five, he took me aside and attempted to convince me that Neil's comments meant nothing, but for me it was the end of the line. "*There's no turning back Alf. No way in a million years would I ever work with this crowd again. That's the finish.*" A good mate, Curly, came across and said, "*Oh, take no notice of that skinny bugger Pud. Anyway, you've got the weekend to forget it. Make a fresh start Monday.*" "*I don't think so Curly,*" I replied. "*This one has sunk in very deep. I can't see me changing my mind.*" I was a very proud person and my pride now was crushed. That I had been made to look like a bludger was a big blow to my self esteem. Resigning was made easier by the fact that dad had found a job, so the payments on the house were covered. Parting company with Alf and Curly I rode home, but said nothing to the family. Les was back, having finished work in Wubin, so we decided to go to the trots at Gloucester Park. Afterwards, on the tram home,

I said to Les, "*Listen, I'm getting on the train on Tuesday for Kalgoorlie.*" "*What for?*" asked Les. "*I'm going to have a go at getting on the mines,*" I said, "*Do you want to be in it?*" "*Yes! Definitely.*" replied Les. "*I'll be in that for sure.*" On the following Monday morning, I fronted for work because I hadn't as yet received my pay. Alf walked over while I was mixing the mortars and said, "*You feeling better today Pud?*" "*No Alf, I'm sorry,*" I replied, "*I want my time and my pay made up today because I'll be on the train for Kalgoorlie tomorrow.*" Poor old Alf left, feeling down in the dumps. Later Jack Hawkins arrived on site and went to his office on an upper storey. Instead of telling Jack about my resignation, Alf came all the way back to me and said, "*Jack's arrived.*" "*Yeah, I saw him Alf,*" I replied. "*You haven't changed your mind have you?*" he asked in desperation. "*No way Alf,*" I said. "*I want you to tell him. There's no turning back.*" Reluctantly he went and told Jack. At knock off time I went to the office for my pay. As Jack handed it over he said, "*I believe you're going to Kalgoorlie.*" I answered, "*Yes Jack, I'm going to give it a go on the mines.*" He shook hands with me and wished me luck, then said, "*Now if you don't get a job up there or if you decide you don't like the work, you can always get a start here with me.*" Feeling that at least he knew my worth, I thanked him very much. Later at the Oxford Hotel for the first time I opened my pay envelope. Inside was ten shillings extra to the normal amount, a handy bonus at a time I needed every penny I could lay my hands on. When my mother learned I was leaving she handed me the bank book in which she had been secretly depositing. It was pleasing to see eleven pounds entered under my name. Les's account held sixteen pounds, so we had a start financially.

...Chapter 18

Next day we boarded the train and travelled to Kalgoorlie - a long laborious trip. The weather on arrival was typical of the goldfields- roasting hot. Rose's brother Sid met us and together we walked to the Halfway boarding house, the rooms of which were occupied by Sid, his father (also Sid) and three other boarders. We settled in with them and started job hunting. Never for a moment did we think we'd be out of work for long. It turned out to be seven weeks. Each morning we plodded round town offering our services in any employment whatsoever but everywhere was the same - no work. Our finances were at a bare minimum. Old Sid was good to us, supplying a bit of tobacco and the occasional pot of beer when he could afford it. Eventually, the piggy bank ran dry. With only two shillings in the world between us we wandered with Sid and his dad out to a two-up school which was being held in the slag dumps of a mine. It was incredible to see the amount of money changing hands there. Completely fascinated by the spectacle I did not notice Les wander off. Minutes later I got a tap on the shoulder and there was Les with a pound in two shilling pieces in his hand. I couldn't believe it. He said, "*I've just won it - eighteen bob.*" Wanting to quit while we were ahead I said, "*Come on, let's go. We've got money.*" But Les had other ideas. "*Let me stop with two bob,*" he said, "*And you take the other eighteen.*" Pocketing the money I quickly biked out of there and went home. Later when Les arrived he told me he had reached eighteen shillings before losing the lot. At least we had something left to live on.

Time ambled on and still no work could be found. Again we were reduced to two shillings. One Saturday Les said in desperation, "*Look, two bob isn't going to get us far so let's back a couple of horses and see how we go. I'll have the first shilling straight out on a horse, Whatever happens, you take the other shilling and do the same.*" Down to the S.P. shop we went. A short time later we were minus a shilling. Les's horse came nowhere. He gave me the last coin and hesitantly I took a stab in the dark and backed a horse called Perodia. "*Don't tell me,*" said Les, "*I don't want to know which horse it is.*" The race started. My heart dropped. Perodia was coming dead last. As the field reached the turn, Les could contain himself no longer. "*Tell me, tell me,*" he demanded, "*So I can help get it home.*" "*You'll have to really be trying mate,*" I answered. "*It's dead last!*" Into the straight they came and like magic Perodia flew up the outside and crossed the line a winner. Jubilantly we collected our takings of nineteen shillings. With money in our pockets again, we treated ourselves to a pot of beer at the Mt Lyall Hotel and replenished our dwindling supply of tobacco. By the following Saturday we had reduced our win to seven or eight shillings. Thinking lady luck might stay with us we tried the S.P. shop again. Sometimes we won, other times we lost. The last race of the day was about to be run. We had three shillings and sixpence between us. *"What do you think we should do?"* asked Les. *"Well I don't know,"* I replied. Our spirits weren't very high by this stage. Les said, *"What would you like to back in the last race?" "Well,"* I replied, *"There's three horses I like - Paternus to win, Septama to run second and Assertive for third. But you don't have to back them. I'll leave it to you."* Les placed his bets and without mentioning which horses he had chosen we walked to the Halfway for tea. As we all chatted over the meal Les's attention was constantly drawn to the wireless. Finally the race was announced. Up jumped Les and with his ear pressed to the speaker, looked in my direction as the race progressed. I could see by the excitement mounting in his face that something good was happening and when he let out a loud, *"You beauty!"*, I knew he must have had a win. *"What did you back?"* I asked. Les replied, *"I had a bob straight out on Assertive which won and two and six for a place on Septama which came second. Your other choice came third but I didn't back that one."* We couldn't get to the betting shop quick enough. Hoeing down our tea we washed and raced off. It was a quiet period at the S.P., being tea time and the interval between races and trots, and the only person there was the clerk. While Les went to the window to collect, I stood looking at results on the boards. The next thing, 1 felt a nudge and Les said quietly, *"Come on."* Thinking it strange that he was in such a hurry I followed him outside. Les whispered, *" He overpaid me. He gave me two quid. Look, here's two pound notes."* Revelling in the unexpected bonus we celebrated over two or three pots in the pub.

Old Sid Coe had said to us at the start that he could not afford to help us with board but if we could find a house - any house - and he could get his wife and family to Kalgoorlie, he'd hold us till we found work. So in between looking for jobs we went house hunting. Eventually the big day arrived. A house became available in Aroyra Street. It was more like a shack actually, the inside being lined mainly with hessian. One advantage it had was a big shed in the backyard where later Les and I dossed down. Sid succeeded in renting the property and immediately contacted his wife to pack up and come to Kalgoorlie. Rose moved with her mother and the rest of the children. There were nine in her family also, except where the Challis' had six boys and three girls, the Coes' had six girls and three boys. I decided to forego meeting the train. Instead I lit a house-warming fire and tried to make the place look presentable. Later Rose told me that when she saw Les on the station, she asked him where I was. He told her that I had left Kalgoorlie and escaped over the Nullabor!! Everyone was happy to be reunited and the condition of the house went unnoticed, though once established, it became a cosy retreat.

Nearly seven weeks had passed since first we set foot in the goldfields. The rear was out of my pants and Rose had to stitch it up for me to go out. Les and I were almost out of money and the future looked very bleak. Lovely people called the Davies lived across the road and we became good friends. Charlie Davies, the father, was foreman in the tool shop on the Chaffers shaft. I still think to this day that he had something to do with getting us a start on the mines because one day two letters arrived to say we were to start work on the Horseshoe 2 shaft which was in the same group as Charlie's. Les was requested to report for the day shift and I the afternoon one. The relief we felt at this moment was unbelievable. Winning the lotteries could not have given us greater pleasure because the lists of blokes needing work were endless and we felt lucky to have been chosen. Knowing we would soon be financial, we went down town and each purchased a Malvern Star bike. The deposit of ten shillings was loaned to us by old Sid.

Les started the following Monday. My shift was straight after his so I was waiting when he came up from underground. *"How did you go?"* I asked. *"Oh good,"* he replied, *"No worries."* Eager to begin, I stepped into the lift along with the rest of the men and we dropped swiftly to the twenty two hundred feet level. Being completely inexperienced I was shown what to do by one of the old hands. The first job I got was trucking sand to build up the stopes. All I had to do was push a ton truck along the rails to the sandpass and open a chute which allowed the sand to fall into the truck. When full I pushed the truck to an opening in the drive called a winze and tipped the truck sideways so the sand fell to the stopes below. It was so easy I felt like I was getting money for nothing, especially after carrying the hod for eleven months. The shift finished and I rode home feeling wonderful and at peace with the world. Les was asleep when I entered the shed but I woke him to discuss the day's work. Thankfully he was happy with his lot and we soon settled into a routine. Our wages were nine pounds a fortnight. On receipt of the first pay I suggested we send something to mum. *"How much do you think we should send?"* inquired Les. *"I reckon two pounds ten each will do."* I answered.

I wrote to mum and enclosed the money. From the next couple of pay packets we had to settle back rent, the deposits for our bikes and buy some clothes which didn't leave us much but certainly enough to keep us in tobacco and a few beers. It was in Boulder I acquired my first tailor made double breasted suit, which I later used on my wedding day.

Around this time Les, Sid and I decided to have a go at taking a course at the School of Mines. Les and Sid were able to go together because they worked the same shift which left me to go on my own. We chose diesel engineering as our subject. After the first lesson I questioned the boys to try and find out what to expect. Both seemed less than enthusiastic, especially Les, and sort of palmed me off with, *'Yeah, well you'll know all about it when you get there.'* Next day it was my turn. With the necessary books in a bag and proudly mounted on my Malvern Star, I cycled to the school. The class consisted of men of all ages, ranging from the sixties down to kids in their teens. Taking a seat, bad memories flooded back of my early school days and how I'd hated them. The lecture started. I was lost from the start. I tried to take notes but couldn't possibly keep up so I attempted a type of shorthand. Later, no-one, not even I could decipher the scratchings on the paper. Then we were asked to show some square or something and calculate something else. The way I understood it was to just draw a square and measure the sides - pretty simple I thought. When told to start, I used my new ruler and drew a square on the paper, measured each side and wrote it in. Sitting back smugly I looked around at everyone working furiously. Thinking I must be the smartest in class I secretly gloated to myself on how I had finished so quickly. Minutes had passed when I happened to glance at the page in front of a young lad next to me. There were figures everywhere. It looked like a jigsaw to me. Feeling less confident about my effort I tapped him on the shoulder and said, "*Listen son, does this look alright?*" "*Oh! No!,*" he replied, and launched into a detailed description of how I should have tackled the problem. When time came to hand our work to the lecturer, he took one look at mine and tried to explain that I should be using fractions. I interrupted and said, "*Well, for a start, I can't do fractions.*" When he mentioned decimals I continued, "*That's worse because I've never done decimals.*" "*Oh,*" he said, "*This is going to make it a bit hard.*" I rode home and told Rose what had happened. We purchased some extra books and that night she tried to teach me fractions and decimals. The next day I went to class again and again ended up with pages of indecipherable scrawl. Afterwards, the lecturer singled me out and said, "*Look, I can get you through as a diesel engineer but,*" - and then the good news - "*it'll take an extra five years.*" On hearing that my feet were on the starting blocks. I couldn't get out of there quick enough. Like a flash I dashed outside, mounted my bike and headed home. Rose asked how I'd managed that day and I said, "*Here's the books. I'm finished.*" "*Are you pulling out?*" she enquired. "*My word I'm pulling out,*" I replied. Nothing would have tempted me to return. Les lasted about a week and Sid not much longer. So instead of three fine engineers in the family we ended up with three dismal failures.

    Life went on with satisfying regularity. The weekends were spent having fun, something I had missed for a long time. Les and I joined our mates for a beer at the Albion Hotel on Saturdays and had a few bets on the horses. We

75 QUID AND AN AXE

were later accepted in to the Boulder City soccer team, a game we both loved. Les was an excellent player and ended up going to the Eastern States for a while where he excelled in the sport.

I purchased a motorbike, the first of two I would own while in Kalgoorlie. The second was a Silver Star B.S.A. - a beautiful machine and the very first to be seen in the town. Most of my wages were gobbled up on board and payments and what little I had over I spent on entertainment. Then Rose and I decided to wed sometime in the future so we got into the serious business of saving for that purpose. Outings were restricted to a picture show once a week. They were held in an outdoor theatre with canvas deckchairs as seating. Rose would enthusiastically inform me of the coming film and I, wanting to please her, pretended to be a keen movie buff. In actual fact I loathed the pictures and still do to this day. Almost as soon as my head touched the deckchair, I fell asleep. Now and then Rose nudged me half awake with a sharp jab of her elbow. Loud laughter from the audience sometimes roused me but for the most part I spent the whole time in dreamland. Our budget for the outing was five shillings. Tickets cost one shilling and sixpence each. A shilling was spent on a bag of cream chocolates and the last shilling was used afterwards to buy two large, stemmed glasses of milk coffee and a round of sandwiches at a little tea shop called Beers. On a couple of occasions we exceeded our budget and bought a cooked rabbit which we devoured as we walked home. As time went on we palled up with a chap named Buller Yates and his girlfriend Lorna. It became a habit for the four of us to meet at the pictures. The friendship grew and any outings Rose and I had were usually spent in their company.

...Chapter 19

I suppose it was close on sixteen months after I started work that the wedding day finally arrived - December 17th, 1938. I was twenty four years of age, Rose twenty one. Rose wore a lovely blue two piece suit and pillbox hat with a net that partially covered her face. I dressed in my suit and Les drove us to the local council offices in young Sid's Chevrolet car. Rose's dad accompanied us but the rest of the family stayed home, preparing for the festivities. At this stage we were living in another house in Clancy Street. A chap took down all our details then married us without any preamble. I paid him seven shillings and sixpence and within minutes we were husband and wife. Back at the house we were greeted by six guests and the family. A few little gifts were presented to us then the party got into full swing - well, let's say we had a couple of beers and something to eat.

For our honeymoon young Sid lent us his Chev. We decided to go to Perth with Buller and Lorna as our passengers. Setting off at 9.30 p.m., I drove all night and reached Egina Street at 8.00 a.m. the following morning. Three enjoyable days in the city followed then we continued on to Kudardup for a short stay with my brother Dave (known as the Squatter). He lived in a marquee on a block where he still lives today. The Chev ran beautifully all the way down and back to Perth. When it came time to return to Kalgoorlie I said to Rose, "*Look, I'd like to take the Wyalkatchem loop on the way back so I can call and see Archie Grossman in Yelbeni.*" "Sure, you do that," agreed Rose. Everything went smoothly till the other side of Wylie when the pump shaft seized. This put the fan, generator and pump out of action. I said to the rest, "*I'll have to wait till we get to Archie's. He's got a greasegun and I can grease the nipple on the pump and free it up.*" Arriving at Grossmans' I did just that and thought all would be fine from then on. Archie made a tremendous fuss of us and insisted on showing the others the fences I had erected and everything else on the farm. Regretfully I announced that it was time we hit the trail. Not far out of Yelbeni the pump seized again. I managed to free it but soon it recurred. Several times in the next thirty or so miles this happened and each time I got it going again. Within a few miles of Merredin I said, "*When we get to town I'll get a mechanic to get to the bottom of the trouble.*" This was a very optimistic statement as it was New Year's Eve and the chances of a garage being open were quite slim. Fortunately one was just about to close as we pulled in. I explained to the mechanic what was wrong. Without further ado he walked inside, grabbed a big hammer and clouted the pump, causing the casting to break. "Well," I said, "*That was a bloody bright thing to do. I could have done that fifty miles back.*" He wasn't at all perturbed by my sarcasm and said, "*You won't get back to Kal now till Monday or Tuesday. I'll have to order a new part.*" I said, "Listen mate, Monday morning I'll be going underground to work!!" "*I don't think so.*" he replied. "*Well I do!*" I retorted. Luckily there was an extra good battery in the car which I hoped, without the generator to charge it, would last the trip. We gathered as many containers as we could find, filled them with water and packed them in every available space in the car. I removed the radiator cap to reduce the heating in the engine. By now it was dark so headlights were a must, putting extra strain on the battery.

    Away we went. The road up till now had been bitumen but from Merredin to Coolgardie, which is only twenty five miles from Kalgoorlie, we would be travelling on gravel, a distance of one hundred and eighty five miles. We had only gone a short distance up the road when suddenly a shower of hot rust coloured water exploded from the radiator covering the windscreen and completely obscuring my view. The side windows were made of celluloid which clipped on but provided little protection from the geyser, so we copped some as well. I stopped, filled the radiator, cleaned the muck off the windscreen and continued the journey. Two miles further on, up it went again. This happened at regular intervals for the whole trip and each time the radiator had to be refilled and the windscreen cleaned. As if that wasn't bad enough, about thirty miles into the trip - bang went a tyre. In those days cars had split rim wheels. After jacking up the car, clips are released on the rim which collapses in two, releasing the tyre. A vulcanising kit is used to patch the punctures on the tube. This involves clamping the patch over the hole, then putting a lighted match to it. The smell given off is vile but it works very well. Just finding the puncture in the dark was a feat in itself, but luck ran with me.

Mobile once more, we again set off. Up went the water - minutes later - bang went a tyre. We were getting punctures at the rate of one every one or two miles. Lorna slept blissfully on the back seat and Rose nodded off now and then in the front. Where I could I switched off the headlights or drove with them on dim to try and conserve the battery power. When twelve o'clock arrived I had the car on the jack, tools all over the place and I was covered in oil, grease and muck. Buller saw the funny side of the situation and said to me, "*It's midnight folks. Do you think we should sing the new year in?*" On we went - fill the radiator - mend the tyre - fill the radiator - mend the tyre - all night this went on. Buller was good company while the women slept and helped keep me awake. By six in the morning I was feeling shattered. I said to Rose, "*Now look love, I'm just about beat. You'll have to stay awake and make sure I don't fall asleep and run off the road.*" "*Okay,*" replied Rose, "*Don't worry - I'll keep an eye on you.*" We bowled along for a while then all of a sudden the car hit some corrugation - the worst I had ever seen. The ruts were at least a foot deep and endless. After a few minutes of bouncing and jolting over this I said to Rose, "*Are we still on the highway?*" "*Yes, I think so,*" she replied, "*You haven't gone off the road*" "*Good God!*" I said. "*I can't recall going over a road like this before.*" Continuing on we bone - shakingly covered ten miles before sighting a camp of several tents and a chap boiling a billy. "*Listen mate,*" I said, "*Are we on the road for Kalgoorlie?*" "*Heck no,*" he replied, "*This is Yellowdine.*" "*God almighty,*" I said, "*What a road!! Can I take a loop* back to the highway?" "*Afraid not,*" he answered, "*You have to go back the way you came.*" Just what I wanted to hear. Into the car we climbed and away we went again. By the time we reached the highway the spokes on all the wheels were bent but one in particular was near collapse. Slowly we progressed with the ever present whooshes and bangs. Finally in the distance I saw Coolgardie. Thinking to myself, "*Thank God, thank God, we'll soon be on a bit of bitumen,*" my joyful reverie was rudely interrupted by yet another puncture. Completely out of vulcanisers I limped into town on the rim. Before reaching the garage - bang went another tyre. I asked the guy at the garage if he would fix the punctures. Casual as you like he said he would but just then his mate turned up and he yarned with him as though we had all the time in the world to wait. Exasperated and running out of patience I barked, "*Listen mate, just give me some vulcanisers and I'll mend the tyres myself.*" With repairs completed we managed to reach Kalgoorlie without any further blow-outs except those from the radiator. The time was three o'clock in the afternoon, making the journey one of thirty three grueling hours - a really great end to our honeymoon! Being responsible for the car I paid for the repairs which left me with thirty shillings, the total amount of money that Rose and I possessed in the world. It never entered our heads to find a place of our own. We were quite content to stay with Rose's family. Shortly after our trip five new houses became available in Whitlock Street. Old Sid applied for one and told me he would get an extra room put on for us. This was to be their final move. Number five is still occupied by Rose's brother Bill since the old folks passed away.

    I bought some lino and furniture for our bedroom

and together we made it cosy and comfortable. In addition to the family, Les and two other chaps were being accommodated as boarders. Looking at the house today, it's amazing where everyone fitted. Rose, being the eldest girl, did the bulk of the housework and was rewarded with free board for the two of us. Still we found it extremely hard to save on the wages I was earning. Most evenings we spent sitting outside in the yard. In summer the temperature in Kalgoorlie regularly rose well over a hundred degrees Fahrenheit but the nights were still and balmy .Gazing up at the Southern Cross one clear moonlit night my thoughts returned to the Blackwood River. I regaled my companions with tales of the fond memories I had of it - the nights and days spent netting in her waters- the camp fires on her shores and the size of our catches. "*One of these days,*" I said dreamily, "*I'll be right back beside the Blackwood River.*" Old Sid laughed and said, "*We've heard that so many times before.*" "*You'll see,*" I replied, "*One of these days I'll get back there.*"

Rose and I spent many wonderful times riding around on my Silver Star motorbike. Rose was quite a bikie in those days and loved hurtling along at full throttle. Occasionally on a Saturday I placed a shilling and threepenny bet on a horse. One mate, Sid Penn, who was a real character, insisted that a horse called Rivette would win the upcoming Caulfield and Melbourne Cups. Despite contradictory predications by his friends he stuck to his guns and one Saturday said, "*I took a double - Rivette to win both races. I put a shilling on.*" The odds of course were terrific. We all jibed and ribbed him about his foolishness but he retorted with, "*I'm that confident of winning, I'm going to take another shilling's worth.*" Which he did. Rivette duly won the Caulfield Cup. This subdued us somewhat even though we were all hoping the double would come off for Sid. Then Rivette won the Melbourne Cup, going down in history as the first mare in a Melbourne Cup to also win the Caulfield. And Sid - well he won too - a hundred and eighty seven quid to be exact, although he did not tell us straight away. In fact he hardly turned a hair after the race - just puffed away on his smoke and drank his beer. S.P. shops were always situated close to the pubs. When Sid went to collect we all went with him thinking probably we might be in the presence of a potential millionaire. The teller in the shop almost choked when he tallied the winnings and we watched in awe as the notes were counted out. Casually Sid checked the money, rolled it into a wad and put it in his pocket. Then he glanced at the race board, returned to the teller and placed a shilling straight out and one and threepence a place on another race. One can only imagine what the teller was thinking having just lost an enormous amount to this person. Back in the pub Sid shouted us a few beers and we all celebrated in grand style.

 Work on the mines continued. Eventually I was promoted to platman, working the cage that took the men to the different levels underground, but before that I slogged it out in the stopes with the rest of the men. The only light down there came from carbide lamps. The carbide, combined with dripping water, forms a gas which, when lit, produces light. Before going below we filled our lamps with carbide but carried some spare in tins in our pockets. If by chance this carbide got wet it became extremely hot. I recall one occasion where the heat emitted by wet carbide was truly put to the test. The day started fine and sunny as the majority of days do in

75 QUID AND AN AXE

Kalgoorlie. I was to go on the afternoon shift but around midday a dust storm hit and boy, was it a beauty. You couldn't see a foot in front of your face. Red dust covered everything. It blew through every crack and opening in every building in town. No sooner had it stopped than the rains came. Kalgoorlie is not noted for its rainfall but when it does occur there is no seepage, due to the hardness of the earth, so the water floods the surface, rushing to wherever the lowest areas existed. By the time I left for work, around, three o'clock, the water in the spoon drains that crossed the roads was up to the hub of my bicycle. I arrived at work to find the cable winder for the cage had short circuited after being hit by lightning. The men from the lower levels had been brought up before the breakdown but those to about three hundred feet were forced to leave by another route. There is, in a mine, a water shaft, separate from the main shaft, which contains a ladder. In case of emergency men can escape this way but it is one hell of a climb because the ladder is vertical with no lean on it whatsoever. All the chaps made it safely above ground and headed for the showers. The shift boss turned to us and said, *"There's no way we can fix the winder for a while so anyone who wants to work can go down the Chaffers and those who don't can go home."* I couldn't really afford to miss a shift so decided to accept his alternative. Mines owned by one company were usually situated within two to three hundred yards of each other. Underground the drives joined up like rabbit warrens so it was just as easy to go down another shaft and walk through to your own area. Only about six or eight of us wandered across to the Chaffers. The rest chose to go home. The Chaffers was the deepest mine on the golden mile - five thousand feet straight down.

Where our cage held eight men, the Chaffers carried twenty four, packed tightly on two decks. I joined the rest of the men and squeezed into the top deck. Down we started. The cage really motored on this shaft and in no time we reached the twelve hundred feet level. Here the water from the surface had broken through and was pouring directly into the shaft. As we passed through it, the roar of the mud, rock and water hitting the cage was deafening as well as very frightening. The lower we descended the higher became the drop of the waterfall and the louder the noise. Mud and slush poured through the cracks in the roof of the cage and filled the spaces between us. Packed in like sardines we were helpless to do anything - even raise our arms. A lot of the men's carbide tins got wet inside and instantly became red hot. Above the tremendous roar of the water came the screams and curses of the men being burned. The cage continued to the twenty four hundred feet level where thankfully we were off loaded. I reckon if it had gone any deeper, none of us would have survived. We left the cage covered in slime from head to foot. A couple of the men were unconscious but soon rallied after being released from their prison. What a sorry sight we looked. Our clothes were soaked through as were most of our so called waterproof draw string crib bags. I think I may have been the only one with a dry cigarette paper. There were several fracture boxes on the platform so we broke them up and started a fire. Then we stripped off our clothes and washed them and ourselves as best we could from the water line. The platman decided to take us to the surface five at a time, in the lower deck of the cage. This way we would have plenty of room and two ceilings above us for protection. Dressed again in wet togs we made the return journey through the cascade. A few men were reluctant to enter the cage but realised it was the only way out. It was an experience I never wished to repeat and thankfully never did. My shift mates and myself went back to the Two Shaft, changed and went home.

The water display around town was incredible. Two cars were submerged under a bridge while kids dived off the top. Cars carefully trickled through the gushing waters in the spoon drains. It was certainly a day to remember. In fact it was brought back vividly to me many years later in Augusta when a friend of mine, Rod Gardiner and I caught up with each other outside the Post Office. We got talking and somewhere along the line I related the story of the flood in the mine. He remained silent till I finished, then looked at me and said, "*Every word you said is true!*" Not understanding what he meant by that comment, I asked, "*What made you pass that remark Rod?*" "*Well,*" he said, "*I happened to be in the cage on that day.*" I was flabbergasted. After all the years I had known him and all the conversations we'd had, never once had that episode arisen. "*Yes,* he said, "*It happened exactly as you said and,*" he added, "*it was my best shift.*" "It wasn't a very good shift as far as I was concerned. What was so good about it?" I asked. "*Well, we got double pay for a full shift*" he replied. The time spent underground that day would have been about half an hour at most. I stared at him in disbelief and said, "*You know something? Us men from the Two Shaft that went down got absolutely nothing. If we'd known you all got paid we could have gone to the union and at least got something.*"

There were a few occasions in the mines when I took chances that could easily have ended my life. I suppose it was the challenges that I found impossible to ignore but whatever the reasons I realise, looking back, how silly I had been at the time. One incident involved a blocked chute, or pass as we called them. I was working the trucks one day with a terrific Slav bloke called Frank. Our job was to truck the ore that came down the passes from the stopes. One particular stope had been worked to within fifteen feet of the level above, making the chute from it to our level about eighty five feet deep. Work was going well until on one run we found the pass empty which usually meant one thing. It was blocked. This was not uncommon. Sometimes the logs that line a chute dislodge and wedge across the opening causing a build up of ore above them. Most times all that is needed is for a couple of rocks to be shifted with a crow bar and the lot can be released. Frank and I decided to investigate. All levels have manways through which men can climb, by means of ladders, to the slopes above. Frank and I ascended the ladder to see if we could spot the blockage. This stope was massive, making our job difficult. We looked around for a while but couldn't find the opening. Just walking around was very risky as the ore could have given way at any moment. I said to Frank, "*I think the best thing is for me to climb the pass and put a shot of explosive in.*" Poor Frank became extremely distressed as this suggestion. He was beside himself. He insisted I follow the correct safety procedure which was to wait for the shift boss to arrive and let him decide the course of action. But me being young, foolish and stubborn, said I'd be okay. I got two sticks of gelignite and a six foot fuse which was the standard length in the mines. I didn't think at the time but blokes had been killed by what we called running fuses. When lit, instead of taking four minutes to burn, the fuse just burns out in seconds, not giving the firer a chance to get away safely. Normally most miners cut a small piece from one end of the fuse and test it but I needed every inch of mine, so didn't bother. With the gelignite and fuse inside my flannels and my carbide lamp in hand I entered the chute. The pass logs had been worn smooth by the constant passage of ore. Added to this, being two thousand feet underground, the sides were wet and slimy. The only way I could climb was to span the chute like a monkey and work my way up by digging the toes of my boots into the crevices between the logs. One slip and I was a goner as there was no way I could have gripped the sides if once I started falling. Eventually I reached the top and surveyed the scene. Sure enough a pass log was wedged across the opening. I knew that it might only take the movement of one or two small rocks to release the ore so I had to be very careful not to disturb anything. I think I may have had a few second thoughts at this moment but decided, as I was there, to go ahead. Gently I placed one stick of jelly above the pass log. Connecting the fuse to the other stick, I slid that in beside the first. The fuse hung down below the log. This gave me a six foot start to my descent. Then I tested my arm's length to the end of the fuse - every inch I could gain was precious. A voice in my head said, "*You're mad, you're mad. You shouldn't be doing this. Once you light the fuse, you're gone.*" Another voice argued, "*Oh bugger it, let's give it a go!*" I reached up with my lamp and lit the fuse. Suddenly I was in complete darkness. The fizzing of the fuse had put out my lamp. Now all I had to guide me was feel and the pressure of my feet against the walls. Down I started. The going was really tough. I knew I was on a time limit and there was no chance of a rest. Below me I could hear Frank shouting. Actually he was panicking. He had his lamp pointed into the chute which gave me some guidance but not a great deal. Six feet from the bottom and totally exhausted, I let myself drop. I hit the sloping floor, slid down onto the base and scrambled out. Of all things my shift boss, Bob Bordanavich, another fantastic Slav, happened to arrive on the scene at that moment. *"Vol you do Pud? Vot you do?"* he asked anxiously. *"You'll know any second,"* I replied. Next thing the gelignite exploded and down came the ore with a deafening roar. Poor old Bob, who was badly 'dusted' (dust on the lungs) from years spent in the mines, stood there with hat in hand and bald head shining in the lamplight. Sweat poured from him. He wheezed, *"Oh! Oh! Oh! You banty bugger. Don't you ever do that again."* Frank was speechless. The fright and concern showed on his face. Me - I was just happy the job was done. I knew quite well that Bob could have said to me, *"That's it Pud, you're finished on the mines."* But in his way I think Bob was quite proud of me. He was like a father to us and we all thought the world of him. Nothing more was said after a stern warning from Bob that I had better not repeat that caper ever again!

    Another time I was bogging out (shoveling) in a stope when I noticed the ore had stopped running from the face where the machinemen were working. A rock weighing about a ton or more was jammed about thirty feet up the stope, preventing the ore above it from moving. Also a couple of fairly large rocks had pinned themselves across the opening of the chute, causing a further blockage. I thought if I loosened those in the chute, I might start the lot moving and if I lost my footing, down I'd go with the ore. Instead of following the standard safety procedures

I climbed down the manway, collected a gimlet pole and some hemp rope and returned to the stope. Near the chute I stood the pole on the sloping floor, then wedged it tightly into the roof. Next I wound the rope around the near centre of the pole so that I'd have a foothold to stand on. After hanging my lantern on a hook in the stope wall and making sure everything was to my satisfaction, I gave the rocks in the chute mouth one big jab with my crowbar. Immediately the blockage cleared and the ore started to run. Like a monkey I leapt across to the pole and put my feet onto the rope. The noise was deafening. As the stope cleared I could see by the lamplight the loose ore coming away from beneath the crescent shaped boulder above me. I knew that sooner or later it had to go. There was no way I could move. Ore was crashing past the post I was on and falling into the chute. The next thing - away it went. I saw it start to move and thought to myself, "*This is it Pud! You're a goner.*" All I could do was watch helplessly as it thundered towards me. It struck near the base of the pole and catapulted me down past the chute to where pass logs are kept inside some uprights. The side of my neck hit one of these posts as I landed. I didn't hesitate for a second. I knew I had to keep going to the bottom where the stope turned up the other way if I was to reach safe ground. Madly I scrambled down and took refuge from the falling ore. By now the chute was almost full and the huge rock was coming to a halt. I looked down. Blood poured from my neck and soaked my clothes. From the top of the stope came a shout. "*Below! Below!*" It was big Paul, the machineman. "*On top!*" I yelled back. "*You all right?*" he screamed. "*Yep, yep. I'm okay,*" I replied. Unconvinced, Paul decided to walk down and see for himself. When he saw the blood he panicked. "*My God! What the hell have you done to yourself?*" he asked. "*I'm alright,*" I said. "*Really, I'm okay.*" I made my way to the platform. For bad accidents, twelve bells are rung to alert the platman who must then drop everything and get the cage to the required level as quickly as possible. Instead I rang ten bells which is the shift boss's signal because I didn't consider my injury an emergency. The cage came and took me to the surface where I was told to go straight to the hospital, so I hopped on my bike and rode there. The doctor said I was a very lucky fellow not to have broken a major artery or snapped my neck. He fixed me up and next day I was back at work.

...Chapter 20

War broke out on September 3rd, 1939. Before long quite a few men from the mines had volunteered their services and joined the army. I worked with a good mate called Jimmie Mitchell. He was a machineman and I bogged out behind him. One day I said to him, "*I think I should enlist and go and do my bit Jimmie.*" "*Now don't be so silly,*" he replied, "*You're a married man and there are still plenty of single men to go.*" Jimmie was actually responsible for delaying my enlistment and it wasn't until Mussolini joined the war and a particular incident occurred at the mine that I ignored his advice and finally got my wish. The morning Mussolini declared war I went to work as usual and entered the change-room. The place was abuzz with talk that if the Italian miners were allowed underground we would all refuse to go with them. Although they were mostly nice blokes the fact remained that we were at war with their country and therefore they were the enemy.

United in our resolve, we walked to the shaft where the shift boss began allocating the different jobs. When he reached me I asked him if the Italians would be going underground. "*Oh yeah,*" he replied, "*They'll be going as usual.*" "*Well,*" I stated, "*You better not worry about giving me my plod because I won't be going with them.*" Around me stood the rest of the shift workers. As soon as the cage arrived and the door opened they were in it like a shot, leaving me standing alone like a shag on a rock. So much for unity. I went to the lamp room, hung up my carbide lamp and went straight to the office. I fronted Billy McMahon the foreman. "*What can I do for you Pud?*" he asked. *"I've snatched my time Billy,"* I replied. Surprised, he said, "*Snatched your time! What's this all about?*" "Well, I'm off down the drill hall and I'm going to join up," I answered. Shaking my hand he said, "*Good luck to you. Matter of fact I don't think it'll be long before I'll be with you.*"

In the months prior to this, when discussing the possibilities of my enlistment at home, old Sid had said adamantly, "*You'll never get in the army with your feet. There's not a chance! And I'll tell you son - if you do get in - by God you'll regret it.*" He continued, "*I saw a lot of chaps in the trenches during the First World War who had flat feet and I saw what they went through. You'll never make it.*" His comments had not worried me at all because up to now I'd had no problem with my feet except for one incident in the mine when a rock dropped on my big toe. I ended up going to see Dr Gillette. He was a terrific doctor who made it a practice to walk round his waiting room and find out each patient's complaint before seeing him or her privately. I was sitting, one foot bare, toe bandaged, chatting away to my neighbour when Dr Gillette began his rounds. Something made me look up. There was the doctor standing back from me staring in my direction but towards the floor. Jokingly I said, "*What's grabbed you Doc? What are you so interested in?* With an incredulous shake of his head, he said, "*They're the flattest feet I've ever seen in my life.*" "*Yes, you could say that,*" I agreed.

At the time I was about to enlist brother Les developed appendicitis. He was in such pain that we asked Dr Gillette to make a house call. When he saw Les he immediately ordered him to hospital. As he was leaving I happened to say, "*Listen Doc - do you remember talking about my flat feet?*" "*Yes, I certainly do,*" he replied. "*Well,*" I said, "*How do you like my chances? I'm going to join the army.*" "*Absolutely no chance,*" he declared, "*None whatever!*" "*You're cheerful.*" I replied, smiling. "*You'll never get in the army with your feet - I can tell you that right now!*" he said determinedly. With equal determination I rode to the drill hall and waited with other volunteers to have my medical examination. When my turn came the doctor quickly put the rule over me then requested I stand on my toes several times. This I did like a prima ballerina. I doubt whether he even noticed my feet before giving me a clean bill of health. The first hurdle had been cleared. Now all I had to do was pass the second examination in the army camp and I'd be in like Flynn. Happily I went home to break the news. Departure depended on the recruitment of enough men to fill a train so I had no idea when I'd actually be leaving Kalgoorlie. Les had his operation and recovered well but shortly after was struck down with pneumonia and pleurisy. He had had every intention of enlisting after the operation and was very disappointed to be back in hospital. It was then I got my marching orders. I went to see Les and he said,

"As soon as I get out, I'm going straight to the drill hall so I can get down with you and then if we are sent overseas, we can possibly go together!" The idea pleased me greatly and I looked forward to our reunion.

Bidding my family farewell I climbed aboard the train. There were one hundred and fifty recruits accompanying me to Northam, (situated sixty miles east of Perth on the Kalgoorlie line) along with enough beer to float a ship. Crates, each holding five dozen big bottles, stood in every available space. As the drinks flowed and the party moved into top gear I took out my accordion and for most of the journey played along as we sang every song we knew. Some of the men got so drunk they fell in the aisles and spent the rest of the journey being tripped over or trodden on by other inebriated characters. By the time we reached Northam in the early morn only about fifty of us were still reasonably sober. The rest looked a mess. There were those with black eyes, bruises and scrapes, dirty wrinkled clothes and bloodshot eyes staggering around wondering where they were. To an outsider the idea that we were supposed to save our country would, at that moment, have seemed very doubtful. Captain Carey met us at the station. Later we became known as Captain Carey's chickens. There was no transport to the camp three miles away so we set off in twos and threes to walk the distance. It was such a straggly spread out mob that when the first groups reached the camp others were still at the station, trying to sober up enough to stand, let alone walk. We were greeted at the camp by cheers and yells of, *"You'll be sorry! You'll be sorry!"* Immediately the last stragglers entered the gate we were hauled over the coals for our behaviour and the two hundred quid's worth of damage done to the train carriages. As punishment we were ordered to contribute towards the repairs — a really great start.

For the rest of the day Captain Carey pampered us considerably, mainly because as yet we had not signed on the dotted line and being volunteers were free to leave. The next day was quite a different kettle of fish. Given numbers we filed through a tent to swear the oath. Emerging from the other side we learned very quickly that now we were in the army. Firstly we were taken to get our uniforms from supply. This turned into a circus when kits, regardless of size, were issued to whoever came next on the line. Much swapping and laughing ensued as small chaps tried on large hats and jackets or vice versa. Clothes flew in all directions as men attempted to find their sizes. Eventually we sorted ourselves out. Hut allocation came next. Each but accommodated twenty eight men. We slept on palliasses covered by three blankets apiece. Northam is well known for it's freezing night temperatures and even with the blankets, many a cold night was spent in those cheerless huts. Regimentation and obeying orders on command became a way of life. When asked what section I wanted to be in I immediately thought of my feet and requested transport. Up to now marches had been fairly light because we were as yet unfit to tackle the long route marches over twenty miles with full kit in hot weather. In transport there were three sections on which I would be examined - driving, mechanics and maintenance. When it came to the practical side of things I was fine but having little education I really had to apply myself to the theory. In the meantime I learned how to salute, slope arms and train hard. Soon we were ready for a long march and that's when I realised what old Sid had said was true. The only thing that kept me going was the band which met us three miles from camp and played us home. I hopped and hobbled along till I reached the hut. When I removed my boots my feet were covered in huge blisters. Determined not to let them beat me, I managed a few more marches before it became impossible to put on my boots. My feet looked like cooked crayfish, red, swollen and raw. Walking across the hut to the sergeant of transport, Dave Griffiths, I said, "*I think it's the end of the line Dave. I don't think I can carry on. Take a look at these.*" He glanced at my feet and said, "*You know what's going to happen if the doc sees them.*" "*Yes,*" I replied, "*I got through before but they'll put me out this time for sure.*" "*Do you want to stay in the army?*" he asked. "*Of course I do.*" I replied. "*Well, I'll keep you off your feet as much as possible in the camp with some jobs here and there. If you can hang out till you get overseas, I'll make sure you get in transport.*" "*Thanks very much, Dave,*" I answered. "*I really appreciate your help.*" True to his word I was given duties that kept me from marching. I knuckled down to my studies and to my surprise, after the exams, I was called out of the ranks on parade and congratulated by a Captain Johnson on achieving top marks. All I can say is there must have been a lot of dunces in my class.

Captain Johnson was a tremendous fellow who later, unfortunately, became the first casualty in our battalion in Syria. He told me to report to the company sergeant who would assign me an army ute. Life became a lot easier now that I was off my feet more. Instead of marching it was my job to take the hot boxes of food out to the men on the march. They were usually found cooling their feet in a creek somewhere.

Relief from the routine of the camp came from leave

passes to the Northam township. A bus ran to and from the camp, departing around seven and returning before midnight. It was a rule that everyone had to be inside the camp by twelve o'clock but several times some of the boys missed the bus and had to sneak into camp. Outside the gates was an A.W.O.L. post set up in a tent. Those on guard duty congregated there with the corporal of the guard called Peter Gorry. The shift was two hours on and four hours off. One night I was assigned guard duty. This was the first contact I'd had with Corporal Gorry. He said to me and a couple of other guys, "*Do you like beer?*", pronouncing it like 'burr'. I didn't know what accent it was but I got the drift and replied, "*My word I like beer.*" Well, from that moment on it was as though he was at the front, working out a plan of attack. I had no idea what he was on about so just followed his orders when he instructed, "*Now be at the ready. When I give the order, I want you to follow me.*" By now it was close to midnight. Buses had been delivering men to the main gate at regular intervals. Suddenly Gorry said, "*Right, follow me!*" With him leading the way in the dark we rushed along behind him, still completely unaware of what we were supposed to be doing. Next came the order, "*Stop! and don't make a sound!*" We found ourselves standing on a track that ran parallel to the road, which was used by latecomers to enter camp. Firstly though, they had to walk through some bush and climb through a fence onto the track. All of a sudden a bus pulled up on the main road. "*Quiet now,*" whispered Gorry. From the cover of dark we watched as the bus disgorged its load of about half a dozen men. It took all my willpower to stop from falling about laughing. Some of the men were so drunk they couldn't scratch themselves. Clutching clinking bottles they attempted to negotiate the distance between the road and the track. Some fell over logs, cursing and giggling, others became tangled in the fence. Loud shushing carried on the still night air as they tried vainly to stay as quiet as possible. Gorry waited till they were within a couple of yards of us before switching on a large torch and bellowing, "*Halt!*" The sight that greeted us was hilarious. There stood this motley crew with the most incredulous looks on their faces. They were frozen to the spot as though in shock. A few carried sugar bags containing their bottles. Gorry commanded, "*Right - hand over the beer!*" This order instantly brought the men to life. "*Aw, come on Corp, give us a go. Be fair Corp - gotta think about the morning.*" To his credit Gorry was quite sympathetic. He only confiscated half of each chap's supply. We apprehended two or three more groups during the night and managed to collect nineteen bottles for ourselves. Then it was the guards' turn to have a little session presided over by our hero, Corporal Gorry.

    Not long after I entered the camp Rose moved to Perth and lived with my parents in Egina Street. Les left hospital in Kalgoorlie and immediately went to the drill hall to join up as he had promised he would. I received his letter on a Tuesday saying he had passed the tests, been accepted and would be on the next train to Northam. I was thrilled to bits. The following Friday a wire arrived which said ' Come immediately - Les not expected to live'. Straight away I thought he must have had an accident of some kind. I applied for leave then got word from Rose that she, my mother and I had been given special permission to travel on the train which was normally reserved for passengers going on to the

Eastern States. Major Potts, the commanding officer of the camp, was a wonderful person. He said, "*I'll give you three days leave but if anything goes wrong, just send a wire and I'll grant you an extension.*" I joined mum and Rose on the train at Northam the next day, arriving in Kalgoorlie at 7 a.m. Sunday morning. Young Sid met us and took us to Whitlock Street. Within an hour of leaving the train we arrived at the hospital to find Les had just gone into a coma. He had been talking to the matron at six o'clock. When mum walked to the edge of the bed he must have sensed we were there because he raised his arm but didn't speak. We were told it was meningitis, contracted when his resistance was so low after his recent illnesses. Although I was unaware of it at the time, the cure was newly available in Perth - the method of drawing fluid from the spine. Our normal doctor, Gillette, was in the army with me. His place had been filled by a young chap, fresh from medical school. I desperately wanted Les flown to Perth, mainly because I thought he stood a better chance of survival with more experienced doctors, but I could not budge the local doctor even though I created quite a stink. I think he was unwilling to take the risk of shifting Les, but to me, anything was better than leaving him to die. Sunday passed with mum never leaving the bedside. The doctor told her not to hope that Les would live because he'd be mentally retarded - not exactly comforting news to give a mother in those circumstances. On Monday morning, mum said to me, "*There's not much point you coming to the hospital for a while. You can't do anything and I'll be there if anything happens. Go and have a few drinks with your mates.*" I still had my motorbike so I rode to the Golden Eagle Hotel where I joined some old friends.

Mr Hunt, our next door neighbour in Whitlock Street, worked on the trams as a conductor. To get a message to me Rose asked Mr Hunt to call into the pub on his way past and tell me I was wanted back at the hospital. He came into the bar and said, "*Listen Pud, if you want to see your brother alive, you'll have to be quick.*" Dropping everything I jumped on my bike and roared off to the hospital, exceeding the speed limit by miles. Rose, mum, Sid, and Les's fiancee Jean were already by the bedside. It was about five o'clock in the afternoon. I sat beside Les in silence. Looking at him lying there I couldn't imagine how my strong healthy brother had been struck down in the prime of his life. It seemed such a waste of a terrific person and my best mate. An hour later, with my hand over his heart, Les took his last breath. We were all devastated by our loss. The household was quiet that night, everyone lost in their own thoughts. It was left up to me to make the funeral arrangements. Mum wanted Les to be buried in Karrakatta cemetery in Perth which meant having a lead-lined coffin for the journey. We travelled down on the train and put Les to rest. I returned to camp and for quite a while felt completely down in the dumps. I had looked forward to having Les join me and the thought that it was now an impossibility filled me with sadness. But life goes on and as time passed the sense of loss eased.

...Chapter 21

It was now October. We were put on alert that at any time we could be on our way overseas. There were a few false starts. One occurred on a scorching hot day. The order came to prepare for departure. This meant assembling our kit bags, sea kits, rifles etc. - all together about ninety pounds in weight. Dressed in full uniform and carrying our gear we formed ranks in the yard. Excitement overrode the heat and discomfort as Captain Duffy led the march out of the gates and down the road towards the station. We got to within a mile of Northam when the Captain commanded us to halt. Thinking we were going to have a welcome break, we waited expectantly for the order to down kit and take a seat. The next words he uttered completely shattered that illusion. "*Right boys,*" he said, "*I want you to go off the road, through that fence and make your way back to camp under your own steam.*" The place he had chosen to abandon us was in a very hilly area covered in large rocky outcrops. Reluctantly we headed bush. As we crawled and clambered our way over the terrible terrain the language fairly flew from the mouths of disgruntled soldiers who thought, by now, they'd be on the train to Perth. Two young lads who we all suspected were underage for the army and would never complete the exercise, surprised us all by reaching the camp along with the rest of us. I still see one of them, Sully, every year at the 2nd 16th reunion. He told me he and the other boy were sixteen when they enlisted. When we entered camp we were a different mob of boys to the one that had left earlier. There were no smiles now. We were exhausted, drenched with sweat and disappointed. But that was the way it was - a preparatory exercise to see how we would perform when the real time came. After a shower, meal and a good rest, we returned to the usual routine of the camp.

   A Sergeant O'Keefe took us for bayonet drill. It was hard work. We formed two ranks facing each other. On the command "charge" we ran through the oncoming rank at full tilt, turned, then charged back again. This was repeated over and over. Although fit, it certainly took the stuffing out of us. On this particularly hot day, O'Keefe had us to the stage where we could hardly breathe. We were staggering. It was okay for the Sergeant. All he'd done was stand there yelling orders. Then he barked, *"The problem with you blokes is you're not half dinkum enough."* I burst into laughter - I could see the funny side of that comment. He came flying down the rank and fronted me. *"There's a war on soldier,"* he said, *"You might have heard about it."* That set me off even more which brought smiles to the other chaps but not the Sergeant. He glared at me but fortunately let the incident pass without punishment.

Another bayonet exercise involved charging and stabbing bags of hay with faces painted on them which were hung in the yard. The bags were held by chaps to make it look more realistic. They had to let go and side-step at the last second as the oncoming soldiers thrust their bayonets into the bags. This day a bloke called Macka held a bag while a big raw-boned Scotsman named Jock bore down on him, yelling and screaming at the top of his voice. The only thought going through Macka's mind, he told us later, was that he be quick enough to get out of Jock's way in time. He said, "*My God, I'd hate to be the enemy with Jock coming towards me!*"

Finally, we were told embarkation would take place the 25th October 1940. Naturally we were a little sceptical after the previous false alarms but nevertheless held high hopes that this time would be it. A mate, Les Dingle, approached me to see if I would share a taxi with him and three others to Perth on the last night. The camp was now closed with an order issued that no-one was to leave. If anyone did, and was caught, they would definitely not be going overseas. We knew the risk but decided to chance it. A plan was devised whereby the taxi would pick us up outside the gates. Just on nightfall we made our way to the rendezvous area. The taxi was waiting for us. In we climbed and away went the car at breakneck speed. To make matters worse one of the boys, Jack (Strangler) Ryan, said to the driver, "*Take your foot off the brake why don't ya!*" The road from Northam to Perth in those days was narrow, very curved and hilly. As we held on for dear life the only noise above the engine came from the tyres screeching round the corners. It wasn't long before we reached the city centre. We arranged to meet there again at 12.00 p.m. I caught a tram and travelled to Egina Street. Rose had been to see me in Northam the week before. We had agreed, as she was pregnant, to say our goodbyes there and then. When I bowled into the house she was taken completely by surprise and was thrilled we could have some more time together. I of course was equally as pleased. A lovely evening was spent with the family before Rose and I went back into the city. All the wives had come to see their men off and the parting was very emotional. That was to be the last time I saw my darling till I returned nineteen months later. The return trip was a lot slower due to the fact a fog had developed which was very fortunate for us. We had no trouble re-entering camp and made our way quietly to bed.

Next day we marched to the train which transferred us to Fremantle. I was glad Rose hadn't come because those farewelling us were fenced off. It wasn't long before we were ferried out to the Aquatania, one of three ships in the convoy. The other two were the Queen Mary and the Mauritania. Once on board we sorted ourselves out and found our sleeping quarters. Altogether there were about three thousand men on the ship - the 2nd 14th battalion from Victoria - the 2nd 27th from South Australia and us, the 2nd 16th. The Eastern States battalions had been picked up before us so they were already settled in. Our escort ship for the first few days was the Perth which was then relieved by the Canberra. We headed directly for Bombay. Time aboard was occupied with cards, two up, reading and generally amusing ourselves anyway we could.

On reaching Bombay we were given leave. Together with three mates I took in the sights and smells of the city. Before leaving the ship we had been drummed time and again not to go anywhere near Grant Road, the red light district. Anyone found there would be in real hot water. After a few beers one of the men suggested we go to Grant Road just for a look. Of course if it had not been mentioned on board none of us would have had a clue where it was but curiosity got the better of us. We hired a gharri - a horse drawn buggy - and said to the driver, "*George!*" [we called everyone George], "*Take us to Grant Road.*" One of our group, 'Rooa', who was as full as a bull, had earlier given his hat to one of the Indian children. Feeling the heat, he produced a spotted handkerchief from his pocket, tied a knot in each corner and placed it on his head. He looked very comical and attracted much attention from the locals. Reaching Grant Road, three of us paid the driver but Rooa started arguing the point about the price. As though from nowhere, hordes of Indians gathered round us. There must have been hundreds of them. From my slightly elevated position on the pavement I glanced at the sea of sombre faces and quietly said to my mates, "*Listen, we better not stick around here or we'll get into big trouble.*" Quickly I went and paid Roo's fare, grabbed hold of him and as a group we made our way quietly through the crowd. What we saw as we walked along Grant Road made us feel sick to our stomachs. Young girls sat in cramped cages waiting for customers. They looked so helpless and sad. I wished I'd never agreed to come. Completely unimpressed with the spectacle we caught a taxi back to the ship.

    The following day we travelled to the British barracks - a nine hour trip from Bombay. This was to be our home for the next ten days. While there we saw a few unusual things; like the way the dead are left for the vultures to eat. It was dangerous to walk along with food in your hand near these vicious birds as they would swoop straight for you. I sampled my first buffalo steak - very tasty too. The days passed pleasantly and soon came time to depart. Back in Bombay we caught our first glimpse of the ship that would take us to the Middle East. My God - what a sight! It was Indian - the Rijoola - and much smaller than the Aquatania. In fact, I think only the 2nd 16th travelled on it. There were no bunks, only hammocks. It was more like a tramp steamer than a troop ship. The first meal on the deck was quite an experience. We sat on long forms with dixies in hand. Along came a couple of blokes carrying large pots. Into our dixies was ladled what could only be described as light brown water with a few meatless bones in it. We looked at each other in disbelief. There were no vegetables, meat or substance whatsoever in the concoction. Next we were handed soccer ball shaped loaves of bread. Thinking we could make a meal by soaking the bread in the water, we broke open the loaves. Inside they were hollow and mouldy green. We went hungry. In our battalion there were two brothers - Alan and Alf Cadlola. Alf was a very quiet chap while Alan was the exact opposite - rough and fiery. As we sat trying to figure out what we were going to eat we saw Alan, three sheets to the wind, staggering up the gangway onto the ship. He collected his dixie and reeled over to our table. Being full, all he wanted to do was tell everyone of his experiences in the city. He took absolutely no interest in what was being placed in his dixie. In went a huge ladle of the coloured water followed by a typical dog bone - one with a knuckle on either end. It didn't quite fit in the dixie so one end stuck up over the side. Alan raved on, unaware of the meal that awaited him. The rest of us saw the humour and found it hard to contain ourselves. Patiently we waited for Alan's reaction. During a lull in the conversation he finally focused on his dixie. Stunned silence - then, "*Surely this is not my tea!*" Oh yes," we replied, "*That's all you're going to get. And you can have a piece of that good bread too if you like.*" Alan sat back and sort of bunched himself up. It was at that moment Colonel Baxter-Cox chose to ascend the gangplank. He was a dapper little bloke who carried a swagger stick and was always, despite the heat, a picture of sartorial elegance in his uniform. The moment someone mentioned his arrival, Alan sprang from his seat, grabbed the bone from his dixie and rushed to meet him. Thrusting the bone to within inches of the Colonel's face Alan shouted, "*How'd you like that for tea Colonel?*" The Colonel was taken aback for a moment but give him his due, he listened to Alan's story, inspected the dixies and declared it was impossible for us to eat such muck. Immediately he ordered we be given emergency rations which, although an improvement, were pretty unpalatable also. To make up for the lousy food I occasionally treated myself to a tin of crab meat and a tin of pineapple.

Two days later we set sail for the Middle East. The convoy's escort now was only a small gunboat. One day while I was on guard duty on the bridge an enemy reconnaissance plane flew over. All men were ordered below decks. Being on guard I stayed at my post and got to see the gunboat go into action. The amount of ammunition it threw at that plane was incredible. I watched the boat actually recoil with the gunfire. Unfortunately the plane escaped. Later I was given a dressing down for being on the bridge but I explained that I thought being on guard duty meant holding one's position. My excuse was accepted.

As we neared the coast allied planes flew out to circle the convoy and provide some protection. As one left, another took its place. On one occasion a mate, Bob Foster, and I sat on the deck yarning. We saw a plane come round the ship and in the distance a relief one approaching. As I said to Bob, *"There's the relief coming,"* the plane closest to us headed for the coast in a line directly in front of us. It was just a speck on the horizon when we saw a huge explosion erupt from that spot in the sky. We never found out what happened but I don't think the enemy hit it as there wasn't a sign of enemy planes in the area. The gunboat raced to the rescue but only wreckage was found floating on the water.

...Chapter 22

On the 25th November, **Rose's birthday,** the Rigoola entered the Suez Canal and slowly made its way along to the half way point of El Qantara where we disembarked. At nightfall we were packed like sardines into fully enclosed trucks. There was hardly any ventilation and standing room only. Making a cigarette was impossible as our arms were held to our sides in the crush. The only relief came during brief intervals at toilet stops. All night we jolted across the desert in the sightless confines of the trucks. It was certainly a wonderful introduction to Egypt.

Finally we arrived at Duellers Camp which was situated on the side of a hill. For two nights, before being issued with beds, we slept in tents on groundsheets. It was on one of these nights that a storm hit. First came red dust then, as the rain fell, dust turned to mud, running down the hill and through our tents. We wrapped ourselves in the groundsheets to escape the mudslide but our belongings did not fare as well. The morning light revealed a chaotic mess. Bayonets and hard-hats stuck out of the mud everywhere. Men trying to walk through the slime grew visibly taller as mud stuck to their boots, layer upon layer. Heat from the blazing sun soon dried the earth and some semblance of order was restored. Beds made from cane and wicker were set up in the tents. Once organised, training began in earnest. The promise that Dave Griffiths had made about getting me a truck fell quite a way short of the mark. There were sixty five transport drivers in the camp and only nine trucks. It turned out I got to drive about one day a fortnight. This meant I had to participate in the long hot desert marches. I managed two or three before my feet became raw. During the marches, Arabs tossed us beautiful Jaffa oranges which helped make the journeys a little more bearable.

One night I was on guard duty at the transport shed. Though everyone loathed the job I enjoyed it because it meant welcome relief from marching. Sitting there thinking, I decided to volunteer for this duty knowing I would meet with little resistance from the other chaps. The following night I was given the same job. As I prepared my palliasse and bedding for the four hour break I would take later, Dave Griffiths walked into the shed. He said, "*Hey listen, you were on guard last night, weren't you?*" "*Yes Dave, that's right,*" I replied. "*Well, what are you doing on guard tonight?*" he demanded. "*I volunteered,*" I answered. "*What for?*" he persisted. "*Well,*" I said, "*There's no way in the world I can march with the state my feet are in. You've seen them so you know what they're like. They're in pretty bad shape at the moment.*" Expecting him to say, '*Fair enough*', I was astounded when he said,

75 QUID AND AN AXE

"I'll tell you this. You won't be on guard tomorrow night. You'll be marching with the boys." Feeling the hackles rise, I glared at him and said, *"Now listen to me David - I might not be on guard tomorrow night but I can assure you of one thing - I won't be marching with the boys!"* *"Oh,"* he said, *"Won't you!"* *"No,"* I replied defiantly. *"We'll see about that!,"* he retorted as he turned on his heel and walked away. Trying to figure out why Dave had acted that way, I decided it must have been because I'd previously had an argument with a great mate of his. It seemed the only explanation for him turning on me like this.

Next morning I went straight to the doctor. He took one look at my feet and said, *"My God, how did you get in the army?"* *"It's a strange thing,"* I replied, *"But a lot of people have asked me that."* He couldn't believe the mess my feet were in. *"You can't possibly march on those."* he said. *"Well, nobody knows that better than I do,"* I replied. *"I've been through plenty."* We got talking and I told him the whole story of how I had wangled my way overseas thinking I would be driving a truck. He listened quietly and when I finished he sat thinking for a few moments. Somehow I think he was on the verge of sending me home which I dreaded, but he must have been weighing up alternatives because suddenly he *said, "Do you reckon you could do a job at the cookhouse?"* *"My word I do,"* I said eagerly. *"All right,"* he replied, *"I'll see you get a start there right away."* And so I became an army cook. Dave never said a word about my appointment. Regrettably he ceased to be my favourite sergeant. The cooks were terrific blokes - Tommy Carter and Tommy Havesham. Eric Fields was the quartermaster sergeant and there were several others on the staff - all nice people. Slotted in as a roustabout I did whatever was asked of me -

cleaning, cutting bread, preparing vegetables etc. I was as happy as Larry.

Christmas arrived and we put on a magnificent spread. The day before, hot boxes containing turkeys and puddings arrived from Tel Aviv. Fresh fruit and vegetables and all the trimmings necessary accompanied them. My pay at the time was ten shillings and sixpence a week due to the fact that the rest, one pound four and six, was being sent to Rose. Out of my pay I had to buy tobacco and toiletries which left me with very little for entertainment. On Christmas Eve the men went to the canteen for a spree but I, being broke, turned in for an early night in readiness for the big day ahead. I was nearly asleep when Blue Maloney, one of my old Kalgoorlie mates, came into the tent. He looked at me in surprise and asked, "*What are you doing in bed Pud?*" "*Oh,*" I said, "*I thought I'd get an early night because I've got a big day tomorrow. We've got to get this Christmas dinner going and everything.*" "*But this is Christmas Eve!,*" he exclaimed. "*Yes I know that,*" I replied. He persisted, "*You've just got to have a drink,*" he kept saying. In the end I said, "*Well, put it this way Blue. I haven't got the price of a drink.*" As soon as he heard that, he said, "*Come on - we'll bloody well make certain you get a drink.*" Sure enough the boys rallied to the cause and my glass was never empty. Next morning I arose before dawn and made my way to the cookhouse. Soon it was a flurry of activity. During the morning a steady stream of officers visited, each with one or two bottles of beer for us. We stacked them up, determined not to drink till the meal was over. There must have been about twenty bottles in all. The time came to serve. Everything went off beautifully. I reckon it was equal to a five star hotel meal judging by the praise we received. With the job successfully completed we relaxed and settled down to knock off our supply of beer - and well deserved it was too.

Training continued as the men prepared for the front. On February 11th I received word that I had a healthy son, Leslie George. A mate's wife was also pregnant but due later than Rose. At times he and I used to discuss the progress of our wives. He was thrilled to hear of my new arrival and looked forward to news of his. Unfortunately he was sent to the front prior to the birth. When the letter came, the dispatch rider went to find him but he had just been killed. He died not knowing he had become a father.

I'm not sure how long we were at Duellers Camp but eventually, after the boys went to the front in Syria, we moved out to Dimra, a staging camp in Palestine. I was assigned to the Sergeants' mess to cook with Len (Rusty) Donovan, a really nice bloke. It was at Dimra that I got to know a lot of men as they passed through on their way to the front. Some of the recruits were so raw and inexperienced they could not even slope arms, the first thing taught in the army. But men were in short supply and were being sent out from Australia with little or no training. Always scratching for a few bob, a mate and I started a swy school. The financial situation altered drastically. Suddenly we had enough money to go on leave, buy gifts for our families and afford a few treats. The first leave I spent in Tel Aviv and Jerusalem. I thoroughly enjoyed wandering around Tel Aviv. Situated on the coast it was a nice little city bustling with activity. To get to Jerusalem from Tel Aviv meant taking a hair-raising trip on a bus driven by an Arab who put his fate and those of his passengers in the hands of Allah.

Hurtling along the road, the bus swayed dangerously as it flew over the seven sisters, a series of very steep switchbacks. It was a very relieved soldier, I can tell you, who climbed from the bus at the end of the journey. Whilst in Jerusalem I took a tour and was shown such things as the footprint of Jesus in the rock, his tomb, the place of the cross and the Mosque of Omar. Here we were given large hide sort of overshoes to cover our boots. Next we were driven through Bethlehem to the river Jordan and the Dead Sea. Being thirteen hundred feet below sea level, the descent was very steep and full of bends. When we arrived at the bottom the heat was incredible, trapped as it was in a forty six by ten mile basin with no breeze whatsoever. The water was the clearest I had ever seen but when we tried to swim in it, the salt content made it almost impossible. My bottom kept popping up and I felt very awkward. As is usual when swimming I copped a couple of mouthfuls of water and the taste was absolutely vile. The combination of local foods I had eaten during the day and the water made me violently ill after the swim, but all in all it was an interesting and enjoyable visit.

    I spent the rest of my months of service in Dimra but found it hard to accept that after all the training and preparation I'd had, I would not see any action. The closest we came to any excitement in camp occurred on two occasions. The first happened just after I arrived in Dimra. It was a beautiful day and everyone was dotted around the camp doing their jobs. Slit trenches had been dug here and there for our protection in case of enemy attack. This day a plane came over very low. We all thought it was one of ours and prepared to give it a wave. As it drew closer we recognised it as German. The men reacted like startled rabbits, caught outside their warren. One minute there were soldiers everywhere and the next moment they all disappeared as if from the face of the earth. It must have looked quite humorous from the plane, which, as it turned out, was only on a reconnaissance mission. The other episode happened one moonlit night when we were sleeping. The Italians were in the war now and some were returning from a raid - we knew Italian planes by their sound. Seeing our camp in the moonlight they must have decided we were the enemy and proceeded to drop the remainder of their bombs on us. Rusty and I slept in a room off the end of the cook house. On being woken by the first bomb we flew outside where we were joined by a little Scotsman and a huge bloke - both cooks who worked with us. Heading for the nearest slit trench, the Scotsman dived in ahead of us. In the dark, the big sixteen stone chap landed on top of the Scotty. Despite being quite a serious situation I had to laugh at the curses coming from the trench as the little fellow mouthed off in his Scottish brogue. We waited till the raid finished then went to check on the rest of the men. Luckily there were no casualties but once again fate had lent a hand. A bomb had landed at one corner of a tent, upending a bed, the only one unoccupied in a tent of four. The soldier who normally slept there was on leave. The other three in the tent were unscathed.

I tried everything to go to the front, even for an hour. One day I thought my big chance had come. A chap I knew from Karridale, Guy New, took over as head of the camp. He was a lot older than me but I remembered him well from my childhood. Making myself known to him, we had a good chat about the old days. Later during a break in the cook house I went to his tent and put my case forward about going to the front. No matter what I said he would not entertain the idea at all. I told him that if I didn't see some action I'd go home in disgrace, not having fired a shot or done my bit for the country. Still my arguments fell on deaf ears. Disappointed, I wandered back to the mess and prepared dinner. Later in the afternoon I decided to have another go in the hope he might weaken. He listened to my pleas for a while then said, "*Now look here Pud, you'd have no show in the world. Even some of the boys with good feet that are there now are packing up on the rough terrain they have to go over, so you'd have no hope of making it.*" "*Well,*" I said, "*If you'll give me a chance to go, I'll get through even if I have to take my boots off.*" "*No,*" said Guy, "*I'm sorry, but I can't allow it.*" Knowing he meant it I did not try again, but resolved to make it there somehow. An opportunity arose when a couple of mates and I planned to join one of the night convoys. It meant being A.W.O.L. but we were willing to throw caution to the wind. The convoy we chose consisted of eleven trucks which were to depart around ten o'clock. With our rifles and bit of gear we split up and each headed for a different truck. Fate must have decided I wasn't meant to go because of all the trucks, I chose the one containing my bosom mate, Arty Milstead, from my mining days in Kalgoorlie. Arty had already been to the front, got wounded and was heading there again. At this stage I didn't know of Arty's presence. Trying to be unobtrusive I climbed in the back of the truck and settled down. For some reason I happened to speak. Immediately Arty recognised my voice and called out, "*Hey Pud. What are you doing? You're not supposed to be on draft tonight.*" Trying desperately to shut him up

I whispered, *"No, no, no, it's okay Arty. I just want a lift up."* Standing his ground, Arty said firmly, *"Look Pud, there's no chance you're going to go. I've already been there and you're not missing out on a thing."* He continued, *"If you get on the truck, I'll put you in. "*— And this was my best mate talking!! Accepting defeat I climbed out and resigned myself to the fact I would spend my war time feeding the troops.

The swy school became my main interest in the camp. Only English pennies were allowed for the game so as the reenforcements came through, to make sure no-one set up in competition, I offered to buy any pennies in their possession. One particular penny cost me six quid, or six thousand mils in Palestinian currency .I wore a money belt which was usually full. Some chaps, due to go on leave, had a dabble to try and make a few extra bob. If they lost everything and it came to my attention , I always returned their stake so they would not miss leave. Because of this I did not make a big profit, but a heck of a lot more than my five bob a day army pay. There were times I had up to a hundred quid in my belt - quite a fortune in those days.

Our battalion eventually returned from the front. Many of the boys had been killed in action. Those left moved out to New Sarat, another camp, before going on to Suez, then home. I remained at Dimra for a short time, then moved to New Sarat as regimental barber. The charge was a shilling a cut. Sixpence went to me, the rest into the canteen fund. It was here I had my wallet, photographs and souvenirs stolen, quite a blow when I was soon due to leave for Australia. On the train from New Sarat to Suez I was again ripped off but in a different way and one I hate to admit. In eighteen months I had never been taken in by the Arabs and their attempts to hawk something or steal belongings. Perhaps the excitement of being homeward bound clouded my judgement on this occasion. I was standing with a couple of mates on the outside platform of a carriage surveying the scenery when an Arab climbed down from the roof and said, "*Do you want to buy a ring?*" "*How much George?*" I inquired. "*Five thousand mils,*" he replied. *No way,*" I said. "*Let's have a look at it.*" He unfolded a piece of rag and exposed a heavy gold ring. I could see it was genuine and knew for a fact that sometimes the Arabs stole jewelry from dead soldiers. I offered him two thousand mils but he steadfastly refused. When I also refused to alter my offer, he gave in and agreed to my price. Handing him the money he quickly thrust the rag in my hand and was gone like a shot back to the roof of the train and away. I unwrapped the rag to discover not the ring I had seen but a completely different one. Turning to a couple of Pommie soldiers nearby, I held out the ring and said, "*What do you think this is worth?*" Taking the ring, one of them licked his hand and drew the ring across it. Left on his skin was a nice green streak. Grinning he said, "*Oh, about two and six I reckon.*" I was ropeable. I couldn't believe I'd been sucked in after all those months in the Middle East. When the train stopped at some station along the way I happened to spot the swindler trying the same caper on a couple of soldiers who had gotten off the train to stretch their legs. I could have caught him if I'd gone quietly to where he was but like an idiot I called out, "*Hey George, come here a minute,*" as though I wanted to buy something else. Recognising me, he took off across the desert with me in hot pursuit. I had no hope of catching him. He could have broken the four minute mile with ease. Back to the train I tramped with my tail well and truly between my legs. I carried that blasted ring home with me even though it had turned a nasty shade of green.

At Suez we boarded a French ship called the Felix Roselle. It was actually a luxury liner before being seconded as a troop ship, so the conditions on board were very comfortable. The officers luxuriated in first class accommodation while the lower ranks occupied the second class berths. We were a motley group, sort of leftovers from battalions all over Australia. There were several Kiwis amongst us also. A Captain Bruce McKenzie was on board. He and I had had quite a lot to do with each other in the camps and it wasn't long before he approached me and said, *"What about being my batman Pud?"* To me, a batman was like being at the bottom of a barrel so I said, *"No, no, sorry sir, but I don't want to be a batman."* *"Look,"* he continued, *"There's practically nothing to do. You might have to polish my shoes now and then but hardly anything really. And you'll possibly get a few privileges."* Finally he persuaded me to take the job but I kept it secret from the other men. A few days later Bruce asked me to cut his hair. Putting on a bit of style I successfully completed the task in his cabin. During the cut he said, *"I've got a pair of clippers here."* He boasted they had once cut General Blarney's hair. *"You can use them if you like,"* he said. *"Thank you sir,"* I replied. *"Would it be alright if I used them around the ship?"* I was still earning a shilling a cut from the enlisted men, my barber shop being the deck. *"Sure,"* said Bruce. *"Just take good care of them."* They were beautiful clippers, the best I had seen. They fitted snugly into my hand and had a broad thumb rest which made clipping a breeze. When Bruce went to dinner fellow officers enquired where he had had his hair cut. Word spread and soon I was fully employed. With my outfit under my arm I entered different cabins where perhaps one or two officers awaited me. I felt like a real hot shot. Most paid me four or five shillings so I made quite a healthy profit in first class.

Life was good as we sailed through the Red Sea to Aden. We docked for a short time but no-one was allowed to disembark. Without movement the ship became a hot box and we were very happy to be on our way. From Aden we sailed to Mombasa in Kenya where we spent three days. It was here I saw a huge fleet of ships move out, bound for battle - a magnificent sight. Leaving Mombasa we headed south, keeping within sight of the coast. Being very humid and hot, most of us slept on the decks using our life jackets as pillows. Among us but unidentified were one hundred and fifty snarlers. These were men whose service was no longer required. In other words they had been drummed out of the army. Below decks, under lock and key, were eighty seven worse offenders.

One night we were having tea when Bruce McKenzie called for our attention. "*Now boys, I've got something to say and I want everyone to listen. I'm calling for volunteers. There's going to be an attempt to take over the ship tonight and I need everyone to volunteer for guard duty.*" Immediately the snarlers were revealed as they were the only ones who did not raise their hands in response to Mack's request. The rest of us were issued with guns and a password and stationed at every door and gangway on the ship. Our orders were that no matter who approached us, if they couldn't give the password, we had to shoot to kill. Throughout the night we took shifts. In the morning I learned that quite a big fire had been started in the bow of the ship in an attempt to burn the vessel. Because we were within sight of the coast I suppose the snarlers thought they had a chance of swimming ashore. The fire was quickly extinguished. I was on guard next day when they brought all the arms out from the cells below. It was amazing to see the amount of equipment that had been smuggled to the prisoners. From Mack I heard the whole story. A snarler had become scared of the proposed mutiny and informed on his cohorts. If he hadn't I'm quite convinced none of us would have survived. The plan was to knock off the guard, release the prisoners, cudgel the men sleeping on the decks and throw them overboard, take over the ship then run it aground on the African coast and escape. A very bold plot and thankfully one that did not come to fruition.

The next port of call was Durban in South Africa. We didn't have a clue where we were headed till we reached each port. While there, a woman called Carol (I can't remember her surname) sang the ship into and out of the port. She had apparently done it for the ships in W.W.I. It was wonderful and moving to hear her voice carry across the water to us. We were in Durban for five days. After the ship docked my mate and I caught a taxi into the city. The first things that caught my eye were the beautifully ornate rickshaws manned by equally ornate Zulus. They stood in lines waiting for customers and the colours looked brilliant in the sunshine. We had a look round for a while then decided to go for a beer. Spotting a pub across the road we stood waiting for a break in the traffic. Next thing an old chap approached us and asked if we'd like to go to his home. Before we could answer he continued, "*What were you planning to do?*" "*Well,*" I replied, "*We were just going to have a beer. We wanted to try African beer.*" "*I've got plenty of beer at home,*" he suggested. I had a quick powwow with my mate. "*What do you think?*" I asked. "*Well, we'll go if you like.*" he replied. Together we boarded a tram and took a short journey to where the old chap lived. Mr Johnson, as he was named, had a beautiful home and a lovely wife who welcomed us with open arms. They explained that over fifty servicemen had been invited to their home from all the services but no Aussies until now. Seated in a spacious lounge we were served a large bottle of beer each and offered cigarettes and cigars. "*Now, just help yourselves,*" we were told. "*If you feel like wandering around, do so. Make yourselves completely at home.*" We felt on top of the world. With a few beers under our belts we sat down to the best home cooked meal I can recall. After dinner their daughter Doreen arrived home. She was a lovely girl who had suffered the loss of two airmen sweethearts. Now she refused to get serious with anyone in uniform in case she jinxed them. A marvellous evening was spent in the company of this loving family before we returned to the ship. Having found out that Doreen worked in a big store, I suggested to my mate that we ring her the following day and offer to take her and her parents to the pictures. As it worked out, Mr and Mrs Johnson were unable to make it but Doreen asked if she could bring a girlfriend along and make a foursome. We were delighted with this arrangement. The theatre was a magnificent building and although I normally hated the pictures, for me this was a rare treat after army life and I actually thoroughly enjoyed the evening. The highlight was an organist who played any songs requested from the audience which consisted mostly of Aussies from the ship. Soon we had a sing-song going with the familiar tunes of home filling the theatre. Later we took a taxi to the Johnsons' where a beautiful supper awaited us. As we ate the ladies asked our opinions of different foods. We thought nothing of it at the time until, on taking our leave, they asked if we would return the following night for a party at which all our favourite foods would be available. Feeling overwhelmed by their generosity, we gratefully accepted the invitation. The next morning we arranged for two chaps to switch guard duty with us if the need arose, leaving us free to attend the party. I was really excited at the thought of having an evening specially put on for just the two of us It was about 9.30 a.m.. I had previously taken Captain McKenzie's washing to the Seaman's Institute to be cleaned and pressed. Suddenly he came rushing up to me, thrust an authorisation note in my hand and said, "*I want you to slip straight over to the Institute and collect my gear Pud because we're sailing at ten.*" This gave me just enough time to grab the clothes and ring Doreen to say we couldn't make the party. I had told our hosts the night before that although I couldn't say we were sailing, it would be the only reason if I rang and cancelled their invitation. Doreen was terribly disappointed as was I. All I could do was thank her and her folks for their hospitality and promise to drop a line, which I did later on. Back on the ship we set sail to the sweet sounds of Carol's farewell songs. Right to the horizon and far out of earshot the words she sang were semaphored to us and repeated over the speakers. As much as I craved returning to my darling Rosie in Australia I still felt terribly sad at having missed the evening with the Johnsons.

Now we were headed for Fremantle and my last port of call. I continued cutting hair and asked Mac on several occasions if I could buy his clippers. Each time he politely refused saying how they meant a great deal to him. One day I said, "*Now look Mac! I'm going to make you a promise and I'll carry it out. When we get off the ship at Fremantle, if you don't ask for your clippers, I'm not going to hand them over voluntarily. I'm going to keep them.*" Laughing he said, "*Forget them? Not a chance! There's no way I'll forget to ask for them, I guarantee it.*" I still have those clippers, with thanks either to the excitement of the homecoming that caused Mac's lapse of memory or his generosity. They still work beautifully and are my pride and joy.

...Chapter 23

We arrived off Fremantle on a morning in May 1942. Due to lack of space on the wharf we were unable to berth till 10 p.m. that night. Naturally the boys were completely browned off. They paced the decks, not wanting to eat, moping around like lost sheep. When the ship finally moved through the heads it was listing quite a bit because every man aboard rushed to the dock side of the ship. Our welcoming committee consisted of army Provos [military police], trucks, and vans waiting to transport the prisoners to jail. The wharf was taboo to the public, not that anyone would have been there as our arrival was not known or expected. Thinking we would disembark within the hour we waited expectantly - all night till 10 a.m. the next day. No one slept, nerves were on edge and the general opinion was that we'd never get off the blasted boat. But eventually the time came and we finally set foot on good old Aussie soil. Our instructions were to go to a place in

Claremont, a suburb of Perth, to collect leave passes and subsistence money. After eighteen months abroad I was being allowed seven days leave, two of which would be swallowed up by travel to and from Kalgoorlie. If there had only been West Australians on board the stopover in Claremont would have been quick but all the Eastern States blokes were allowed leave and all wanted their money too.

The day was stifling hot and we each wore full uniform with about ninety pounds of gear on our backs. Arriving at the address and dripping with sweat we were informed that they could not deal with our requests and we would have to go to Rockeby Road in Subiaco, quite a distance from Claremont. My one thought was to be on the 5 o'clock train for Kalgoorlie. We caught a train to Subiaco, left our gear on the station platform and went outside. The queue stretched for at least half a mile from the station right up Rockeby Road to the office in question. I took one look and decided there was no way I'd make the 5 p.m. train if I had to wait here. Seeing a sergeant nearby I put my story to him, whereupon he suggested I go to Nicholson Road, not far from Rockeby Road, where the queue should be a lot shorter. A mate and I quickly walked there but to my dismay the line was still too long to be dealt with in the few hours I had left. My other worry was finding time to dump my gear in Egina Street so I would not be burdened with it for the journey. Added to all this was the fact I hadn't eaten or drunk anything since the day before. Fortunately, while standing in the queue wondering what to do next, some girls came along with buckets of water and I was able to quench my thirst. I decided not to waste any more time. I left the queue and walked over to a lieutenant. After hearing my tale of woe, he said briskly, "*Come with me.*" Straight to the front of the line we went. "*Fix this fellow next,*" he instructed the chap behind the desk. "*He's got to go to Kalgoorlie.*" With a new lease on life I sprinted back to the station and travelled into the city. Thinking I'd still have time to take my gear to Mt Hawthorn I tried in vain to hail a taxi but with the place full of Americans and servicemen I didn't stand a chance. The only alternative was the tram which seemed to take forever getting to Coogee Street. From there I humped my gear several streets to my parents' home. By this time I was saturated from head to foot and totally exhausted. I staggered down the path to the rear of the house but was unable to climb the steps onto the verandah. All I could do was stand there. My sister Win spotted me first and shouted excitedly to the rest of the family. Within minutes I was stripped of my gear and led into the kitchen where mum poured me a drink of wine. Unable to relax because of my need to make the train I explained my intentions, which were immediately howled down. Everyone wanted me to stay and said I was in no condition to travel. I gave in, had a meal and a bath and fell into a very welcome sleep. The next day was spent talking and watching the clock till it was time to go. Once on the train I paced back and forward all night willing the loco to keep moving. I couldn't get home quick enough.

    I arrived in Kalgoorlie the following day at around 10 a.m. There were no taxis available so I quickly walked to where the tram could be taken to Whitlock Street. Passing a pub, an old mate saw me and tried to persuade me to have a drink but nothing at this stage could deter me from wasting one more second than I had to. With a rapid apology and brief explanation that I had a wife and new son waiting, I sprinted off. Finally I reached Whitlock Street. The feeling I had as I walked along towards the house was like floating on air. I was so excited I actually passed the house and went on to a neighbour's place a couple of doors away. Kathleen, their little daughter, saw me from the front yard and yelled, "*Pud! Pud!*" Realising my mistake, I hushed her and instructed her not to say a word. Back I went to the house, along the side and round to the rear. Rose's three younger sisters, Mary, Betty and Sue and my son Les were playing on the verandah. As I turned the corner the girls stared at me with mouths open, then, as one, made a rush for the door. "*Rosie, Rosie, George is home!*" they screamed. Out ran Rose and the rest of the family. My happiness was complete. Les found it all very confusing. All he had seen of me was a photograph. I carried him inside, pointed to the photograph hanging in the front room and said, "*Who's that?*" With a quizzical look on his face he stared first at the picture, then at me, then back to the picture again. He must have noticed some resemblance because he seemed to accept the fact he had a real flesh and blood father and not just a picture on a wall. Rose told me she had had a premonition about my arrival. She had been knitting a jumper for herself and a few days before I appeared on the scene she felt a desperate urge to finish the jumper so she would look nice for me. The day I arrived she almost asked her mother to keep lunch for me, so sure was she of her sixth sense.

 That night, after a marvellous dinner and lots of talk, the time came for bed. Rose had placed Les's cot in our room during the time I was away but many times he had snuggled in with her. He was asleep when we quietly crawled into bed, leaving the light on and whispering to one another. Suddenly Les woke up! What a performance he put on! He went berserk. I stuck it for awhile and then suggested I go sleep on the verandah. *"No way,"* said Rosie. *"You're not going anywhere."* The screaming continued unabated till I'd had enough. I got out of bed and went into the kitchen. Through the slightly open door I watched to see what would happen. Immediately, Les stopped crying, then when Rose lifted him onto the bed he went to the bottom of it, surveyed the room to make sure I was gone, crawled back beside his mother and fell asleep, still sobbing softly. We managed to move him to his cot later and I was able to stay in the room but it was quite a while before he fully accepted my presence. The next day, seeing familiar faces and places was an absolute thrill for me. The time passed much too quickly. On leaving for Perth with Rosie and Les, I felt angry and upset that such a short leave had been granted after so long away. Also the welcome back to our country had left a lot to be desired, although I must admit it would have been difficult to arrange anything when no one knew we were coming.

...Chapter 24

Arriving in Perth I found out through a friend that a particular doctor was willing to issue a medical certificate to those wanting extra leave. I went along to see him early in the morning and explained my situation, leaving nothing out. He listened patiently, then after a moment of thought said, *You don't look well! You've got—"*, and he gave some name to my supposed condition. "*I think you could be right Doc,*" I replied. He wrote out a certificate which authorised me to take three days' leave. As he handed me the slip of paper he said, "*Now when you go through the waiting room, don't throw your hat up in the air and shout hip hip hooray, will you?*" Even though that's exactly what I felt like doing I assured him I'd behave myself. Rose was thrilled to hear the good news and we spent the time very happily in each other's company.

Eventually the time came to return to camp in Claremont but I wasn't too worried as I felt I'd got what

75 QUID AND AN AXE

was due to me. At the gate I handed my leave pass and medical certificate to the guard then went to see where I would be sleeping and so on. Shortly after, I noticed a bit of hurried activity amongst the boys and asked what was happening. *"Oh, there's leave at eleven o'clock."* It had been around nine when I arrived so by now it was fast approaching that time. A corporal said to me, *"If you get in the office quick enough before they stop issuing passes, you'll possibly get one."* Absolutely delighted by this news I entered the office and explained my situation to the corporal behind the desk. *"Oh yes,"* he said when I'd finished. *"You'll be right for a leave pass."* At that moment, a sergeant barged into the office and said, *"Are you Private Challis?"* *"Yes,"* I replied. *"Well you're under open arrest,"* he declared. Completely stunned, I said, *"You must be mistaken."* *"No, I'm not,"* he replied, *"You're under arrest."* *"Ridiculous!"* I retorted. *"Well,"* he replied, *"That's the order."* *"Where do I go from here?"* I asked. *"If you're quick,"* he said, *"They're putting a mob through now, otherwise you'll have to wait till ten o'clock tomorrow. And,"* he added, *"if you get in now, you'll still be in time for leave."* Feeling lousy about my predicament I walked across to join the throng of men waiting to explain themselves to the brass. I heard from a few of the blokes that the chap in charge, Colonel Flanagan, didn't have a very good name and really dished out the punishment. It was all very formal. When it came to my turn two sergeants escorted me to the door, whipped off my hat and marched me in. I was ordered to halt, right turn and stand at ease. Colonel Flanagan eyed me off for a moment, then said, *"I believe you've been A.W.O.L. Challis?"* *"Not really sir."* I replied. *"How do you make that out?"* he asked. *"Well sir,"* I answered, *"I've been sick and I put in a medical certificate with my leave pass. It was from a doctor who examined me so I don't really see how I could be A.W.O.L."* "*Did you come back from Kalgoorlie on the day you were supposed to?*" he questioned. "*Yes sir, definitely,*" I replied. "*I was in Perth and ready to come back to camp.*" "*Well,*" he said, "*We have a hospital now - Hollywood - and what you should have done as soon as you landed in Perth was notify the hospital. They would have sent an ambulance for you.*" "*Look sir,*" I replied, "*I've only been back from the Middle East for approximately ten days and I've never heard of Hollywood Hospital.*" He thought for a while, then said, "*Have you ever been in trouble before Challis?*" "*No Sir,*" I replied. Luckily I had a completely clean sheet. Flanagan quietly thumbed through my record book to see if there were any red lines denoting misconduct. Meanwhile I stood waiting, my stomach churning and feeling like I was about to receive the death sentence. I can understand how it must feel to stand in a dock with a jail term hanging over your head. At last, after what seemed an eternity, Flanagan sat back, crossed his arms, stared at me and said, "*Challis, I think you're telling the truth. Case dismissed.*" Breathing a sigh of relief I shot outside, where a sergeant said, "*Now slip across quick and you'll get your leave pass.*" Within side of half an hour I was on the train to town.

For quite a while I was stationed in Claremont. Being a returned soldier I was allowed leave every day from 11 p.m. till 8 a.m. This suited me perfectly as it was like holding down a normal job. Later I was moved to Works and Parks in Karrakatta where I did maintenance work on army vehicles. Myself and another chap called Pringle were the only two returned men in this unit. The first morning we went on parade. We hadn't been there long when lessons began in sloping arms. Having learned this at the start of my army training, I flatly refused to join in with the rest. Instead I stood with the rifle in my hands, the butt resting on the ground. The sergeant was on me like a rocket. "*Righto soldier,*" he said, "*What's wrong with you? Paralysed or something?*" "*No Sergeant,*" I replied, "*I'm not paralysed. But I've got no intentions of sloping arms.*" "*For what reason?*" he enquired. "*I learnt it years ago,*" I answered. "*It was my first lesson when I joined the army. I've just done fifteen months in the Middle East so there's no way I'm going to learn to slope arms again. It's an insult.*" "*All right,*" he said, "*You can go into the hut and take your webbing off but you're going to hear about this.*" Completely unperturbed and prepared to stand on my digs no matter what, I went at the appointed time to see the Captain. He said, "*I believe you disobeyed an order?*" "*You could say that, yes sir,*" I replied. When asked the reason I again explained how I felt about sloping arms. "*That's fair enough,*" he said when I finished, "*but you've got to remember - you did a lot of things after learning that skill. And there's a lot of things you will have forgotten.* He asked me about my time in transport, then said, "*It's been a while since you read a map. How do you think you'd go at that now?*" "*I think I'd go all right sir,*" I replied. Producing a map he laid it on the desk. I could see at a glance that it was quite complicated. I was in a corner, so I said, "*Look sir, to give me a break, I feel if you start me on any one route that I'm supposed to take I could go on from there.*" Obligingly he gave me a clue and as I worked, all previous knowledge flooded back to me and I moved across the map with ease. "*That's very good,*" he said. "*I won't penalise you this time but try in future not to disobey any orders.*" He gave instructions that I was to be omitted from the lessons, which pleased me greatly.

...Chapter 25

It wasn't long before I was ordered to catch up with my battalion stationed in Maroochydore in Queensland, which was about three thousand miles away. This meant another farewell to Rose and Les with no promise of when I would return. On the train there were quite a few men in the same boat as me. Also there were several army prisoners being sent to the East. Pairs of us were assigned the prisoners to guard on the trip.

My partner and I were put in charge of a little chap called Tim McCoy. What a character! His crime had been to jump ship in Perth before leaving for the Middle East. Funnily enough it was the Aquatania, the ship that had picked us up. For two years he had worked around the wheat belt but was always on the look out for Provos or someone that might recognise him - not the greatest way to live, he told us finally he decided to give himself up. His few possessions he carried in a sugar bag. When he presented himself at the gates of the camp in Claremont the guards thought he was a hobo and wouldn't let him in. It took a lot of persuasion and record checking before they would admit him. Now he was under arrest for desertion and on his way back to Melbourne. Despite this we thoroughly enjoyed his company.

When we pulled in to the station at Port Pirie in South Australia we discovered we had eight hours to kill before the train departed. The Railway Transport Officer instructed that leave to go to town was permitted to all those who were not in charge of prisoners. The rest of us were to remain at the station. Unhappy about this situation I approached the Officer and said, "*Now listen Sir, I'm not very happy about all these others getting leave. What have we done? Golly alive, we've been given a job to do but I can't see why we should be deprived of a few hours break because of it.*" "Sorry but that's the orders," he replied. "*We've got to make sure the prisoners don't escape.*" "*Right!*" I said, "*How about we make a deal. You allow us to go on leave and take our prisoner with us and we'll be responsible for his safe return.*" "Sounds all right to me," he replied. "*Just remember, the onus is on you!*" "Sure," I answered. "*I'm quite happy about that.*" Off we went. Tim was really excited, despite the fact he hadn't any money. On reaching the town, which is quite a distance from the station, we entered the nearest pub and had a few beers. Every now and then I'd say to Tim, "*Now look here you little bugger. Don't you try and get away.*" "*Look mate,*" he'd answer, "*There's no way in the world you'll lose me.*" "*That's all very well, but you make certain you keep your word because we're going to be in the sh— otherwise.*" "*She'll be right,*" he assured us. We took him to a cafe and had a good feed. He thought we were the greatest. When we arrived back at the station we could hardly scratch ourselves. Tim was almost legless and I wasn't much better. The first sight that greeted us was two smartly dressed American officers. Having never seen their uniforms before I lurched up to them and said, "*You'd be a couple of Yanks, right?*" Politely they confirmed my statement. Cheekily I asked what all their insignia represented as they were covered in it. Again they politely answered my questions. Finally I said, "*What rank do they stand for?*" Grinning slightly, one said in a drawl, "*I'm a major and my friend here is a colonel.*" Sobering up very quickly I said, "*I'm sorry if I talked out of turn. As a matter of fact I've just got back from the Middle East and I haven't sorted you blokes out at all.*" "Don't worry about a thing Aussie," they said, "*We're all here to do the same job.*" Bidding them farewell we boarded the train again, Tim safely in tow. By this stage he could not have escaped if he'd wanted to.

After leaving him in Melbourne we continued on to Sydney where again we had an eight hour stop. My mate and I had a look round and took a taxi across the bridge before catching the train on to Brisbane, then Maroochydore. I reached the camp in the afternoon and it was great to see my old mates from the 2nd 16th. Arty Milstead, my bosom buddy, was there to greet me as were many others. We'd been chatting for half an hour or so when a runner came and asked if I was Challis. He said I was wanted in the OIC's office which was actually a large tent. I didn't know what to think as I walked over to see him The Captain said, as I fronted his desk, "*Challis, it's taken you a long time to catch up with the boys, hasn't it?*" "Yes sir," I replied. "*Quite a long time.*" "*Well I've got a bit of bad news for you.*" Immediately my heart sank as I thought something must have happened to one of my family. He continued, "*Now that you've managed to catch us up I'm afraid I have to send you back to Western Australia to see a medical board.*" Normally I would have been disappointed but the thought of going home pleased me no end. My flat feet had once again stopped me from seeing any action. When I told my mates, they all agreed I was a very 'lucky sod'. That night we decided to have a little celebration before the parting of the ways. The beer flowed freely and Arty, not being one given to vocalising, sang over and over the only song he knew - 'Jeannie With The Light Brown Hair'. In the end we all fell apart laughing every time he launched into another rendition. I left the next day and began the long haul home.

In Adelaide I discovered I could not get a ticket to Perth. It left me with no option but to report to the barracks at Wavell. While there I was given a medical. Several doctors agreed that my feet were not made for the army. One said, "*If you lived here we'd give you an immediate discharge but we can't do that so you'll have to have another medical in Perth.*"

Every day for six long weeks I went to the station in the hope of getting a ticket. Luckily I was given a free pass to come and go as I pleased. I joined up with a couple of guys from the camp and we managed to fill the days. Then my money ran out. For the first time since joining the army I was forced to write to Rose and ask for ten pounds to be sent across. When it arrived I did something I should never have done. Always fond of a punt, I joined in a poker game. There were six men in the school originally but one went broke and pulled out. I was asked if I'd like to sit in. Unable to resist, I took my place. In the first hand I had a pair of kings. Throwing out the three rags, I waited for the deal. As was my habit when playing poker, I placed the pair on top of the three new cards and left them face down on the table. The betting started and quite a large pool grew in the centre. When it came to my turn to bet, I picked up my cards and took a look at the bottom one. It was a king. Knowing I had two more in my hand I said with my best poker face, "*Oh, I'll kick it.*" I placed some money in the pool. Around went the bets again. This time when it reached me I felt slightly worried as no-one had pulled out. Taking another peek at my cards I was delighted to see a fourth king nestled there. Casually I kicked the pool for the second time. The chap next to me said, "*My God, you must be alright mate.*" A few blokes pulled out and the rest decided to look at my hand. I placed the cards down and said, "*Four butchers!*". It won, and I happily took possession of at least ten pounds over and above my original ten - a small fortune and a most welcome one.

...Chapter 26

Eventually I managed to get on a train bound for the West. It was wonderful to be home again. I wasn't discharged from the army, just downgraded from 01 to B2. My next assignment was to the 5th Graves Commission. Part of my duties included chauffeuring a Lieutenant and a Captain around in a big Pullman Chevrolet staff car. The Captain, named Gregson, had sons who later became the owners of the biggest auction rooms in Perth. Lieutenant Davies owned a lovely home on a farm in Gosnells which produced gladiolas for commercial use. My job as driver was very enjoyable and easy. The Pullman was the only army vehicle in Perth allowed to carry civilians, they being the next of kin of the deceased.

After a short stint there, I was transferred to Parkston, just outside Kalgoorlie, as a cook for the troops passing through. It was a good job as I didn't have any drills or parades and was able to go home every night. I even managed to go to the mid-week race meetings now and then. Rose was pregnant again and on the twentieth of October 1944 gave birth to a beautiful son, Bobby. He was not well from the start. He had hernias which today would have been treated easily but in those days were very serious. Rose spent hours trying to get him to suckle and the only time he slept was on Rose's stomach. The poor little mite suffered for four months before passing away. We were desolate. I continued working at Parkston but for some time I had no interest in anything much. It was so hard for Rose. She had spent every minute of the day with Bobby and to see a baby in pain the whole time must have been agonising for her. It left a big hole in our lives but we just had to push on.

Every month I got four days' leave, so to supplement my income I took a job carting wood at two quid a day for a chap called Bill Trurin. When that cut out I went to see Dinny, the foreman of the mines. He was an old friend and was very happy to give me some work. Not that you could call it work. Dinny realised I needed a few extra bob, so as long as I went out of sight underground, he didn't really care what I did.

As time passed and fighting continued in the Pacific, reinforcements became increasingly hard to find. Word came through that any men who could be spared were to return to Claremont for a medical. Smithy, our O.I.C., left it up to the heads of each section to select which men were to go. Straight away I thought I'd be a certainty because I had earlier crossed swords with the mess sergeant. I hadn't liked him from the start. He used to come in the kitchen when we were preparing the troops meals and tell us not to worry much because they were only going overseas to get knocked off anyway. This riled me and it showed. Then something happened which later gave him an opportunity to have a go at me. It was over an incident involving a big pug faced cook called Bishop. The saying 'Who called the cook a bastard?' followed by, 'Who called the bastard a cook?' really applied to him. I used to keep the kitchen spotless and had often been commended for it. One day I cleaned up after lunch and went to my tent. Shortly after Bishop came to me and told me I'd better go and clean the kitchen. "*What do you mean?*" I demanded."*Oh,*" he said, "*I've just done a job down there and there's a bit of clearing up to do.*" When I entered the kitchen I couldn't believe my eyes. It was a wreck. It looked like he'd emptied a flour bag and then shaken it all over the place. I was livid. I marched back to his tent and really did the block at him. After a stream of abuse I said, "*Don't you dare think I'm going to clean the kitchen.*" I didn't either. He had to go and clean his own mess. That night, Bishop and the sergeant came into the kitchen together - they were good buddies. The sergeant said, "*I believe you refused to clean the kitchen today.*" Immediately my hackles went up and I had my say again. I received no backing whatsoever from the sergeant. The matter was dropped - but not forgotten. So now, when we assembled to hear who had been selected for overseas duty, sure enough my name was called out. My mates were disgusted, even though I'd previously told them I'd be going and why. The fact I was married and had not long before lost Bobby, meant nothing. The sergeant wanted revenge. Smithy announced that anyone wishing to swap places with those chosen were free to do so. I was mobbed by several of my single mates who wanted desperately to see some action. They pleaded with me to give up my posting. "*No way in a million years,*" I said.

"I couldn't possibly stay in the camp with that bastard. There'd be a tragedy for sure."

Once again I bade farewell to Rosie and Les and took the train to Perth. In Claremont I had to front a panel of officers before going for a medical. When I walked in I recognised an officer as one from the 2nd 16th. We shook hands and he made quite a fuss of me. Another officer sat behind a table and two or three others stood nearby. The one seated did the questioning. He said, *"Challis, I believe you have a lot of trouble with your feet. Now what would you do if you were accepted? What do you think you are capable of?"* Pulling no punches I answered, *"Look Sir, I've been in the army for nearly four years. I've been overseas and done my best. I really think I'd be a lot more benefit to the country if I was back in civilian life."* He didn't say much and I was dismissed. Outside on the lawn were a group of young blokes waiting to see the board. They eagerly asked me how I'd gone but all I could say was I didn't know. Hardly had my behind touched the lawn when a runner informed me I was wanted back inside. Thinking it rather strange I went in and crossed to the table. The Colonel said, *"Challis, we've decided to discharge you."* I'd heard some sweet words in my life but none quite so sweet as these. *"Very good sir,"* I replied, trying to keep the smile off my face. It was the 22nd March 1944 - a date never to be forgotten. Those leaving the army are usually supplied with a suit, hat, shirt and shoes etc., but for me there were no suitable clothes that would fit, so I was forced to wear my uniform back to Kalgoorlie. The train reached Bullabulling, a small place not far from Coolgardie which basically consisted of the Rock Hotel and little else. Two Provos, who had been checking on the servicemen in each carriage, were now seated in the same one as me. Before we pulled into the station I said to the chaps around me, "*Well, when we get to the Rock I'll be able to try a nice Hannans Beer.*" One of the Provos overheard me and said, "*Sorry mate, but I don't think you'll be sampling any beer.*" "*Why not?*" I asked. "*It's out of bounds completely now,*" he replied. "*It has been for a while.*" "*Oh yeah,*" I said, "*And for what reason?*" "*All drink has been banned on the train,*" he replied. I heard after that apparently a Provo had locked horns on one trip with a soldier who, with his mates, had held the Provo out the window and would have dumped him if the emergency whistle hadn't been pulled. The order went out that no booze was allowed on the train and the pub was off limits. Casually I said, "*Well I think I might be getting a drink.*" The Provos thought this rather humorous and replied, "*I don't think so mate.*"

    When we pulled up to take on water I left the carriage and strolled towards the hotel. All along the train guys were yelling encouragement and whistling. As I neared the pub, five Provos who had been standing talking, spotted me and moved in to encircle me. One said, "*Now listen soldier, get back on the train. You're not supposed to leave it.*" "*How do you make that out?*" I asked. "*Are there any restrictions on civilians getting a drink?*" "*No,*" he replied. "*Then get out of my road,*" I said. "*What do you mean?*" he asked. "*I happen to be a civilian,*" I replied cockily. "*You can't be,*" he persisted. "*You're in army uniform.*" "*That's because they couldn't get me a bloody suit to come home in,*" I responded. I pulled out my pay book and pass and showed it to them. "*Move back,*" I said, "*I haven't got much time.*" I knew I was being a smart arse but I didn't care. It was lovely not having to obey orders and I was relishing the last chance I'd have to give a bit back. I'd had a few run-ins with Provos in the past. Because of my feet, special factory shoes had been made for me. At first they put arch supports in them which was like walking on two rocks. Then a pair made to allow for my condition were produced which were perfectly comfortable. Unable to wear gaiters with these shoes, on leave pass I was sometimes a target for Provos who patrolled the city. One such time happened when I was standing outside the Perth station with my brother Bill. Across the road we watched an army bus pull up and discharge about ten Provos. Losing interest we continued chatting, when all of a sudden I got a tap on my shoulder. Two of them had crossed the road, come over the bridge and down the steps behind me. "*What's the trouble?*" I asked. "*Where's your gaiters soldier?*" he demanded. "*I think they're back in the camp somewhere,*" I said. "*You know you're supposed to wear them?*" he asked. "*Possibly I am,*" I replied, "*But I just don't have to wear them now.*" I pulled out my leave pass on which was printed, PERMITTED TO WEAR SHOES OWING TO MEDICAL CONDITION. Maybe it was their attitude or the authority they represented, but I always got a kick out of being able to get the better of them. Into the Rock I went, downed a quick pot and purchased a gallon of beer. Back on the train I managed to smuggle the bottles to the different carriages for the boys to have a sip.

    Rose was delighted with the news of my discharge and for two or three weeks we did nothing but enjoy ourselves. My intention still was to return to the banks of the Blackwood as I had promised myself. One day I went to the mine to thank Dinny for having given me the four days work each month, and say goodbye. He responded by offering me any full time job I'd like to do. Appreciating the gesture I declined the offer and said, "*I'm going to have a shot at making a go of it in the South West. I don't know how things will turn out, but if it doesn't work I'd be grateful for a job if I come back to Kal.*" "*No worries,*" he replied. "*There'll be a job waiting for you anytime.*" Walking from the Chaffers past the Two Shaft, I saw my old foreman who offered me the same deal as Dinny. It gave me a feeling of security to know I had something to fall back on.

...Chapter 27

While in the Middle East I had written to Mrs Cosgrove and asked if I could have first refusal on their block if ever they decided to leave. She had answered assuring me I could. Unbeknown to me I was just in time because Harry later offered to buy the block when the Cosgroves announced they were shifting to Cowaramup, but Mrs Cosgrove stood by her word. He then asked if he could put a twenty pounds deposit on the property so that if I couldn't manage the sixty pounds purchase price, he would have first option to buy. She agreed to this and accepted the money but it was returned when I produced the full amount. Anyway Harry and Dave already owned the block next door.

Harry was married now to Mary who had just given birth, in Perth, to their first son, Jimmy. I had the pleasure of bringing the glad tidings to Harry when I came down. My old dad, unable to work much due to heart strain caused by lifting heavy rocks on the Perth foreshore, was taking a break from the city and living in a small humpy on what we called the 'flats' which was a block situated between the original homestead and Cosgroves'. When I arrived on the scene Harry and Dave were fishing, which provided their only source of income. I joined them and we operated as the Challis Bros. I'd left Rose in Kalgoorlie till I could get on my feet. We purchased another boat for nine quid. I handled it while Harry and Dave worked on as before. We lived mainly on kangaroo, wild duck and fish and managed to eke out a living. Cosgroves' house had long since disintegrated and the block was just virgin bush. I had seventy five quid and an axe to my name. The first job was to build a home for Rose. I chose the site where my house stands today on a slight rise about a hundred yards from the river. By hand, when not fishing, I cleared seven acres around the proposed building site. The days were long and hard. Most nights were spent on the river with short naps snatched whenever possible. Harry had done a course in plastering and had qualified. Along the way he'd picked up enough information to know how to go about erecting a house. I cut the stumps while he set out the plan. With him as the mastermind of the operation and me labouring for him, the house slowly took shape. When it reached the stage of being weatherproof I wrote to Rose and told her we had a bit of a house put together but it wasn't lined or anything. Rose didn't care - she was itching to join me and said as long as it was dry and she could cook a meal, it was okay by her. A few days later she arrived and we set up camp. I had managed to rustle up a few pieces of furniture and a stove. Washing was done in a copper in the yard.

With Rose able to lend a hand, I went into top gear,

determined to make the property productive. Seven to eight hours a day I spent on the axe, ringbarking and clearing. When nightfall came I ate dinner, took a crib and went fishing, sometimes till daylight. After two or three hours sleep I headed back to the bush. Eventually after weeks of back breaking slog, seventy acres were ready for pasture. Every penny I earned fishing was used to buy equipment, things for the house and food. Our only transport was Harry's ute, so trips to town were infrequent. It's hard to explain what it's like to have a dream and know exactly what you want but not have the resources to finance it. Everything had to be achieved slowly and it was just a matter of plodding along one step at a time. I didn't mind though because I loved work and revelled in it. To sit idle for any length of time drives me crazy.

Harry picked up some extra income doing renovations on buildings in the district. Dave and I continued fishing, working a boat each. Dave had taught himself to yodel and he was a natural. Some mornings we'd be on the river - it'd be mirror calm with the sun just beginning to rise. I'd be a mile or more away from Dave when he'd start to yodel. It sounded so fantastic floating across the water in that idyllic setting that I'd stop work and just listen.

One aspect of fishing that did not thrill me at all was when I had the misfortune to be stung by cobblers. We always worked in bare feet and the mud on the riverbed was a favourite haven for these fish. They have three barbs on their bodies. One under each side fin and one on the back. My dad was the first to tread on one back when the family lived on the old homestead. The moment the barb breaks the skin the pain hits and it's agonising. Poor old dad. We got him home and mum tried everything to relieve the pain. She almost cooked his foot in boiling water. Dad was a tough old bugger but even he was reduced to tears. Later he said to me - I was about seventeen at the time - "*Look boy. It doesn't matter what anyone says to you, there's nobody can describe the pain of a cobbler sting unless they've had one.*"

Quite a long time after, Bill, Les and I were on the river one night. Bill was in the boat watching the net as Les and I hauled it ashore. Les worked the top line while I pulled the lead line, using my foot to keep it on the bottom. I felt a fish roll against my foot, stopped, and called to Bill, "*Did you see anything in the net?*" "*Yes,*" he yelled back. "*There's some beautiful whiting in it.*" Pleased, I plonked my foot down to continue hauling and landed fair on top of a cobbler. The dorsal spine pierced the skin under my big toe. As the cobbler thrashed around one side barb stabbed my instep and the other just broke the skin of my heel. Instantly I was paralysed with pain. I couldn't speak. I nearly went berserk. Les wanted to light the lantern to have a look but all I wanted was to get home which was at least half a mile from where we stood. As I took off, Les said, "*I'll go ahead and tell mum to get the water ready.*" Normally I would never beat Les in running but that night it took him quite a while to catch me and only then because I started to weaken and begin vomiting. Mum had the water ready when I reached the house. I plunged my foot into it, not noticing the heat, but feeling only the slight relief it brought. It was now about half past eight at night. I sat in a deckchair while Win changed the water to keep the temperature up. She stayed with me till nearly midnight when I told her to go to bed as I could handle the water myself. I managed okay till around one o'clock and then fell asleep. Mum found me like this in the morning, my foot still in the bowl of now cold water. She asked how I was and I replied, "*Good, there's no pain at all now.*" With that I lifted my foot from the bowl. It was cooked. There were huge blisters between my toes, round my ankles and everywhere the flesh was raw. I didn't walk on it for six weeks. As dad had said, it's hard to describe the pain. Suffice it to say it is so bad you can put your foot in boiling water and not even notice the temperature.

Ten years after that incident, when I was in the Middle East, a corn came up under the base of my big toe. Now and then I'd get a razor blade and cut it back. One day a mate, Bill Edwards, was watching me do this and he said, "*There's some pus in there.*" "*It looks like it, doesn't it Bill,*" I replied. I got a needle and pricked the skin. Out came some pus, leaving a neat hole in the centre of the corn. Intrigued, I squeezed and out of the hole popped a cobbler barb about half an inch long. I couldn't believe it. For a start, to break a barb takes tremendous pressure as it's like bone, but to carry it inside me for ten years was quite amazing. Since that first sting I've had thirty five more over the years but it was after about six that I learnt the secret for pain relief. It was discovered by a chap who was up the river in his boat line fishing. He was having a great time pulling in whiting and was loathe to stop when it dropped dark. Unfortunately he hauled in a little cobbler and the spine pierced his finger. In agony and panicking a bit, he went to the rear of the boat to start his little Seagull engine. To do this he first had to tickle the carburettor to get the petrol flowing. Then he fired the engine and headed for home. Five minutes later the pain had completely disappeared. He worked out it must have been due to the petrol dripping on his finger when he tickled the carby and he was correct, because I have used it on every sting since and it certainly works.

With mostly all work and no play while fishing and clearing the block, I made a few enquiries about maybe having a dance. Several people said attempts to organise dances had fallen through due to lack of interest. I said, *"Golly alive, surely there's enough old-timers and people round the place who'd like to have a dance."* Determined to revive the get-togethers, I managed, during the short breaks I had from work, to put one on at the school house. I was the band, playing my accordion, and also M.C. Quite a crowd turned up and a good night was had by all. Encouraged, I repeated the event a couple of weeks later except this time two ladies came who could both play piano. It gave me a bit of relief from the accordion and enabled me to have a dance. The third time, the place was packed with hardly room for the ladies to sit. Everyone looked forward to the outing after that as it was the only chance for some to socialise with people outside their families. Soccer had ceased to exist in the district with Aussie rules now being the game of the day. Later my young brother Harold became a star in this sport and I excelled in barracking. I've always had a loud voice and I put it to good use at the local matches.

Slowly the property improved. It was around this time we bought our first Seagull engine for the boat. Until then we rowed everywhere. It was nothing for me to start about three in the afternoon and row fifteen miles to Alexander Bridge. That was only, of course, if I'd had no luck fishing closer to home. I'd go ashore, boil the billy and have a bite to eat. When it dropped dark I'd head slowly for home, listening for the fish as they broke the surface of the water. Everything was done by ear and in blackness. Winter brought the rains which in turn brought fresh water to the river. Most years we'd get a flood which suited us because it took a lot of fresh water to flush mullet from the salt water pockets they occupied in the upper reaches of the river. Some pockets were over a hundred feet deep. To get first bite of the cherry when the mullet made their move, we'd go to meet them around Molloy Island which is the biggest river island in Western Australia. Often we'd camp on Molloy to eat and snatch a bit of shuteye. After the mullet came the whiting, so thick that a net could be strung anywhere night or day and come up chock-a-block full.

The highest flood I remember occurred in 1945 when the mouth of the river had closed due to silting. An island in the river named Thomas Island - known to us as Piggy Island - was completely covered. All that showed were the tops of the paperbark trees. I rowed my boat right across it looking for nets that may have been swept down with the tide and become tangled in the trees. At home I could take the boat to within forty feet of the house. Because access to the ocean was closed, the river just built up and up. There were no tides which meant we could set the nets anywhere, even in normally unsafe places. And this is what we did. We strung every inch of net we owned from the shore to Piggy Island then tied the boats to blackboys quite a way inland but now under water.

Prior to this, a meeting had been held between local fisherman and some of the businessmen of the town to discuss whether to reopen the bar where the original mouth of the river was, or open one nearer the town. The businessmen, able to see the benefit to tourism in the latter idea were keen to push ahead with it. I suggested the fishermen do the shoveling and the businessmen dob in a few bob for the labour. Not willing to come to the party there and then, they said they'd think about it and give a verdict next day. So there we were that night, with our nets out, hoping for a big catch. Unbeknown to us a, couple of guys, after the meeting, took spades and dug a small channel through to the ocean. No-one considered notifying us so when we woke in the morning the river was back to normal, our nets were gone and the boats left high and dry. The volume of water pushing through the bar must have really been a sight to see. For us it was a disaster. Our livelihood was gone and with it the chance to get more net as we were only permitted so much a year and no more. I travelled to Perth to see the Fisheries but all they had was eight cuts of three and a half inch mesh, completely unsuitable for river fishing. Still, I bought it regardless and headed for home. As luck would have it a chap called Matt Brennan who seldom fished, offered us completely brand new hauling net on the condition we replace it when next we got our quota. We were delighted. Never was a net tanned and hung so quickly. We had the corks and leads sewn on in record time and were ready for action once again. When eventually we did get our new net Matt refused to accept it saying he had all he wanted, so we paid him out and kept it.

...Chapter 28

Time passed. Work continued on the farm and the house but the river remained my greatest love. The bird life on the Blackwood is fantastic. I've sometimes wondered what the river would be like without birds and the answer is - empty. There are pelicans, cranes, ibis, ducks and cormorants. I'm not a great fan of the cormorant, mainly because they are so crafty at stealing fish from nets. Hundreds and hundreds of pounds of meshed fish have disappeared down their gullets over the years. But the pelican is a different kettle of fish. They don't worry the nets and appreciate any offering thrown their way. One time I noticed a big pelican with one of its wings broken - possibly by a gunshot. It was unable to fly so when time came for the annual migration it could not lift itself from the water. The other birds took to the air, spiralling higher and higher into the sky before drifting off into the distance. As I watched, two pelicans returned and settled beside the injured one. They pushed up against it, one either side, as though trying to get it aloft. Several attempts were made before they abandoned the exercise and left their friend to its fate. I don't know whether it survived or not because I didn't see it after that.

Over the years I became pretty adept at spotting fish and often from quite a distance. One of the hardest to see is skipjack. Although they travel in large schools they hardly disturb the surface but I eventually learnt to read the telltale signs and netted some big catches. On one occasion I was down at the landing putting the nets on the boat. Harry wandered over from his place to have a chat. Next thing I spotted a school of skippy coming round the corner. The river was very calm and the fish were just high enough to break the surface of the water. Anxious to catch them before they hit deep water I went into overdrive. Harry said, *"What's wrong Pud?"* *"I've just seen a school of skippy. I want to get them,"* I answered. *"I'll hop on the boat with you,"* he offered. Away we went. I had the net half way round when Harry, who was standing on the front, yelled, *"Hold it, hold it!"* I pulled up but I was panicking a bit because you don't get much time to put a net round when fish are on the move. *"What's the matter?,"* I asked. Harry said, *"There's another school coming across the front of the boat."* I held back till he gave me the okay then closed the circle. I finished up with about three quarters of a ton, some of the fish weighing up to eight pounds. This was a Sunday. The only train leaving that day was from Margaret River, twenty five miles away. Fortunately skip jack are beautiful to handle - big and clean and easy to box. We loaded them all on Harry's ute - there would have been a ton in all with the weight of the boxes included - and left for Margaret River with Harry at the wheel. At Kudardup we got a puncture. Using the spare we proceeded on our way with me in the driver's seat. At McCleod's Creek, another puncture. We were stuck. No spare, a ute load of fish and no-one in sight. It wasn't long before a truck, driven by a chap called Archibald, came along. He pulled up and said, "*What's the trouble boys?*" "*We're in the 'nure properly,*" I replied. After explaining our predicament he said, "*Well there's no problem. Just load them on the truck.*" Soon we were on our way again. I said, "*By gee, we'll be battling to catch the train now.*" Archie casually asked, "*What if we don't make it?*" "*I hope we do,*" I answered. "*Otherwise, what am I going to do with all these fish?*" "*Oh well,*" he drawled, "*If we don't catch it at this station we'll go to the next and if we don't catch it there we'll go to the next and if we miss it again I'll take the buggers through to Perth for you.*" With a generous offer like that I relaxed somewhat. Needless to say we managed to get to the station on time.

There was a comical little incident once, concerning a fish box and my son Les. He wasn't very old, perhaps three or four. Having spent a lot of his life in Kalgoorlie being raised with Rose's three younger sisters he was dying to get back there to see them. One day he was pestering me about this so I said, "*Well I don't know. The only way I can get you to Kalgoorlie is in a fish box.*" "*That'll be alright,*" he answered happily. "*That's a good idea.*" So I got a box and said, "*Righto, hop in and I'll tack you down. Later on I'll put you on the train.*" Happy as larry he squatted in the box while I loosely tacked some hessian over him. He stayed there for about half an hour. Every now and then a little voice would ask, "*When am I going on the train?*" "*Won't be long,*" I'd reply. Finally I had to come up with some alibi about the train not running that day otherwise I'm sure he would have stayed in there for hours.

...Chapter 29

On the 26th January (Australia Day) 1946 Rose gave birth to our first daughter Julia Rosina, and what an event that turned out to be. Harry had told me to take the ute when the time came but like a fool I didn't think to actually park it at our house. Rose's mum and dad were staying with us and it was around midnight that Rose started having contractions - amazing how babies always seem to choose the middle of the night to arrive on the scene. I dashed next door, got the ute, bundled Rose and ma into it and sped off for Margaret River. We'd passed Witchcliffe which is about six miles south of Margaret when suddenly the ute conked out. Desperately I jumped out and tried to locate the problem. Meanwhile Rose got out and leaned against the back of the ute. By now she was in full labour. Having no luck whatsoever at getting the engine to fire I was relieved to see headlights coming towards us. It was a furniture laden truck - perhaps someone doing a moonlight flit. I stood on the road waving my arms but the swine went straight past, ignoring me as though I wasn't there. Looking in the engine again, I discovered the fan belt had come off so it wasn't long before we were back on the road. After depositing Rose at the hospital, ma and I waited till about 2 a.m. when a nurse called Norma Cross came to inform me I had a daughter. Relieved and happy ma and I headed for home. Oh! Sweet revenge! Who do we see on the side of the road and waving us down but the furniture truck driver. I said to ma, *"There'll be a body splashed across the road if he doesn't jump quickly because there's no way I'm stopping."* Planting the foot we whizzed by, causing him to leap backwards to avoid being hit. Normally I'd never leave anyone stranded but in this case I felt justified and satisfied.

After Rose came home life settled back into a routine. I was fishing in all weathers and working the block during the day. It was around this time that a humorous incident occurred. During my mining days I had worked with a bloke called Bob Jones who was from Karridale. We knew each other really well. One day, underground, we were eating our cribs with a few other guys when the talk turned to fishing. Bob turned to me and asked, *"Hey Pud, how high can a mullet jump out the water?"* *"Oh, about three or four feet,"* I replied. Bursting into laughter he said, *"Three or four feet! You must be joking."* *"No,"* I replied, *"That's about right."* Well, he really rubbished me. *"Go on,"* he said, *"There's no way a fish could jump that high!"* *"Alright,"* I replied, *"Possibly I'm wrong, but I've seen mullet jump and I reckon I'm right."* I remembered a time when a mullet had flipped out of the water and hit a big chap called Donovan in the chest while he was standing in his boat. Anyway I said to Jonesey, "*If you don't want to believe me, that's fine.*" The subject was dropped but now and again in the months that followed I'd cop a serve from Bob. He'd laugh and say, "*Don't believe him, he thinks mullet jump four feet out of the water.*" I saw Bob briefly while in the army, then lost contact till we both settled in the South West. One day he asked if it would be possible for me to take them for a trip up the river. He wanted his dad, Bob senior, to go. I loved the old boy, so I told Bob to fix a time and I'd take care of it. I ended up with about six adults and two or three kids on board. Bob, his dad and I sat at the rear where we smoked and yarned as we chugged along. I took them round Molloy Island and entered a lagoon where the Scott River branches off from the Blackwood. Suddenly - ping - out of the water shot a large mullet. It hit old Bob right under the jaw, then dropped at his feet. Jonesey was speechless for a moment. Then he looked at me and said, "*Challis, you never bloody lose do you!*" Now it was my turn to do some rubbishing. "*Oh no,*" I chortled, "*Mullet don't jump three or four feet -remember Bob?*" The whack on old Bob's jaw must have been pretty solid but all he said was, "*I think I ought to be able to have that fish.*" "You certainly will mate," I replied, "*I'll clean that specially for you.*"

...Chapter 30

Twenty one months after Julie arrived, our last child Carol, was born, this time in Kalgoorlie. I'd taken Rose and the kids there for a short holiday and she decided to stay till after the birth. I returned to the farm and went flat to the boards to make the house really nice for Rose's return. Between fishing, wielding the axe and renovating I hardly found time to sleep. Then I got very ill. I'd cooked a stew in an aluminium saucepan and left it in the pot. Eating a helping on the second or third day resulted in me being poisoned by the aluminium, though I did not know that at the time. I woke during the night, sweat pouring out of me and my heart palpitating wildly. I realised it was food poisoning because I'd had the same experience when I worked for brother Bill on the old homestead. We'd picked a bucketful of mushrooms and eaten most of them in one hit without any other food. That night we were going out somewhere so I had the copper going for a bath. After washing up I told Bill I'd have my bath first. When I sat in the tub, my heart started racing and the sweat began pouring out of me. Not knowing what was happening, I panicked a bit and struggled to get out the bath. And it was a struggle - I felt terrible. Walking to the verandah to tell Bill, I found him out to it on the bed. The last thing I remembered was falling on to my bunk. We were both fine the next day but it was thirty years before I'd touch another mushroom. Now here I was in the same predicament feeling like death. Like before I hit the cot and slept it off.

The big day of Rose's return arrived. The house looked good - I even put flowers on the table. I went to pick her up from the train and saw she'd brought her sister Mary with her. We drove home. Expecting a reaction and pat on the back for my domestic efforts, I was surprised when Rose showed little interest at all. Instead she said, *"I'm not feeling well love. I'm aching. All my joints are so sore."* Immediately concerned I got her to bed and spent hours massaging her arms, knees, feet and hands. Thankfully Mary helped with the kids although Rose had to cope with the baby. After a terrible night with no improvement I went and rang the doctor who told me to bring her to see him. Explaining she was too sick to move he came to the house and after an examination said she would have to go to the hospital. Rose took the baby in with her and then her ordeal began. She was in agony. I could only get to see her once a week and each time I begged the doctor to get Rose to Perth to see a specialist but his standard reply was, *"Just give it another week."* He made it obvious he thought she was malingering. He used to watch the nurses put hot poultices on her joints and wait to see if she reacted. He finished up ordering her to walk down the long steep hill from the hospital and up the main street. The only comfort Rose got was from a lovely Sister Thorpe who, through the night, massaged her joints and brought her cups of tea.

    Young Mary went back to Kalgoorlie and I put Julie with her godmother, May Price, in Kudardup. Les stayed with me. He'd always had trouble with his tonsils and it was during Rose's stay in hospital he had his worst bout. One night he was pretty feverish but I, being so desperate for a quid, had to go fishing so I asked Harry to sit with him. I said, "*Look, I'll stay in the bay and if anything goes wrong just come down to the foreshore and wave a lantern.*" Just before midnight, with the nets in the water, I spotted the lantern. Quickly I hauled the nets on board and headed for shore. When I got home Les was lying on his bed, frothing at the mouth and fighting for every breath. I remembered an old remedy mum had used as a last resort on Dave one time when he couldn't breathe properly. It was a mustard bath used as an inhalant. I prepared one just in case, then moved Les's bed in front of the fire. Harry said, "*I've got some Wands Wonder Wool at home. It's supposed to be very good for breathing troubles.*" I'd never heard of it. "*Would you mind dashing home and getting it?*" I asked. Meanwhile I rugged up Les's hot struggling body and prevented him from throwing off the coverings. Harry raced in several minutes later and I wrapped the wool round Les's neck which of course made him hotter. Now he was fighting to get free as well as for breath I told Harry to go home and get some rest. I sat with Les till daybreak, by which time his breathing was back to normal and he was sound asleep. When he had his tonsils out later a doctor said he could easily have died during one of these bouts.

75 QUID AND AN AXE

The weeks passed and I was getting angrier and angrier about the treatment Rose was getting. Then the great doctor announced Rose had pyorrhoea, a disease of the gums She had beautiful teeth. The top set were completely removed. Nothing improved. It was six weeks since Rose had entered hospital finally I demanded she see a specialist. Reluctantly the doctor gave in. She went by ambulance to St John of God hospital in Perth. Dr Troop, the specialist, took one look at her and said, *"This woman has got rheumatic fever. Have that baby taken from her immediately. She's not to lift a finger."* And there had been the other idiot doctor forcing her to walk the streets. If she hadn't been such a strong woman she would surely have died at Margaret River in the hands of that butcher. Rose stayed in St John's for two weeks during which time she made a good recovery. Dr Troop was a bonzer chap who cared a great deal about his patients. He warned us that rheumatic fever affects the heart but Rose could be fortunate because her heart at that moment was very good. We returned home and things got back to normal but the partnership with my brothers was not working out too well. Earlier we had purchased a property from Mrs Horrocks. Dave lived there and milked the cows, so he stopped fishing. Any money made from the milk and cream went back into the farm. Harry was busy renovating homes which left me doing most of the fishing. Dave and I had a falling out and he insisted we break up the partnership. This suited me fine because I just wanted to be on my own. I didn't care what I ended up with. I would be happy. Dave got the farm on which he still lives today. Harry got his farm and a block which belonged to our mother. I got the boat, nets and two hundred and fifty pounds from each of them, paid out over quite a long period.

...Chapter 31

It was around this time a chap called Wally Paynter asked me to join a salmon fishing team. I was reluctant but he persuaded me with the promise of making good money. We started in Hamelin Bay, a beautiful beach about fifteen miles from home. Every opportunity I got was spent in the surf swimming. One day a mate, Bill Overton, and I were in the watchtower on our shift looking for salmon. Bill had fantastic eyesight - I used to call him Hawkeye. Suddenly he spotted a shark ambling along inside the reef. *"Look at that Noah's Ark,"* he said. I picked it up through the binoculars and watched if for a while but wasn't particularly interested. Later Bill, another mate, Hubie McDonald, and myself were standing talking next to the Whitely, a big square 4WD steel army bus we used to pull the dinghy out of the water. I said, *"Well, I'm going for a swim."* Where I normally swam was a bit of a channel close to the shore outside which was a bank, then the surf. I plunged in, came out of the channel and walked about waist deep in water across the bank. Something made me look back to the shore. Bill and Hubie were gesturing but I couldn't make out what they wanted. Apparently, ahead of me, they'd spotted a dozen or so salmon, the forerunners of a school. Unaware of this I continued wallowing around in the surf. Again for some reason I glanced back at the shore. This time Bill and Hubie were standing on top of the Whitely going berserk, jumping up and down madly and waving their arms. Thinking they must have spotted some salmon, I started for the shore. On reaching the bank, I stood up and had a look round. As I did, a big swell came in. Above me and inside it, like a goldfish in a bowl, was a large grey nurse shark. It turned sideways then away from me as the swell dropped. I didn't panic. I remembered an old sea-farer from Flinders Bay telling me as a kid that if ever a shark attacked when you were standing in water, never to swim away. Instead, front it and kick up all the racket you can. Nine times out of ten, he'd said, they'll swim away. Luckily I didn't have to prove his theory and managed to get ashore safely. Bill and Hubie were a mess. They had seen the shark well before me. It had been swimming by when it must have detected my presence because they said it suddenly turned and headed in a bee line towards me. What made it turn away at the last moment I'll never know but I doubt whether I'd be telling the story today if it hadn't.

We'd been at Hamelin about a month and had not caught a salmon, though not from lack of trying. Bill said he knew of a bay further round which he thought would be a good fishing spot, so one cold morning before daybreak, he and I set off to have a look. It was quite a hike along the beach but eventually we made it to the point of the bay. He suggested we light a fire while we waited for any signs of salmon schools. Hardly had I got it going when he yelled, "*There's a big lot coming round the corner.*" He added, "*I'll stop here and you go and drum the boys.*" I raced back and alerted the men. We drove along the road to where we could see the bay. Now came the job of pushing a road through the bush to the beach, which we later christened Stinky Bay, so named because of the salmon heads rotting on the beach. Officially, it was put on the map as Foul Bay.

The terrain from the existing road to the bay was very steep so we had to dig out the side of the hill on an angle to get the vehicle down. The boats were brought round by sea. Camp was set up and army phones positioned at points around the bay so spotters could communicate with one another. Of course with all the preparation work we had to do, we naturally missed the school Bill had seen, but we were confident more would come. After settling in, I tried to persuade Wally to anchor the boat out past the surf as it took the whole team of ten men to launch it from the beach. He didn't go along with the idea at all. When the first lot of salmon - about five ton - came along, all but Wally went into action. "*No need to panic,*" he said casually, "*Plenty of time, plenty of time.*" There were two places suitable for netting. By the time we got the boat in the water the salmon had passed the first. With Wally in the boat and Bill and I on the oars we started running the net round the second spot. Wally yelled, "*Turn to the shore, turn to the shore.*" Both Bill and I knew it was too soon because we could see the salmon ahead but Wally kept on at us and him being the boss, we had to obey. We did not catch one salmon. I was furious. When we reached the shore, I did the block. "*Another episode like that,"* I threatened, *"and you'll only have nine men on the team. That's the worst display of fishing I've ever seen in my life."* My words must have had some effect because from then on he more or less let me take over the reins. The boat was anchored out each day and soon the catches began, the biggest being twenty two ton. I only stuck the job for one season - it really wasn't my cup of tea at all. I suppose I missed the river and being my own boss.

Rose and I decided to take a three week break and go to Kalgoorlie. The annual racing round was on and despite the fact we had very little money, I thought it would be great to have a small flutter on the horses. At this stage we owned an old Buick, a car which had been cut down to a ute. I took it to Charlie Taylor in Witchcliffe and asked him to put a canopy on the back. He did a marvellous job along with fixing a few other things that needed attention. We put a mattress in the back for the kids, packed, prepared plenty of food, took a billy and set off. The first stop was in the tuart forest the other side of Busselton and about sixty miles from home. It was a gorgeous sunny day. We had something to eat and the kids had a run around, then it was back on the road again. After a couple more pit stops we went through Perth and continued on to Meckering, situated eighty miles or so along the Kalgoorlie line. By now it was dark. The local garage was open so I fuelled up and filled some containers. I'd scrounged some extra petrol coupons from Harry and different ones before leaving home because the Buick only did about thirteen miles to the gallon - you could hear the horses neighing when they saw a bowser. After purchasing a bottle of beer and some smokes, I drove on with Les and Julie asleep next to me and Rose and Carol sound as a bell in the back. Sipping quietly on my beer I resolved to drive straight through to Kalgoorlie even though I'd been at the wheel since six that morning. However by one in the morning I was starting to wander off the road so I pulled over and climbed onto the mattress with Rose. We woke to blue skies and sunshine. Luckily I'd stopped right next to a crystal clear pool of water from which we were able to wash and fill the billy. I lit a fire, we had breakfast, then on we tootled. Two or three more stops were made before we trundled into Kal at two in the afternoon. The break did us both good and it was nice to catch up with friends and family On the return journey I broke all records by reaching Perth in twelve hours, not bad for four hundred miles when the old girl only averaged thirty to thirty five miles per hour. Two days were spent in Perth before driving on to Kudardup. When we pulled up at the house, the car was ticking over like a Rolex watch. The only thing I had to do to it for the whole trip was replace one plug. I eventually sold it to Bill and I'm not sure what happened to it after that but as a vintage car today it would have been beautiful.

...Chapter 32

Earlier, during the partnership period, I'd tried to get Harry to take on building war service homes but he wouldn't have a bar of it. "*Golly alive,*" I'd said, "*It's a good job. Even if you only take one house you can't possibly lose on it.*" He knew all about building having erected his own and my home and also through the renovations he'd done. I kept urging him knowing he could do very well if he once started. At the finish, in desperation, I said I would help if he wanted to give it a go. So now I was in the building game. We worked like Trojans. First we had to dismantle the existing old houses on the war service blocks, salvage what we could from them, then erect new ones. I worked for Harry for fourteen months then went back full time fishing. Harry went on to own the biggest building company in Augusta.

In 1950 my dear old dad passed away. My mother had been to England for a holiday, paid for by her brothers. Not long after she returned, she left again for a second trip. I knew in my heart that dad would love to have gone too. He had said many years previous that he'd like to end his days in the old country. One by one I spoke to my sisters and brothers who all put something towards his fare and spending money. At the wharf I stayed on board till the last possible moment. As I shook his hand I said, "*Now listen dad, whatever you do, make certain that you're absolutely happy you've seen everyone and everything you want to, before coming home. If you run short of money, drop me a line and I'll get the hat round and send you some.*" The ship pulled away from the wharf and as it moved out of the harbour dad's hat blew off into the water. I felt very upset about that because like me he loved wearing a hat. I was more upset that the ship did not stop to pick it up. That was the last I saw of him. He wrote three times, the last letter arriving after his death. In that letter he said he was leaving for Australia in four days' time having spent nearly four months in England. He was so excited to be coming home even though it was without mum who wanted to stay on. During those four days something happened to cause his death - perhaps a heart attack - I'm not sure. But he died in his bed in my aunt's house. Rose gave me the news when I returned from the siding after delivering a bundle of fish. It was a shock even though he hadn't been well for a long time. My best mate in the world was gone.

...Chapter 33

On Saturdays, for about two years, I had cut hair in the betting shop in Augusta at two shillings a time. Two chaps, Andy Rocchi and George Jones, were running the shop but Andy became very ill. One day he said to me, "*Listen Pud, I've got to get out of this and I'd like you to take my place. I'll tell you what - you can buy in for a hundred quid but you needn't pay me till you've made that as profit in the bookmaking.*" Knowing I could not get a fairer deal than that I decided to give it a whirl. Once involved I started a two-up school in the shop. Then George and I got a trotting licence to field in the country which meant travelling to towns such as Bunbury, York, Harvey, Bridgetown and so on. Some trips took me away from home for three or four days but Rose backed me all the way and never once complained. In fact, in the beginning, she agreed to let me put every bit of money we had - a hundred and twenty quid in all - into the venture. George matched it and said, "*That'll be plenty to start with."*

I'll never forget our first race meeting. It was Caulfield Cup Day - everyone was backing a horse called Grey Boots at seven to one. One chap had ten quid straight out on it. Sure enough the damned horse won. By the time we paid out we were a hundred and thirty quid in the red. The sweat was pouring out of me. I was really distressed. All the money I'd worked so hard for was gone and here I was in debt. I went to George who had paid out the extra money and said, *"Look George, I can't go any further than this I'm afraid."* He could see the panic I was in. *"Don't worry,"* he assured me, *"It'll be okay, you'll see."* Unconvinced I continued writing out tickets. We did the Perth and Sydney meetings, then the trots at night. When we tallied up on the day I was absolutely delighted to find we had recovered our dough and made a profit of sixty five quid each. This called for a little celebration and I must say the beer sure tasted good that night. In between trips and when I wasn't cutting hair, I took every opportunity to put the nets on and go fishing or spend time working on the farm. I sold the Buick and bought a Ford Pilot car. It was a heavy vehicle with roll down fringed blinds on the windows and a spare on the boot. We were going up in the world!

The bookmaking lasted two years. I gave it up for a couple of reasons. Due to the fact I was hardly exercising but drinking and smoking much more than I normally would, my weight ballooned from thirteen stone to fifteen stone three ounces. It made me feel sluggish and unwell. Also I was becoming a stranger at home, especially with the kids. Sometimes I only got to spend an hour with them before going off to another race meeting. I thought if I stayed on I might get caught up in the gambling world for good, get fat and lazy and be incapable of physical labour, and that did not appeal to me one bit. So I made my decision, went to George and said, "*I don't know whether this is good or bad news but I'm pulling out mate.*" After explaining my reasons for leaving he shook my hand and said, "*Look Pud. It's been a fantastic partnership and I've never had a better mate. I appreciate your sentiments as to why you want to leave and I give you full credit for it.*"

I went back working for Harry for about three or four months, then took up fishing again. The catches were large and plentiful. In four days I caught two thousand pounds of whiting. Another time I netted everyday for six weeks catching between two hundred and fifty to a thousand pounds a time. The price at the markets was pretty weak though - only one shilling and sixpence a pound, out of which came freight and commission. At one stage I hired a chap to cart them to Perth for me and paid him sixpence a pound but still the actual profit was quite small. Despite this I was back doing what I loved best.

Having to work on tides and weather often meant being out all day and most of the night. If everything went according to plan I would finish a couple of shots by three in the morning, boil the billy and have an hour or two sleep on a bag by the fire. Usually I was cold and wet but too tired to care. When waders came on the scene and I discovered waggas which are made from bags slit open and sewn together, conditions improved dramatically. Now I could stay dry and warm while in the water then flop on a wagga in the rushes. Sometimes I worked myself to a standstill - I'd be so exhausted, stars would flash in front of my eyes. The longest stretch I remember fishing without a break was thirty seven hours. I started on a Monday morning, worked all day and came home with five fish which I'd caught in a particular spot at about five in the afternoon. Knowing the same spot could produce a lot of fish with the turn of the tide, I urged Rose to quickly prepare me some crib and away I went. Shortly after dark I hauled the nets again. By one in the morning I was still plucking whiting. My food and smokes had run out so, leaving the nets in the water, I shot back to the landing, woke Rose who prepared some more food, rolled myself some twirlies and headed back to the river. I finished plucking between ten and eleven that morning, got to shore and then had the job of washing, boxing and transporting the fish to the freezers in Augusta. The haul netted five hundred pounds of whiting, three big kingfish and a hundred pounds of mixed. On returning home Rose said, "*You must be feeling absolutely shattered love!*" "*To be honest,*" I replied, "*I'm not. If I had to go out again I could.*" I suppose I must have gone past the point of tiredness by that stage though when my head finally hit the pillow, rest assured, it didn't take very long to enter the land of nod.

...Chapter 34

My brother Harold decided, during this period, to come from Perth and work for Harry. He boarded with us for a total of four years. Whenever he could, he helped me with the bigger hauls of fish. At work, he picked up the building trade with ease and became a first class tradesman. He also took up football and mastered that too, receiving many trophies along the way and the nickname 'Roughchops', or 'Roughy' for short. I was on the football committee for several years, organising cabarets, barbecues and fund raising events. Around this time I decided to extend the house. Two bedrooms, a lounge, bathroom and sleepout were added to the original building, the kitchen was enlarged and cement verandahs back and front completed the picture.

Rose and I sometimes played tennis at Kudardup. One day while playing, Rose almost collapsed. She couldn't seem to get her breath. Worried, I took her to see the new doctor, Paddy Barrett. He referred her to a specialist in Perth. We drove up and after he examined her he said to me, "*Your wife's got a bit of a murmur in her heart but its nothing really to worry about. If she doesn't overexert herself she'll live quite a normal life.*" Relieved and happy with this diagnosis we went home to Kudardup. But Rose just got worse, often gasping for breath after merely sweeping the floor. I went to Paddy and said, "*Look, I'm not very happy about Rose's health at all. The other guy said there was nothing to worry about but, by God, 1 think there's a lot to worry about.*" "*I'll tell you what I'll do,*" answered Paddy. "*I'll give you a referral to a young doctor - he's just done two years in Harley Street and has set up a practice in Yorkshire House in Perth - he'd be one of the top heart specialists in Australia.*" Feeling as though some headway was finally being made, we went to Perth and saw Dr Cullity. On completion of his examination he said, "*I'll be blunt. Rose, if you don't have a heart operation you will not live beyond five years and in three years from now you won't be able to lift a teatowel.*" Taken aback I said, "*Well, where do we go from here?*" Turning to Rose he said, "*Outside of your heart you are a perfect patient for this operation.*" The operation he spoke of had been performed less than ten times in Western Australia so candidates were more or less guinea pigs at that time. But what alternative did we have? Dr Cullity set out the risks involved and made sure we understood the procedure. Rose had a leaking valve in her heart which had to be cleared.

Shortly after the visit, Rose was admitted to the Royal Perth Hospital. The kids were billeted with their Godparents which took a big load off our minds. Harold insisted on coming with us. In fact we used his car. The night before the operation Rose sat up in bed, cheerfully chatting away as though she was on holiday. Neither of us really had any idea of how huge the operation was going to be. I kissed her goodnight and said I'd see her the next day. At eight in the morning she went in to theatre. Roughy and I arrived about half an hour later and while he sat on the steps outside the hospital I spent most of my time trying to get some information. I saw two nurses entering a lift so I dashed up and said, "*Excuse me, you wouldn't happen to know how a Mrs Challis is would you? She's having a heart operation this morning.*" One of the nurses said, "*Yes, your wife is back in her ward.*" "Oh," I replied, "*She's through the operation then?*" "Yes, that's right," she replied. Happy as a sandboy, I told Harold, then went up to the seventh floor to see Rose. A sister on the ward said, "*Dr Simpson, the surgeon, would like to see you.*" Entering a small room I was confronted by Dr Simpson, still in his theatre gown and cap, covered in blood. He had a little smile on his face as I shook his hand and thanked him profusely. Then he said, "*We mustn't get too carried away. It'll be at least three weeks before we can say your wife is out of danger.*" Still not comprehending the gravity of the situation I said, "*Okay. I'm sure she'll be fine. Can I go and see her?*" "Well," he replied hesitantly, "*You can see her but my advice is it wouldn't do you or your wife any good. I think it would be better if you left it till later.*" "What time do you think would be alright?" I asked. "*About four o'clock,*" he said. It was now about 9.30 a.m. When I returned to the hospital I was expecting to see Rose sitting up in bed. The matron told me to stay no more than two minutes. I thought that was a bit stupid, until I saw my darling, and then two minutes seemed like an eternity. Rose lay unconscious and barely breathing, tubes coming out of her body everywhere. Completely stunned and thinking there was little chance of her surviving I left and went to Egina Street where good friends, Mr and Mrs Cardie, were staying in mum's house. "*She won't make it,*" I said to them. "*Of course she will,*" they replied. "*Don't worry, she'll come through.*" "*No,*" I said sadly, "*I'm afraid not. I only hope you're right, but I don't think so.*"

After dinner I went to see Harold. I found him, legless, in the pub. I'd never seen him so drunk in my life. He adored Rose and must have been under a lot of strain but had kept it to himself. Now he had cut loose. The pub was about to close. I saw a friend and went over to have a few words. Meanwhile Roughy disappeared. Outside I found him lying on the back seat of the car, his legs hanging out the window. At Egina Street I managed to get him out of the car, amidst protests of '*Leave me here! Leave me here!*", and we both went to bed. Next day I went back to the hospital but there was not much improvement. Rose was heavily sedated and hardly opened her eyes. But slowly, through sheer willpower, she made progress. They had literally cut her in half. The scar ran from under her left breast, round under her arm and across her back to below the right shoulder. The doctor had put his finger into her heart to clear the valve. Rose was in Royal Perth for six weeks before I took her, lying on the back seat of the car, to Margaret River Hospital where she spent another seven weeks. Ma and Pop Coe came from Kalgoorlie to look after the kids who had been gathered up and brought home.

It was during Rose's convalescence that I did a bit of matchmaking for my brothers, Roughy and Dave, or the 'Squatter' as we called him. One day I took Pop, Harold and his mate Len to see Rose. After a short chat the three of them left to have a sip in the pub. Immediately they'd gone a lovely red-headed nurse called Joyce came into the room. The first thing she said was, "*Oh! Who was that gorgeous guy with you?*" Thinking she was talking about Len I said, "*What, the blonde bloke?*" "*No, no,*" she replied, "*The one with the beautiful eyes!*" Amused I said, "*You fancy him a bit do you?*" "*Mmm,*" she replied ecstatically, "*What a dream.*" "*Would you like him to take you out?*" I asked casually. "*Would I ever,*" she replied. There happened to be a show on at the local men's club that night that women were allowed to attend. "*How about if he takes you to the Club tonight?*" I asked. Slightly confused she said it would be great but impossible as she hadn't even met him. "*Look, you just be ready at eight o'clock and he'll be here to pick you up,*" I replied confidently. Acting as though she'd won charities but at the same time doubting her luck, Joyce kept saying, "*Oh you won't be able to get him to come - you won't be able to.*" "*He'll be here,*" I assured her. "*You just be ready.*" Later at home I asked Roughy what he thought of the nurse he'd seen at the hospital. Never one to say a lot he replied, "*I didn't think she was too bad a drop.*" "*How'd you like to have a run out with her tonight?*" I asked. He looked blankly at me, not sure what I was getting at. "*Well,*" I continued, "*It's like this. I've booked you in for the Club. I told her you'd pick her up at eight.*" Roughie's reaction was typical of him. Showing no real excitement but not saying a definite no either, I thought there might still be a chance for my plan to work. The day wore on and I began to worry a bit. If he decided not to go I'd be in the 'nure. As I got ready to see Rose in the late afternoon Harold was having a lie down. He'd had a few beers earlier so there was a chance he'd just drop off to sleep and miss the deadline. I went to his room on my way out and said, "*Now you better do the right thing otherwise I'll really be in it. You definitely will turn up won't you?*" "*Oh yeah,*" he replied casually, "I'll *be there at eight.*" Arriving at the hospital I was almost knocked over by one very anxious nurse. "*Is he coming?*" Joyce asked. "*Yes,*" I replied, "*He'll be here - no worries.*" "*I don't think you're dinkum,*" she said. "*You just be ready,*" I answered. "*He'll be here.*" Time ambled on. At about seven, Joyce went to the nurses quarters and got changed. She rushed in to ask Rosie if she looked alright. "*You look lovely,*" Rose assured her. Time ticked on. At five to eight Joyce came across from her room and said, "*I think you're having me on. I don't reckon he's coming.*" "*It's not eight o'clock yet,*" I answered. "*It's only five to.*" Completely unconvinced she waited impatiently as the seconds went by. Good old Roughy. He left it to the last moment to arrive - dead on eight o'clock. Joyce was over the moon. Before leaving for the club they asked me to join them after my visit with Rose. I called in later but stayed on the verandah yarning with some mates. Joyce came out and tried to get me inside but I was quite happy where I was. When I left around eleven, Joyce and Harold were still dancing the night away. That was the start of the romance. They have now been married over thirty years.

Dave's story was quite different. In fact it was by accident that he met his bride-to-be. On a visit to Rose I mentioned a barbecue Harry was having that Saturday night. A lovely nurse called Mary overheard me and said how she'd love to be going. "*What's stopping you then?*" I asked. "*Nothing really,*" she replied. "*Okay,*" I said, "*When I come up that afternoon I'll take you back. I can't give you a lift home but I'll make sure you get one."* The Squatter had just bought a new Chev which I hoped he would put to good use after the party. Saturday arrived but Mary wasn't at the hospital. A change of shifts or something. Another nurse, Grace, explained Mary's absence after I enquired about her. I said, *"She's supposed to come down with me to a barbecue tonight at my brother's place."* "Oh yes," answered Grace. *"Would you like to come instead?"* I asked. Absolutely delighted she smiled and said, *"I'd love to."* *"Well get yourself ready,"* I replied, *"I'll take you there and you'll have no worries about getting home."* At the barbecue I introduced Grace to Dave. Then later I took him aside and said, *"Now listen, this little girl wants to get back to Margaret River tonight. Is there any chance of you taking her?"* The rest is history. That night started them down the same bridal path as Joyce and Harold. My bachelor brothers were well and truly hooked - and happily so.

Rose was finally allowed to go home. She was fed up with hospitals and I had missed her terribly. Now she was a new woman, able to do things with little effort. The operation, doctors and hospitals ended up costing a thousand pounds, a figure naturally way beyond our means. I went to each of the parties involved and arranged to pay them by installments. Ten pounds a month went to the Royal Perth Hospital, five to Dr Cullity, five to Dr Simpson, five to Paddy Barrett, five to the anesthetist and five to the Margaret River Hospital. It took over two years but eventually every penny was paid.

...Chapter 35

A chap called Ernie Lilley moved into the district and was driving an old bulldozer for a bloke called Chapman. I needed some dozing done on the property but at five pounds an hour found it hard to raise the capital. Harold came to the fore and lent me two hundred pounds. Ernie did my job, some for Harry, then moved on to Prices', the Godparents of my daughter Julie. While there I went to see him and said, "*Listen Ernie, have you ever thought about taking on a relief driver?*" "*Actually,*" he replied, "*that's something I've been telling Chapman for a while - that I need another driver.*" "*Well,*" I said, "*I'm interested in doing the job. I've never driven a dozer before so I'll tell you what I'll do. I'm prepared to do a fortnight for nothing as long as you teach me the ropes. Then if I'm satisfactory I'd like you to give me a start.*" "*That's a fair enough offer,*" replied Ernie. "*Okay. I'll come up tomorrow then,*" I said. By the end of the next day I was hired at fifteen pounds a week,

75 QUID AND AN AXE

starting immediately.

As time went by I discovered that Ernie was earning a pittance of a wage for the work he was doing so I suggested we go into partnership and buy a new bulldozer. Ernie said he could hardly afford a set of spanners, let alone a dozer. He was living in a caravan and had a young family Apart from my block I had very little myself. "*If we could get a deposit and some guarantors,*" I suggested, "*I can't see why we couldn't get a start.*" Ernie was enthusiastic enough but very doubtful that the idea would actually come to anything. "*Right,*" I said, "*I'll make the first move.*" I broke the news to Rose on the way home from Prices'. "*Ernie and I are going to buy a new bulldozer,*" I said. "*Oh yes,*" she replied casually, "*And how much will that cost dear?*" "*Ten thousand pounds.*" I said casually. Rose nearly fell out of the ute. "*Ten thousand pounds!*" she exclaimed, "*You haven't got ten thousand pennies.*" "*She'll be right,*" I assured her.

I went around to a few people and got five to act as guarantors. Then I went to the bank. Three men worked there, Aikenhead, Dawes and Tapper. I needed three and a half thousand pounds as a deposit. I knew Dawsey wasn't too happy about the situation because he was in on a deal for dozers to do war service work and didn't want competition. The manager, Mr Aikenhead, was quite obliging but said final approval would have to come from head office in Perth.

I waited...and waited. Nothing. This day Ernie and I were going to see brother Bill, who was one of the guarantors. I suggested we go to the bank afterwards. We were only a couple of miles past the Kudardup store when along came Aikenhead and Dawes. We both pulled up and I strolled across to their car. I asked about the loan. Aikenhead ummed and ahhed for a bit, talking about head office, then Dawes butted in and said, "*To cut a long story short the whole thing's been declined.*" "*Has it!*" I stated. "*Okay - thanks fellas.*" I turned on my heel and went straight back to the car. "*We'll shoot out to Bill's now,*" I said to Ernie. When we got there Bill told us that the bank Johnnies had just been there. They had told Bill and his wife Vi that if they got involved in our venture and we went broke they'd be up for ten thousand pounds. Bill explained he would have to pull out as guarantor because he could not possibly meet that sort of debt. "*Look,*" I said, "*There's no way you have to front that amount. It's the deposit of three and half grand I'm asking you to go guarantor for.*" But my arguments fell on deaf ears. Bill was too frightened to be in it and chose to believe Aikenhead and Dawes until I got proof in writing. Ernie said, "*Well we may as well drop the idea. There's not much point in going any further. What are you going to do now?*" asked Ernie. "*We're off to Perth,*" I said. "*What are you going to do in Perth?*" he asked. "*Don't worry,*" I answered, "*I've got a few cards up my sleeve.*" We accepted a lift with an old retired wheat cocky who was staying at Bill's but was going to Perth the next day. Arriving in Pinjarra, a town about fifty miles south of Perth, I rang the R & I Bank and made an appointment to see the manager, a Mr Basisto. The wheat cocky had had a lot to do with the R & I Bank and Basisto over the years. He said, "*When you go in to the bank, if Basisto says 'I'm sorry, nothing doing', grab your hat and come straight out because there's no way you'll change his mind. But if on the other hand he decides to help you he's the greatest man in the bank to deal with.*" "Fair enough," I said confidently, thinking I had enough ammunition to get my point across. The appointment was for ten o'clock. While waiting we were given a cup of tea, which I thought was a nice gesture. Then we were shown into the manager's office. Mr Basisto sat in a large swivel chair behind an equally large desk. He was a fairly old chap who, after asking us to take a seat, sat back with his hands behind his head and said, "*Well chaps, I'm afraid from all the information I've got there's no way 1 can help you.*" He continued. "*You have no security and very little collateral*"...and on he rambled, saying how sorry he was etc. By now my hair was starting to crackle. I was really getting wound up. He finished talking, ending with, "*I don't think we can go any further.*" I leapt out of my chair, banged my fist on his desk and said, "*Right Mr Basisto, you've had your say. That's your side of the story. Now are you prepared to listen to mine?*" "*Certainly,*" he replied, "*Go right ahead.*" *I* put my case to him in full, about Dawes and Aikenhead and the fact I had five guarantors who were prepared to back me all the way. He sat back and said, "*That just couldn't be true Mr Challis.*" I wasn't in the habit of lying so the comment really hurt. "*Look Mr Basisto,*" I said, "*Evidently you don't believe me but if I walk into this office tomorrow morning with the five people I have nominated would you believe me then?*""*I'd have no option would I?*" he replied. "*No,*" I said, "*And if that's what I've got to do then I'll have them all here at ten o'clock tomorrow.*" He realised then I was dinkum Suddenly there was action. His secretary was summoned, details were taken and the loan approved. Ernie and I were absolutely delighted. As we were about to leave I said, "*Just one more question, Mr Basisto, I'd like to ask you!*" "*Yes Mr Challis?*" "*If anything unforeseen happened - say we were killed or got sick and couldn't operate - and *we went broke. How would our guarantors stand? What amount of money would they be up for?*" "Three and a half thousand pounds," he replied. "*Now that is the maximum amount, is it?*" I asked, wanting to make sure of the facts. "*Definitely,*" he answered, "*That and not a penny more.*" "*Look Mr Basisto,*" I said, "*Would it be possible for you to put that in writing and sign it yourself?*" "*No trouble,*" he said obligingly. Within minutes I had three typed copies, signed, sealed and delivered into my hand. We shook hands, thanked him very much and left.

That was a Friday. Saturday was spent in Perth and on Sunday we headed home. I said to Ernie and the cocky, "*There's a little detour I'd like to make on the way home if you don't mind.*" "*Where to?*" they asked. "*I want to see a little fellow called Mr Aikenhead,*" I replied. Being Sunday, we drove to his home, where we saw him dressed in overalls in the front garden. When he saw me step out of the car he came to the gate and with a cheerful, "*Hello George*", asked me what he could do for me. "*Oh not all that much,*" I replied. "*There's just a letter here I'd like you to run your eyes over.*" I took it from the inside pocket of my jacket and handed it to him. As he read it, it was like watching a crayfish cook. He went bright red. Without looking up he slowly folded the letter. "*I'll have that thanks Bill,*" I said, "*And I'll see you.*" Three weeks later there was movement at the station. The staff of three were transferred from the R & I Bank in Margaret River to parts unknown. Obviously Mr Basisto did some checking after our meeting and discovered the lies that had been told to stop us getting the loan.

Work started coming in at a steady rate. Fortunately we managed to get the bulk of the war service work in the area. In the beginning we worked three hours on and three off but this meant both of us being on the job all day so we altered it to twenty four hour shifts, the change over being at twelve midday. The one working the afternoon shift did the following morning shift as well, knocking off at midday. This allowed us time at home to do other things. I took charge of the paperwork and the maintenance of the machine. Every Monday for the best part of the morning I gave the dozer a major overhaul to make sure it was kept in peak condition. Normal maintenance was done by torchlight at 4 a.m. on my morning shifts. It was hard, dirty and sometimes dangerous work but I enjoyed it. There was no such thing as air-conditioned cabs or ear muffs as there are today so in the heat of summer it was like climbing into an oven. The noise took it's toll on my hearing over the years which left me slightly deaf. Most days I came home black from head to foot, the only white skin being that on my eye lids.

We had a good run apart from a couple of altercations with nasty customers who were immediately struck off the books. The partnership last seven years. Ernie came to me one day and said that his eldest son Georgie had asthma and they would have to shift to a warmer climate. *"Fair enough,"* I said. *"Do you want to buy me out?"* asked Ernie. *"Oh yeah, at the right price,"* I answered. *"You'll have no worries about work,"* said Ernie. *"You'll have the full monopoly of the place."* After a deal was made I went to the bank and made the necessary arrangements. At this time both Harry and Ernie were on the Roads Board. It was after a meeting later on that Harry said to me, *"Is Ernie Lilley going into bulldozing Pud?" "Into bulldozing,"* I exclaimed, *"He's going out of bulldozing." "Well,"* said Harry, *"I thought it pretty strange last night. I* heard Ernie say to some guys that he wouldn't be able to make a meeting because he was going to Perth to tee up on a dozer." "*That's news to me,*" I replied. "*He told me he had to leave because of his kid being sick.*" I couldn't for the life of me think why Ernie would do this to me. I'd always been straight with him and made sure he got the easy end of the stick as much as possible. Maybe that was the problem. Straight away I drove down to see him. "*I believe you're teeing up on a dozer,*" I said. "*Yeah,*" he replied defensively, "*I'm entitled to if I want to.*" "*Who told you you're not?*" I replied. "*And what's this tale about your kid being sick and having to leave and me having monopoly and so on!*" "*Oh well, I've decided to have a go myself that's all,*" he said. The money had not yet come through from the bank so I said, "*Well I've just decided I might not buy you out.*" Ernie nearly collapsed. I found out later he had already been round the district trying to get bookings for work ahead of me. Now he was depending on my money for the deposit. "*Anyway,*" I continued, "*I'll give it twenty four hours and think it over. But I might just change my mind and not sell.*" In my mind I knew there was no way we could work together again but I felt pretty hurt and wanted him to sweat a little. After talking it over with Rosie we decided I'd be better off on my own in the long run. The transaction went through and Ernie and I parted company over a meal and a few beers. He stayed in competition with me till he died but by then he was broke. He had two dozers at the time and they were repossessed after his death.

While working with Ernie I managed to clear quite a bit of my property on which I grazed Herefords. I also dozed a road through to the new golf course for the price of the fuel. Both Ernie and I had become keen golfers and this was part of our contribution to the club. It was a rough and ready old course when first I picked up a club, but like a magnet it drew me in. A basic clubhouse was erected with outside toilets. Often we'd have a get together there with me on the accordion. They were great days. I even managed to improve my game enough to twice become club champion. Rose still plays every week. She has won many trophies over the years and the honour of getting a hole-in-one.

Bulldozing could only be done for about nine months of the year. In winter it was just too boggy. So the other three months I spent on the river. It was always a welcome break from the dust and heat. Whereas the river seemed like a companion to me, dozing was the opposite - it was a lonely type of job being out in the bush all day with only my smokes and the roar of the engine for company. I'd always had a dog of some sort round the house but one time I got a dog that went to work with me.

He was a beautiful blue heeler and I called him Skipper. He used to sit on the front seat of the ute and was often mistaken for a person. While I worked he stayed mostly by the vehicle but would always let me know when it was time to knock off. Having had a couple of close shaves with falling trees he kept wide of the dozer, circling round till I spotted him. We became really good mates and I enjoyed having him with me. One morning I rose as usual at three o'clock. While Rose prepared my crib and thermos I went out to load a drum of fuel on the ute. Normally I'd feed Skipper next, then he'd go straight to the ute and wait for me. This morning he was there for his food but when I came out again he was no-where to be seen. I called and whistled for a while but still no sign of him. I said to Rose, *"I'm buggered if I know where the dog is but he's not around here. Would you keep an eye out for him?"* I went to work, not particularly worried, thinking he'd be home when I got there. But I was mistaken. *"Did Skipper come home?"* I asked. *"No,"* said Rose, *"I haven't sighted him."* *"That's strange,"* I replied, *"Well I'm not going to work in the morning. I'm going to do a run and see if I can find him."* Next morning I went to the old homestead which was now owned by Brindleys. As I entered their property Alan and his wife were driving out. *"Listen Alan,"* I said as we pulled up alongside each other. *"You haven't seen my dog have you?"* Casual as you like he said, *"Yes, I shot him."* *"Shot him!"* I exclaimed, *"You must be joking."* *"No,"* he replied, *"It was a bit unfortunate actually. I didn't shoot to kill him. I shot to frighten him but I hit him in the back. I had to put him down then."* It was a good thing that Mrs Brindley was in the car because I was so angry I think I would have killed Alan had he been alone. That was the last dog I ever owned.

    I continued bulldozing for nine years after Ernie and I split. The farm was eventually fully cleared and stocked with breeding cattle. Les, having spent two years at Busselton High School, got a job. Julie, and later Carol, both graduated from teachers' college and took up country postings. Carol worked part-time as a singer in a band. Les, the most musical of the family, learnt to play the drums at the age of fourteen and later the piano accordion. He also played in a band for years.

...Chapter 36

In 1966 Rose started getting breathless again. A visit to Paddy showed another murmur in her heart. A week or so later we received a letter from Dr Cullitty. He said he'd been in Margaret River and had spoken to Paddy about Rose. Paddy had told him he wasn't pleased with the test results. He went on to say that he knew it would be difficult financially for us to pay if another operation was necessary but not to let that interfere in our decision to go ahead. He said he'd like us to see him in Perth as soon as possible. If an operation was needed both he and Dr Simpson would give their services free of charge. This was an extremely generous offer from two wonderful men who obviously thought a lot of Rose. He finished by saying that we should not let things slide as time was very important. A few days later we went to Perth where Dr Cullitty examined Rose. He was unable to reach a decision without further tests and said he wanted Rose admitted to the Royal Perth Hospital for about ten days. As the days passed and nothing showed up on the tests, our hopes rose. One day I went to the races then on to the hospital. Dr Cullitty was there by Rose's bed when I arrived. "*Well,*" he said, "*I've got a bit of bad news for you but I don't want you to worry. I'm afraid Rose will have to have another operation.*" I was rocked. I had convinced myself it wouldn't be necessary and the news came as a real blow. Rose on the other hand reacted as if she'd just been told we were going on a picnic. She didn't turn a hair. I expressed my fears of the first operation but Dr Cullitty assured us it would be a lot different this time. Fourteen years had passed and the procedure had been greatly improved. A day or so later Rose underwent surgery. Admittedly she recovered a lot quicker than before but the initial sight of her in intensive care still left me shaken. Rose was out of hospital in three weeks and on the golf course in six. Her will to live and strength of character were the main factors in getting her through. One problem had arisen after the operation. It was an irregular heartbeat. The doctor had tried a few things to regulate it and told me he had one last treatment left after which he would have exhausted every avenue. I was absolutely delighted one day on a visit to listen to Rose's heart and discover it had been corrected, but later at home it went out of whack again and remained that way, thankfully with little effect on Rose's health.

Bulldozing continued till 1969. I'd been at it for sixteen years and I'd had enough. I wanted to semi-retire, sell fish locally and run the farm. My one main ambition was to get enough money together to take Rose for a long holiday to England. Over all the years we'd struggled she had never once complained about our lack of finances.

Whatever I could afford to give her was always enough. One time in Kalgoorlie Rose managed for three weeks on ten pounds spending money which was all we could afford at that stage. Now I wanted to see her spend freely without giving a thought to the budget. An added bonus was that Julie had gone overseas in '67 and later in '69 married a Welshman whom we had yet to meet. This trip would allow us to spend time with them. Carol and Les also got married in the same year as Julie, a very busy and pleasant time for us. I told Rose that whatever we got from the sale of the dozer would be used for our holiday. A couple of efforts to sell attracted offers of only three thousand pounds which I felt was not enough for a machine in such good condition. Then one day a Yank came round to negotiate a deal. I asked for six thousand but finally accepted five thousand six hundred pounds. He wrote a cheque and for the first time in my life I actually had money of quite a considerable sum with which I could do anything I wanted. We had no debts, the kids were off our hands, the world was at our fingertips.

At this time the share market was booming. Quite a few of the locals had invested and were showing profits. I said to Rose, "*Now this is entirely up to you love. You have to give me a yes or no and whatever you decide I'll go along with it. I've always said that money makes money and if ever I had the opportunity I'd like to be in a position to invest. If you're not panicking about going on the trip I'd like to have a go for twelve months in the share market. It's a risk. If I do the lot, there won't be a holiday, so the decision is yours.*" Without hesitation Rose replied, "*You just do as you please. If we don't go for another year it won't make a bit of difference.*" Over the next twelve months the money I invested more than doubled itself. In fact after six months in England I returned with the original sum intact. For the trip, we booked to go over by ship and fly home. Rose took sick on the way to Fiji and was quite ill, but recovered later in the journey. We loved the sea voyage and were overjoyed when Julie and Tom came aboard after we docked at Southampton. Tom worked in travel and had been given a special pass. They had a car and soon we were on our way to London.

Being in England after forty eight years was indescribable. I'd always, since leaving at the age of eight, longed to return to the village where I was born. Dozens of times I'd had dreams where I was back in England on the farm where dad worked, with my mates. The dreams were so vivid I used to say to myself in my sleep, "*It's true this time. I'm really here.*" Now that I was actually here, I kept expecting to wake up and find it was all just another dream. We spent a few days seeing the sights of London before journeying on to Essex and my cousin's house outside Finchingfield. Tom and Julie had to return to Wales but we joined up with them there later on. Ron, my cousin, and his wife Joan, were wonderful to us. We were treated like V.I.P.'s. Our picture was published in the local paper. Relatives we had never met made us feel completely at home. My memories of the village and surrounding districts were so good that I needed no directions to find my way round. When told where my dad was buried I directed Ron to the church in White Notley. I showed Rose the grate in the street which had fallen on my hand. We walked to the place where I used to pick bluebells and peggles. I looked up school mates who still lived in the area. We visited Rose's relatives in London, travelled through Scotland and Wales and enjoyed every single minute of it all. After six months we were quite happy to be going home to the farm, having achieved everything we'd set out to do.

...Chapter 37

My intention to settle down to the quiet life was knocked on the head when Harry approached me about skippering a ferry on the river. Prior to this, after I got back from England, I'd heard a few whispers about a new ferry coming on the river and how a syndicate of local businessmen, including Harry, had been formed to finance the venture. The chap in charge in Perth intended selling his house and moving to Augusta to run the show. I knew all the local syndicate members well but not one had said a word to me about the venture. Evidently, when the time came to bring the ferry down on a low loader, the Perth guy pulled out, leaving a white elephant that no-one wanted to manage. Looking for someone to fill the bill they elected me as first choice. Harry came, explained the situation and asked if I'd be interested in skippering the boat. "*To be honest,*" I answered, "*I'm not really anxious to do anything. As far as I'm concerned my working life is* *over and I wasn't contemplating taking on anything more."* Harry's son Jimmy stepped into the picture and said, *"There's really nothing for you to do uncle George. We'll buy your uniform. All you have to do is drive the ferry. You know the history of the place so you can just give a bit of a commentary." "What's it worth?"* I asked. *"Eighty dollars a week,"* he replied. For a seven day week the money was not at all worth the effort but not wanting to see people I knew as mates take a dive, I agreed to do it. Little did I know what I was letting myself in for.

Out of all the things I'd done in my life this job gave me more worry than any other. Often I would be sitting up at midnight drinking a glass of wine to settle my nerves. Apart from the worry there was also a lot of hard work involved. There was no mooring, no landings, no tourist trade. Not able to bear the thought of failing I jumped in, boots and all. The syndicate gave me no help really. It was left up to me to organise everything. The first job was to build a jetty in Augusta and a landing at Alexandra Bridge where I hoped to arrange for tourist buses to transfer passengers to the ferry for a trip down the river. Two mates and I erected the jetty. With a post hole digger I dug every pile hole to a depth of seven feet through heavy clay. Each time I left the water I was a total wreck. While doing this I also ran short trips to the mouth of the river. This meant changing out of my wet gear into some clean togs, doing the trip, then going back in the water to continue digging. Day after day the slog went on and all for the princely sum of eighty dollars a week. There were lots of teething problems with the boat. The steering went one time, leaving us stranded on a bank. It dragged its moorings into the shallows in front of the house. The rudder was inadequate and too deep. Until I had stabilisers put on either side, the boat, being flat sided and blunt nosed went where it liked in windy conditions. Something always seemed to be going wrong.

As time went by I began to see a light at the end of the tunnel. I visited coach tour offices in Perth and organised time schedules. Rose took care of the canteen on board which provided passengers with morning or afternoon teas. Soon we were providing a beautiful scenic trip on the Blackwood complete with music and commentary. Rose was a wonderful asset, mixing and talking with everyone on board. Together we made a good team. The only trouble was - Rose was working for nothing and I for not much more. Seeing no future in the wages I was receiving, I asked the syndicate, after three years, if I could lease the boat from them. They agreed and once again I was in business for myself. We employed a couple of ladies to relieve Rose and they proved to be naturals like her.

One little highlight of the trip involved two ducks we christened Sid and Sadie. They belonged to an American family who had a beautiful home right on the banks of the river. I had a hooter on board and used to give a toot as I approached their place. The ducks got used to it and would paddle out to meet us and get their reward of bits of bread or cake. The word spread and people would wait expectantly to see the performance. One lady even wrote a poem about it. Most people that travelled on the ferry said it was the most enjoyable part of their tour. In spring the banks were lined with wattle, creepers and wildflowers. Birds perched and swam everywhere. Apart from the American's house, no others interrupted the view of natural bushland. I must say I never tired of doing that trip nor telling everyone the history of the area. I was on my river and I was happy.

Not long after I leased the outfit, I took on a partner called Grant Buller. He was just the right sort of person for the job and we got on like a house on fire. There was one hairy episode that occurred when cyclone Alby hit Augusta. I did the morning trip that day, picking up passengers at the bridge and returning to the jetty. It was still a beautiful day when I handed the reins to Grant who had almost a full load to take back to the bridge. I drove home and was eating lunch when a sudden gust of wind through the front passage nearly lifted me out of my seat. I couldn't imagine what had happened till I looked out at the river. I said to Rose, "*Oh my God! I'm off!*" Dropping everything I dashed down to my boat to secure it. The battle I had to manoeuvre it in the wind was almost beyond me. I could not credit how quickly the weather had turned. As soon as I got back to the house I said, "*I've got to go straight to Alex Bridge. When Grant gets there we'll have to leave the ferry at the landing. There's no way in the world we can bring that back.*" Rose went with me. A coach was already there waiting for the pick up. I explained to the driver what would have to be done and said there were sixteen people on board who were not coach passengers. When I talked of taking them in my car the driver offered to carry them all on the bus. With everything teed up I waited for Grant. Being a narrow part of the river surrounded by dense growth and tall timbers, the water was flat calm at the landing, perfect for ensuring the safety of the ferry. When the boat arrived I told Grant the situation and then I said, "*You'd better not take her back. There's no way you're going to land her in Augusta.*" "*Oh she'll be alright,*" he replied.

I'd made a stipulation when we started the partnership that it was 'one ship, one captain', so Grant, being in charge, had the final say. It was a rule I wished, later that day, I had broken. He kept the sixteen passengers on board and set sail. Rose and I raced back to Augusta. When I saw the waves breaking over the jetty I knew we were in real trouble so I flew out to Molloy Island hoping to stop him there. The road was covered in branches and leaves and the wind was screaming. By the time I arrived he had passed. I was too late. We started for Augusta again. Between the time we got to Molloy, turned around and headed back, a tree had fallen across the road. After surveying the leafy end I asked Rose to hold a couple of branches back so I could get the car round. She had a terrible job as the wind nearly blew her over. Nevertheless we managed to get back on the track and on our way again.

Grant had reached the jetty before us. Abalone fishermen and others were trying to hold the ferry with ropes while the passengers disembarked. Eventually, with them safely ashore, I jumped on board and said to Grant, *"We'll have to leave the jetty straight away because she'll pull it away if we tie her up."* He backed out and we were blown almost across to the opposite bank before he could turn around to head for West Bay Creek, a mile or so up the river. Harold was fixing tiles on someone's roof at that moment and he told me later he watched us head into the waves. He said as we went from one wave to the next all but the very rear of the boat was off the water. The thumping we got inside was bone jarring. One of the windows broke and sliced my arm. When I got the anchor out to moor the boat I was very lucky not to get my foot caught as it went overboard, which would certainly have torn it off. Finally the boat was safe in the lee of the bay. Someone came out in a punt and picked us up. At home Rose dressed my arm and I changed into dry clothes. Soon the winds died. We were in the eye of the cyclone. Where before the blow had come from the North, when it started again about nine o'clock, it came in from the West. At one in the morning I got a phone call from Merv Newton, a local fisherman. "*Listen Pud,*" he said, "*Your ferry's swung round on the mooring and has beached itself on the other side of the bay.*" "*Well as far as I'm concerned Merv,*" I replied, *It can bloody well stay there. I'm going back to bed*" "*I just thought I'd ring and let you know,*" he said. "*Thanks a lot for that,*" I replied, "*But right now I couldn't care less.*" Next morning the cyclone had gone. With the help of a couple of abalone boats and my own engine power it wasn't long before the ferry was safely moored at the jetty. It was not an experience I would ever want repeated.

Another episode turned out to be quite comical. Due to a very late coach I ended up leaving the bridge in the dark. Unfortunately there was no moon that night so the trip had to be done mostly by guesswork and my knowledge of the river. I warned the passengers, "*You'll have to take a chance on this one. I have to take you through a channel and it isn't very wide. I have no spotlights on board so it could be very interesting*". Everyone was happy to go along and rather excited at the prospect of a little adventure into the unknown. Everything went fine for about fifteen miles. I reached the channel and hugged the bank, feeling my way along as the boat nudged the edge. All would have gone well if I'd chosen the other side of the channel because it went directly into deep water. The side I was on branched off into an old channel and once the boat headed off the course, with a strong tide running, I had no hope of getting back on line. We went aground. Luckily Bill Hadley, a good mate and fellow fisherman, happened to be setting a net nearby. He saw the inside lights go on in the ferry and realised there must be something wrong. He took a few people in his boat to Augusta where he recruited several other boats to come to the rescue. Rose made everyone a cup to tea while they waited for their lifts. The passengers thought it was a great joke. To them it was something different and would be a good topic of conversation for years to come. Another time the leg broke on some rocks near the mouth of the river. A chap and myself had to chair lift most of the passengers ashore. They thought it was wonderful, but not me. The mud was deep and some of the ladies were heavy. It was back breaking work.

I suppose the worst thing that happened in the eight years I had the boat was when I put it up on blocks on the beach so I could paint the bottom with anti-fouling. I'd done most of it and had about twenty minutes work left to do. I'd found a piece of square pine driftwood which I'd cut in half and stacked under the bottom of the boat. When it came to painting that area I added blocks further forward to raise the boat above the pine logs. Before getting glass windows fitted on the boat there were roll down plastic blinds. These were all down on this particular day making a perfect wind buffer. It was lovely and calm when I crawled under the boat. I almost took the pine blocks out to give me a clear working area but something told me to leave them where they were. Shortly after starting work the wind came up, hit the flat side of the ferry and toppled it off the jacks. I was on my side at the time and although I felt it going there was nothing I could do. The eight ton came down on my shoulder, pinning me to the ground. Luckily the bulk of the weight rested on the pine blocks. Without them I would have been crushed to death. If I'd thought for a moment and waited for help I would possibly have escaped injury but being alone I went for the big struggle to free myself. I felt my shoulder go but kept pushing till I was out. Suddenly there were people everywhere. I knew my shoulder was broken but I'd ordered a low loader to come and get the ferry back in the water and I was the only one qualified to drive her to the moorings. So against the wishes of several people that I go straight to hospital, I said I wanted to wait for its arrival. But repeated urgings from a nurse finally had me at the doctor's being x-rayed. He showed me where two bones in my shoulder were now separated. "*I've still got to go back to the boat John,*" I said, "*so stick a bandage on it and I'll shoot through.*" He strapped me up and I returned to the beach. Two mates finished the painting then I directed operations as the ferry was put back in the water and onto her moorings.

Seven hours had passed since the accident. I was home when the doctor rang. "*Now look Pud, you'll have to have that shoulder fixed you know*" "*Okay,*" I replied. "*What do you suggest?*" "*Well I think I'll book you in to the Fremantle Hospital,*" he said. "*When do I have to go?*" I asked. "*You'll have to go tomorrow morning,*" he said. Next day we headed off to Perth. The doctor informed me that my shoulder would have to be pinned. Alternatively, he said if I wore a sling for six weeks and kept my arm rigid the bones would knit of their own accord. "*I can't see myself running around for six weeks with my arm in a sling,*" I answered. "*No, you get stuck into it and fix it up.* "It's going to look a little odd," he said, "*There'll be a bit of a lump on your shoulder. But that won't matter too much. How old are you now?*" When I said fifty six he remarked, more or less, that the shoulder wouldn't see much more activity anyway. "*Listen, mate,*" I said, "*That shoulder's got a lot or work to do yet in my lifetime. You make a bloody top job of it.*" He gave a chuckle and left the room. The operation was a great success and soon I was back to normal, lump and all.

...Chapter 38

Grant and I continued to run the ferry for the next six years. In 1978 Rose and I decided to go to England again. This time we went with Tom and Julie. We spent time in the States, six weeks in Britain and two in Greece - another memorable journey. When we arrived back, Grant, who had been in control while we were away, suddenly opted out of the partnership. I don't know to this day what happened to warrant this but he obviously had his reasons. I handled the ferry for two more years before selling out to another buyer. Now I was fully retired and determined to remain so. Rose and I spent a lot of time travelling. One trip was on the Canberra via the Suez to England. Rose became gravely ill on the ship due to a virus that laid low the majority of the passengers. There were times I thought I would lose her as the medical care on board left a lot to be desired. I expect with so many people sick they were pushed to the limit. In fact seventeen people did lose their lives on that trip. Many others were flown back to Australia when we docked in each port along the way. Once in England, it took a couple of weeks for Rose to recuperate before we could move from her aunty's house.

Other trips included a tour of Europe, New Zealand, Cocos Islands, Tasmania, two trips round Australia and one to England and Africa which I did with my two sons-in-law and my brother Harry. Every year Rose and I make the trip to Kalgoorlie for the racing round. My two girls divorced and remarried two nice chaps. We now have five grandchildren, one married, all healthy and well.

The greatest blow to our idyllic life-style came in the middle of 1988 when Rose was seventy years of age. A regular checkup revealed that she would have to face a third heart operation, this time to have an artificial valve inserted in her heart. As always, she took the news calmly. After being admitted to Royal Perth, surgery was delayed for a couple of days. Right up until she was sedated on the day of the operation she sat laughing and chatting with us all, as though on holiday. This time she was cut through the chest cavity. Her body resembled a railway shunting yard. Within four days she was sitting up talking to us and it wasn't long before she was back on the golfcourse. On the seventeenth of December that same year, we celebrated our Golden Anniversary. We had decided to have a family dinner at the hotel which is partly owned by Jimmy and Harry and their wives. I kept checking with Kaye (Jim's wife) to make sure everything was being arranged according to plan. "*Yes, Uncle George,*" Kaye assured me. "*The room is booked, the menu set and everything's fine.*" The kids and grandchildren arrived the day before and the house buzzed with activity. On the evening of the seventeenth, Julie, whose husband couldn't make it, said as she drove us to town, *"We're going to have a few drinks at Harold and Joyce's before going to the hotel. Also, we got you a present which was too big to bring to the house so we've set it up in a room at the sports centre. We'll have a quick look at it after the drinks."* Although very curious as to what the gift could possibly be, I was more anxious about being late for dinner. I'm a stickler for time. We arrived at Harold's, had a couple of drinks, then on my urging we climbed into the cars to head to the hotel. The sports centre was directly opposite Harold's place and Julie insisted we see the present first. All was in darkness when we pulled up outside the building and climbed out the car. Suddenly the doors opened, lights went on and we were greeted by cheers from a roomful of friends and relations. We both stood there like stunned mullet. It took us several seconds to register what was happening. After greeting everyone, the music, played by Les and his mate, began, and the party was soon in full swing. We discovered that all the cars were hidden in the dark behind the centre. Several friends and relations who had travelled from Bunbury and other places had stayed inside the hotel all that day in case we came into town and spotted them. Carol and Lena (Les's wife) had brought all the supper with them from Perth We were absolutely amazed that in such a small place like Augusta not one word had reached our ears about the planned surprise. I must say, and I know Rose would agree, it was one of the loveliest nights of our lives. As for Kaye, I told her I'd never believe another word she said!

    Now I am eighty and Rose is seventy seven. We both enjoy good health and mobility. I still fish on the river and Rose occasionally goes to golf. Our lives are full and active… To me, being where I am is the closest thing to heaven on earth. I've had a marvellous life with a wonderful partner and there is nothing more I could wish for.

THE END

PHOTOS

Frederick and Martha (Rose) Challis

Original house with outhouse

Where George, Winnie, Harry and David were born

Bill, George, Fred and Rose (from left)

Accommodation at Pierce's farm

75 QUID AND AN AXE

Front of homestead

The Challis family

On the squeezebox

Bill, George, Dave, Harry and Harold (from left)

Skipper of the Miss Flinders' ferry

Finchingfield, Essex

George

75 QUID AND AN AXE

Pulling the net in the Hardy inlet

Barrabool

George on the dozer